Reading Stephen King

Reading Stephen King

Issues of Censorship, Student Choice, and Popular Literature

Edited by

Brenda Miller Power

Jeffrey D. Wilhelm

Kelly Chandler

University of Maine

National Council of Teachers of English
1111 W. Kenyon Road, Urbana, Illinois 61801-1096

Staff Editor: Zarina M. Hock

Interior Design: Doug Burnett

Cover Design: Doug Burnett

NCTE Stock Number: 39051-3050

Library of Congress Cataloging-in-Publication Data

Reading Stephen King: issues of censorship, student choice, and popular
 literature / edited by Brenda Miller Power, Jeffrey D. Wilhelm, Kelly
 Chandler.
   p. cm.
 Includes bibliographical references.
   ISBN 0-8141-3905-1 (paperback)
   1. King, Stephen, 1947– —Study and teaching (Secondary). 2. Horror
 tales, American—Study and teaching (Secondary). 3. High school
 students—United States—Books and reading. 4. Censorship—United
 States. 5. Canon (Literature). I. Power, Brenda Miller. II. Wilhelm,
 Jeffrey D., 1959– . III. Chandler, Kelly, 1970– .
 PS3561.I483Z8 1997
 813'.54—dc21   97–34367
                                                                          CIP
                                                                           AC

For Ed Brazee, who learns from and advocates for adolescents

Contents

Acknowledgments

In *Bird by Bird,* Anne Lamott writes, "We are not here to see through one another, but to see one another through." It would be impossible to thank all the people who have seen us through this project, but a few deserve special thanks.

The steering committee for the Reading Stephen King Conference—Rosemary Bamford, Ed Brazee, Phyl Brazee, Robert Cobb, Ethel Hill, Virginia Nees-Hatlen, Jan Kristo, Paula Moore, and Tom Perry—worked for eighteen months to develop an inspiring event that led to this book. A special thanks goes to Kay Hyatt, who coordinated media relations, and Susan Russell, who took care of myriad daily details. This book would not have been possible without the care and commitment of these people in planning the original conference.

Stephen King's participation challenged us to do more than celebrate his work. His provocative views and humor encouraged us to lighten up about issues of choice and censorship and bear down at the same time to get new perspectives on old concerns.

The contributors to this volume made one impossible deadline after another in drafting and revising their chapters. Their commitment, drive, and good sense illuminate many pages in this volume.

Michael Greer and Karen Smith at NCTE provided the enthusiasm and confidence that sustained us over the past year. We are grateful for their willingness to publish work that will move debates in English education in new directions and for their savvy in balancing political and practical agendas.

Finally, we thank the many teachers who will read this book with open minds and make changes in their thinking and instruction. We know how tough it is to navigate the fault lines between popular literature and popular culture in adolescent reading programs, and we're grateful that so many are willing to try.

List of Illustrations

Introduction

1

Reading Stephen King

▼

An Ethnography of an Event

BRENDA MILLER POWER

My first and only experience with reading a horror novel remains vivid. I am fourteen, and baby-sitting the next door neighbor's children. I reach the last chapter of the book at 2 a.m.—the parents are at a party miles away, the kids are long asleep, the house is dark save for my reading light, and quiet but for the tick of a grandfather clock. Suddenly, a few pages from the end of the book, I have an overwhelming need to crawl on my hands and knees, below the view of windows and doors, making sure yet again that everything is locked up tight and that all the curtains are closed. I am shaking with fear as I read of butcher knives and walls sprayed with blood, but I finish the book. And I vow never to read horror again.

I was not the most likely candidate to direct the Reading Stephen King Conference. But I did serve as the director of that conference in October 1996. Those of us who organized the event hoped it could provoke some unusual learning and insights for participants because of the unique qualities of King's writing and its appeal to teenage readers. This book is an outgrowth of the learning from those conference events.

Inspiration comes from the most unlikely places sometimes. In 1992, the University of Iowa hosted the Reading Nancy Drew Conference. This conference was designed as a tribute to the "original" Carolyn Keene, a woman who is eighty-seven and lives in Iowa City. What began as a small, quiet honor for one person evolved into an intense celebration of a particular childhood reading obsession that many white, middle-class women share. "Reading Nancy Drew" attracted an amazing amount of media attention. National news shows covered the event, and over 500 stories about it appeared in newspapers and magazines. Some of the conference organizers presented their findings about reading gleaned from participants at the next year's National Reading Conference, which I attended. The energy of this event and what it taught everyone about literacy stayed with me.

Maine is a long way from Iowa, and I'm not just talking about geography. I live in the real landscape that inspires much of Stephen King's imaginary terrain. Everyone who resides near Bangor, Maine, knows the same landmarks. On my way to work, I drive by Route 15, the pastoral country road heavily traveled by logging trucks that was the model for the highway in *Pet Sematary*. Our family can't attend a sporting event at the Civic Center without driving by the huge, hideous statue of a hatchet-wielding Paul Bunyan that appears in *It*. And on Halloween night, my young daughter treks past the wrought-iron fence topped with gargoyles, up the steps to the blood-red mansion, to wait in line patiently to get her piece of candy from the Man Himself.

I kept images of "Reading Nancy Drew" in the back of my head as I continued to teach at the University of Maine, where King had been a student leader years before. And then one day it came to me— "Reading Stephen King." Why not? King has been reading the local community for decades, turning ordinary events of rural life into epic fantasies of good and evil. His books have special appeal for teens, an audience of readers increasingly challenging for literacy educators in a post-literate age. I worked with others to form a planning committee, and we called Stephen King to ask if he would participate. We weren't surprised at his enthusiastic response, since he speaks with pride and concern about his past experiences as a high school English teacher. The event "Reading Stephen King: Issues of Student Choice, Censorship, and the Place of Popular Literature in the Canon" was born, with its subtitle defining how we would use King's work to look at adolescent reading programs.

Our goals for the conference were rooted in the local culture. The University of Maine is close to Bar Harbor and other enclaves of summer folk who have vacationed in Maine for generations. There is a real distrust locally of anyone who "puts on airs." Lobster is a rich person's treat, but it's the meat and potatoes of local economies that rise and fall with the market price. People are reserved in accepting people "from away"—you have to live here years before you truly feel embraced. Local folks want to know you're going to stick around and accept the hardships of long winters and constant economic strife before they let you into their lives. Even then, there will always be a bit of distance between you and the natives. My husband, who was born in Maine, is still not considered a native by locals, because his mother was born in Massachusetts. A native friend explained it to us well in the local lingo, "If your cat crawled into the oven and had kittens, you wouldn't call them biscuits!"

In this environment, Stephen King *is* a native. He and his wife Tabitha were born and raised in rural Maine, and met as students who eked out an education at the University of Maine through grants, scholarships, and lots of menial labor. In their first years of married life, they lived in a trailer, with King writing his novels in the boiler room late at night before leaving early the next morning to teach at a high school.

King not only hasn't forgotten his roots, he continues to champion the rights and needs of those who struggle around him. He and his wife are blunt and strong advocates for youth programs, for political candidates who help citizens help themselves, and for library and hospital improvements that can feed minds and heal bodies.

And so we planned an event which would celebrate the imaginative landscapes of King's books and the social culture of rural Maine, a place which pretty naturally can foster and promote an equality among readers and their opinions of books. We wanted to develop a conference plan that would bring together readers of all ages and backgrounds who enjoyed King's work, in an atmosphere that could make them comfortable with sharing their thoughts on King specifically and reading generally.

During our eighteen-month conference planning period, our steering committee of teachers, faculty members, and administrators at the University of Maine made diversity of participation our primary aim. We solicited presenters, advertised widely, and developed a structure for the event. But we struggled to understand who would come and what the shape of the discussions would be.

The quality of King's work, like the characteristics of his fans, is not easy to define. Both the sheer volume of King's writing and the large number of fans defy pigeonholing. Yet it seems that every English teacher has an opinion about King's writing, whether she or he has read it or not. When opinions are formed with little knowledge of the writing, it's no wonder stereotypes are formed about the readers. What we did at the Reading Stephen King Conference was try to figure out what King's books meant for readers of all ages. The common ground for participants, along with a devotion to King's work, was concern about adolescent reading programs in schools.

We didn't want a conference that was a fan-gathering of folks who view King as a pop culture icon. Neither did we want a conference that was wholly given over to esoteric discussions of postmodern feminist deconstruction of characters in *Rose Madder*. We wanted fans to attend, and we welcomed literary scholars. But the focus of the conference was to use King's writing as a springboard into literacy education issues. The problem with most discussions of censorship and choice is that they are dominated by people who think the answers are simple. Both groups—those crusading against censorship and those promoting book banning—are often shrill, dogmatic, and uninspiring. We wanted to get at some of the complexities of dealing with these issues, using King's work as a lens to focus our attention. We couldn't know when we began planning the conference in 1994 that Stephen King would be at the peak of his popularity in October 1996 when the conference was scheduled to begin. The conference was held two weeks after the concurrent launch of *The Regulators* and *Desperation*, and just after the final summer installments of *The Green Mile.* King's phenomenal success in 1996 sparked a media frenzy that spilled over to the conference. There were over 700 newspaper articles before, during, and after the conference; C-SPAN ran Stephen King's keynote address repeatedly on its "Booknotes" program, and radio and television reporters descended on campus.

But garnering attention doesn't mean you've succeeded in your goals. If anything, the attention was a distraction from what the conference organizers wanted to accomplish. The moment I knew we were successful in our modest aims of bringing together different kinds of people for a different kind of conference was when I sat in the back row of an auditorium filled with people waiting for Stephen King to speak. As I scanned the crowd, my mind flitted on a quote from a review of one of King's novels in *The New York Times Book Review* years before. The reviewer attacked not only King's work, but those who enjoy it:

> *Needful Things* is not the sort of book that one can readily recommend to the dilettante, to the dabbler or to anyone with a reasonable-sized brain. It is the type of book that can only be enjoyed by longtime aficionados of the genre, people who probably have a lot of black T-shirts in their chest of drawers and either have worn or have dreamed of wearing a baseball cap backward. Big, dumb, plodding and obvious, Mr. King's books are the literary equivalent of heavy metal. (Queenan, 1991, pp. 13–14)

These words are the classic snobby rant against Stephen King's writing and his fans. I wondered what the reviewer would think of the clothes in this conference crowd. Certainly, there were baseball caps and black T-shirts—Stephen King himself wore a Harley Davidson T-shirt. There were also professors in tweed jackets, women in business suits, fresh-scrubbed students in polo shirts and khakis. As I scanned the audience, I also wondered what the *Times* critic would think of Leslie Fiedler's recent assessment of King. Fiedler is perhaps the most revered literary critic in the country today, and he believes King will endure long after our current literary titans have passed from our culture's consciousness. (Geier, 1996, p. 31)

Participants at the conference ranged in age from thirteen to eighty-one, from twenty-seven states and Canada. Librarians, teachers, scholars, students, homemakers and a few unusual professionals were all represented. One of my friends at the conference, a local teacher, told me about the others who sat at her table at the Friday night banquet. Her tablemates included three other high school teachers, two ghostbusters from rural New Hampshire, an English professor from the Midwest, and a mother with her two teenage daughters. That mix accurately reflects the diversity of the conference. These

folks easily sat together and chatted at meals, workshops, and plenary sessions.

　　We talk a lot in education about diversity—opening ourselves
up to different viewpoints, reflecting and accurately representing other
cultures in the decisions we make. But the truth is, most gatherings
in education are clearly dominated by one culture. I remember some
years ago directing a group of young college students to an NCTE
conference site about an hour from our university campus. The students didn't know exactly where the convention center was on the
street I pointed to on the map. Finally, I said, "Just look for about a
thousand women in blue suits and jersey dresses with scarves. They
will all look just like your favorite high school English teacher. Follow them." Every one of my students found their way to the conference, and they noted later that they each followed a gaggle of women
dressed exactly as I described. (I suspect that at the MLA conference
there are fewer blue suits and far more birkenstocks and tweed.)

　　It's very rare that you have a gathering where there is a real mix
of people not only viewing an event, but participating in it with equal
voices. Inevitably when parents and students are invited to most literacy education conferences, they are a minority. We plunk them down
into discussions centered on our concerns and needs and talked about
in our most current jargon. No wonder outsiders to our academic
cultures rarely participate in these meetings and have little to say
when they do attend. No wonder the discussions of critical issues
like censorship and choice so often seem stale and recycled.

　　During the Reading Stephen King Conference, we did more than
bring a diverse group of readers together. We designed an event where
participants wouldn't just go their separate ways (teachers to cur-
riculum-focused presentations, students to films and writing workshops, and scholars to literary paper presentations). During the two-
day conference, every other session involved whole-group
participation. The evening session on Friday included a banquet and
Stephen King's talk. The Saturday morning plenary session was a
series of roleplays developed by university faculty, preservice teachers, and high school students to highlight different controversies
around King's books. After the roleplays, a panel including a high
school teaching principal, an elementary teaching principal, a drama
theorist, a middle-level curriculum planner, and the president-elect
of the National Council of Teachers of English discussed issues brought
up by the roleplays. Audience members of all ages and sensibilities
also participated in the discussions.

　　Between the whole group sessions, we did have workshops and
seminars that we thought would attract more homogeneous groups
of people. But many teens attended the curricular sessions with teach-

ers, and spoke up about what represented quality teaching practices to them. We were stunned at how mobbed some of the arcane literary analysis sessions were—attendees ignored the "postmoderns" and "deconstructions" in the titles, concentrating instead on the fact their favorite books (such as *The Stand* or *Dolores Claiborne*) were being discussed.

At the Saturday luncheon, we had open-mike testimonials about reading King's work. The lunch had a baseball theme, in deference to King's love of baseball. Amidst peanuts in the shell, popcorn, cotton candy, and a sea of baseball caps worn backwards, conference attendees went to the mike one after another. A doctoral student from North Carolina talked about reading the latest installment of *The Green Mile* series instead of attending a study session for a major examination. When she went to the professor and asked for a copy of the study guide, he bartered a loan of *The Green Mile* in exchange for it. A high school student talked of getting a couple of poems published after being inspired to write by King. A woman talked of meeting her best friend in college when she saw her reading *Four Past Midnight* on a bench outside the dorm, and how they bonded over a delight in King. Another teen talked of how her family always went to a clown-themed restaurant for dinners, until she read *It* and became afraid of clowns. She thanked Stephen King for writing *It*, because now she really doesn't care to go out much with her parents—and he saved her from that.

Because the conference attendees were so diverse, there were also random moments of real tension. An adult reader's theater workshop, carefully and joyfully prepared for weeks, was marred by the insistent giggling and chatting of some teenagers in the front row. I can still feel myself squirming through a seemingly interminable luncheon testimonial from a woman who took it upon herself to read a story she composed that included fifty-seven references to King's work ("There once was a man who had two daughters, named *Carrie* and *Christine* . . ."). About ten minutes into her testimonial, I leaned over to a friend and whispered, "Perhaps this is the sort of conference activity that works better with Nancy Drew readers!"

But as I listened to the testimonial, I remembered sneaking a flashlight in the back of the station wagon as an eight-year-old so that I could get through the latest Nancy Drew book during long trips. I remembered reeling off titles with friends to compete over who had read the most, just as many testimonial listeners vied to see who could recognize the most King references in that woman's narrative. There is something elemental about the connection between readers who are turned on to reading through the same author, and it cuts across gender, race, and socioeconomic class.

We hope with this collection we've managed to capture just a bit of the energy and diversity we experienced at the conference. After this introduction, you'll move right into reading King's provocative statements from his keynote speech about reading, choice, censorship, and teaching. We close this introductory section with some voices and opinions that are no less challenging and articulate—a conversation with students and a teacher from Noble High School (Berwick, Maine), who attended the conference and presented their work.

The key themes of the conference are highlighted in separate sections of the book. In "Choice," the authors show that considering the role of choice in adolescent reading programs is not easy. Teachers have a lot of murky territory to navigate in considering how, when, and why students should choose their own reading materials, and what issues these choices raise.

In "Popular Literature," the contributors present different ways popular literature can be used in adolescent reading programs. Essential questions about balancing the quality of the literature used with the quality of the reading experience are explored.

In "Censorship," the contributors take readers through test cases of censorship based on King's work. All contributors in this section emphasize that it's important for teachers to think about censorship issues and develop plans of action before these plans are needed. The book closes with some helpful and practical appendixes of resource materials for developing censorship policies and using controversial literature in adolescent reading programs.

What we can't capture well in these pages are all the moments of insight the conference provided for so many participants. These were different for every person who attended the conference, so I can only write clearly about my own personal discoveries. Since October 1996, I've often asked myself, What surprised me in directing the conference? What did I learn?

First of all, I learned the best way to get to the hard issues in literacy education is through the pleasures we share as readers and writers. Sometimes we forget that—many of us became English teachers, avid readers and writers, through the influence of one writer, read with a flashlight in the back of a station wagon. Often teachers opened us up to that passion. We can use that love as a springboard into the tough issues of censorship, choice, and even what classrooms should look and feel like.

Second, authors should not have to be advocates for their work. Stephen King argued eloquently at the conference that it's his job to write, not to defend his writing. A corollary of that for me is that it's not our job to defend our students' tastes in reading—but it is our job to try to understand those tastes, so that we can build upon them and expand their understanding of what reading can be.

Third, teens can still surprise me. From the thoughtful grace of their roleplays at the Saturday plenary session, to their pleas to "leave King alone if you're only going to ruin it by teaching it in schools," student participants demanded they be listened to and that we change our practice through listening to them.

Finally, what stays with me from the conference is its powerful effect on the participants. As Annie Dillard writes,

> It's a challenge to bring off a powerful effect, or to tell the truth about something. You don't do it from willpower, you do it from an abiding passion. . . . Caring passionately about something isn't against nature. It's what we're here to do. (1989, p. 47)

Those who came to "Reading Stephen King" have an elemental connection to his work that translates into avid reading. For two days, I walked among people who have a pervasive love of Stephen King. They were moved. And if we want to see movement in education, we have to tap into that elemental connection between author and reader, between ideas and feelings on the page and the hearts and minds of readers. If we don't like what students are connecting with in their reading, then we have to acknowledge there is probably something in our culture we need to deal with.

Some critics have argued that what troubles us most about Stephen King's writing is what troubles us most about our society. As noted King scholar Michael Collings writes,

> King is perhaps not a horror writer at all. His monsters, when they occur, often function more metaphorically than literally. Even if no one believes in haunted hotels . . . or vampires, one must believe—because the evidence is all around us, on every street, in every newspaper, on every television news broadcast—in educational systems that destroy rather than build; in parents who destroy their children; in cancer, that insidious disease that systematically destroys living tissue; and in political negligence that destroys society and civility. In all but a few of King's works these are the real monsters; and humans appear as their avatars. (Beahm, 1992, pp. 209–210)

Perhaps by tapping into what appeals to students in King's work, we may begin to get at in our classrooms some of those "larger monsters" of popular culture and societal ills that his novels encourage us to face.

Maybe the book will help you get to a deeper level of understanding reading, what King would say cannot be taught. I hope the contributors can take you back to the days you snuck a flashlight into

the backseat or under the covers to read one more chapter past bed-
time. I hope they help you become a better teacher and to respect the
emerging passions and tastes of readers which cannot be taught, only
observed.

Works Cited

Beahm, G. (1992). *The Stephen King story.* Kansas City, MO: Andrews and
    McMeel.

Dillard, A. (1989). *The writing life.* New York: Harper and Row.

Geier, T. (1996, September 23). The obsession of Stephen King. *U. S. News
    & World Report,* p. 31.

Queenan, J. (1991, September 29). And us without our spoons. *New York
    Times Book Review,* pp. 13–14.

––––––––––––

For literature references, please see "Reference List of Literary Works."

2

I Want To Be
Typhoid Stevie

STEPHEN KING

Readable, interesting novels don't begin with a desire to teach but a desire to please. The writers of such books aren't always successful because of any particular skill, but because their loves, obsessions, and objects of fascination overlap the loves, obsessions, and fascinations of their readers. This may happen for a writer many times, as has been the case with writers as disparate as Robert Ludlum, Danielle Steel, V. C. Andrews (who continues writing bestsellers even though she's dead), and John Fowles . . . or just once, as in the case of William Peter Blatty's *The Exorcist* or Robert James Waller's *The Bridges of Madison County*. One of the most interesting things I ever heard said about Waller, who has sold his own CDs on cable TV and has a remarkably tiny head for a man of letters, is that every book he has written since *Bridges* expresses a weird inverse ratio: each is better written and sells fewer copies. The last barely kissed the bestseller lists.

I have been fortunate enough in my career to have struck a number of those chords in my readers—points where my perception of the world seems to overlap their own, thus offering up that shock of recognition that sometimes only a book can provide. I can still remember my first intimate acquaintance with that shock: sitting in the second-floor lounge at Gannett Hall on sleety winter nights, reading the early novels of Ross MacDonald and finding in them, over and over again, observations and insights which exactly expressed my own thinking, but which were set out in a way more elegant than I could ever have imagined. These books made me feel elevated. They made me feel glad to be alive.

That is something I always wanted to pass on as a writer, and in some cases I have, but mostly not because of any extraordinary ability on my own part. I have become wealthy and well-known to a very real extent because I happen to be an average American of my time with some narrative ability and some visualization skills. To be well-paid for what I do is great; to be honestly enjoyed by so many readers is greater. Nor is that a false modesty. The desire to please— or to try to—seems hard-wired into my system. When I was a kid, my mother sometimes used to say, "Stevie, if you were a girl, you'd always be pregnant." The way I have tried to repay this good life and fulfilling career is to give as completely as I can of what I have, to entertain people as well as I can, and to try to play the game squarely.

The best thing I ever read on that subject was attributed to Frank Norris, author of *McTeague, The Octopus*, and *The Pit*. Responding to critical indignation over the rough and squalid lives depicted in his fiction, Norris said, "What do I care what they think of my work, or how they rate it? I never truckled. I told the truth." I would be perfectly happy to have that last part—I never truckled, I told the truth—on my tombstone. I may have told a few whoppers about ghosts, goblins, vampires, and the living dead, but I like to think that I have told the truth, as best as I've been able to manage it, about the human beings that the books are mostly about. As for the more outre subject-matter, there's something Ben Mears says in *Salem's Lot* that I've always liked: "The world is coming down around our ears—why stick at a few vampires?"

I write each book twice. The first time, when it comes out of my head and onto the page, what I'm mostly concerned with is the emotional gradient. That writer has absolutely zippo interest in theme, allegory, symbolism, politics, ethics, sexual roles, culture, or dramatic unity. What I want is to reach through the page and grab the reader. I don't want to just mess with your head; I want to mess with your *life*. I want you to miss appointments, burn dinner, skip your homework. I want you to tell your wife to take that moonlight stroll on the beach at Waikiki with the resort's tennis pro while you read a few more chapters and see if Jesse Burlingame is going to get out of the handcuffs or if Gage Creed is going to come back from the dead and eat his mother. I want you afraid to turn off the lights. I want you to be sorry you ever started the goddamn thing in the first place, and I still don't want you to be able to stop. With me, that first time through, it's personal, and it's really more about you than it is about me. I want you sweating bullets and looking behind doors. Nothing about this seems in the least abnormal to me, I'm afraid. Compulsive reading is a sickness, and I have always wanted to be Typhoid Stevie.

But there can be more to a book. I don't say there *has* to be more—there's room for Clive Cussler in my philosophy, as long as I don't have to read him—only that there *can* be. I do know that a book which lives only on an emotional spectrum is a disposable item—the mental equivalent of a stick of gum. I found out early on that there can be a second and more resonant level even in popular fiction. This came to me in the writing of *Carrie*, when I realized that the book was, in addition to a story about a sad little girl with psychokinetic powers, a story about blood, and what blood means to us. An actual substance, it also provides powerful metaphoric connections to such things as religion—"Washed in the blood of the lamb"—and adulthood, which for girls is symbolized in part by first menstruation. Blood also symbolizes powerful family connections which we sometimes hate and find we still can't ditch.

The blood imagery in *Carrie* doesn't make it a great book. As I have pointed out somewhere, with my customary delicacy, "You can frost a dog-turd, but it's still a dog-turd." I'm not saying that *Carrie* is shit, and I'm not repudiating it—hell, that kid made me a star—but I am saying that it was a young book by a young writer. In retrospect, it reminds me of a cookie baked by a first grader: tasty enough, but kind of lumpy and burned on the bottom. But the vibration of that blood imagery still pleases me, and it gives the book what echo it has.

So, ever since *Carrie*, when I worked purely by instinct and achieved what little I did mostly by accident, I have written once for emotion and rewritten for something else, something that's harder to name without sounding too pompous or too humble. I guess you could say that whole-body rewrite comes in an effort to satisfy my own intellectual curiosity.

Every book has to be about *something*, and if the writer did an honest job—didn't cheat, didn't truckle, in Frank Norris's terminology—then the result is bound to be something the writer cares about. And, if the writer works very fast (as I tend to do on first draft), there are apt to be some interesting connections which form almost on their own, like snowflakes.

With *Salem's Lot*, it was the connection between small-town life as I understood it and the whole idea of vampirism. With *The Shining*, it was the connection between alcohol abuse and child abuse; it was also the idea that, while hotels may or may not be haunted in the off-season, human lives are almost *always* haunted by the lives of others. When I wrote *The Shining* the first time, the wasps' nest Jack finds in the roof—the one where the wasps come back to life and sting his son in the middle of the night—was there strictly as something that intensified the suspense, that made the tale-telling more personal and vital between me and the person I call Constant Reader. Later on, thinking about what I'd written in a cooler frame of mind, it struck me that the wasps served as an adequate symbol for the pass-it-on nature of abuse. What we are able to live with as adults—what won't sting us—will sometimes sting our loved ones, as we ourselves were stung when we were younger. And the nest that comes back to life when it's supposed to be dead also expressed the nature of the Overlook for me.

It's this second level—the one where *The Tommyknockers* is a book about technological abilities which have far outraced moral ones, the one where *Pet Sematary* is a book about the corruption of love, or the one where *Misery* is a book about the redemptive and liberating qualities of imagination—that is the level most commonly taught in schools, because that level can be taught. That the teaching is in many ways irrelevant is an ironic counterpoint. You can teach the lyrics to a Bruce Springsteen song like "Atlantic City" in a high school poetry class with some success, because it's a song of ideas, but that still ignores the fact that "Atlantic City" has this absolutely *bitchin'* E-minor, G, C chord progression. Songs are about how you feel in the dark, not what some teacher says while standing in front of a blackboard, and some stories are like that, too.

I write twice because I want to know what I think as well as what I feel, but I write to begin with because my heart demands it and would break without it. So I can say that *It* has a coherent, thematic core—you cannot be an adult in this or any society until you have finished with your childhood, and one most commonly does this by raising children of one's own. But there is nothing thematic about the way the book *feels* to me; like *The Body*, it is about what I remember most and treasure best in my own childhood: love and terror and finding a hand to hold when things get hard and living in the world hurts.

I think that young people who don't ordinarily read are attracted by that combination of emotional heat and honest, if sometimes simplistic, intellectual investigation. I think that even those who wouldn't know a thematic unity if it bit them in the ass sense that books are better when they're about something, and best of all when the something they are about pertains to their own lives. Often those who come new to the idea of reading for pleasure become the most heartstruck fans and partisans, because the power of fiction catches them utterly by surprise.

In some cases, of course, my readers are R. L. Stine fans who have recently gotten past the point where they believe that (a) snapping a girl's bra-strap is suavely romantic; (b) a loud fart in study hall is the most hilarious occurrence imaginable; and (c) no rock group can express the angst of the modern junior high schooler as well as Pantera or White Zombie. In others, I like to think they managed to skip the Stine experience entirely—deep woods mummies, vampire football coaches, and all. I have nothing at all against R. L. Stine, but I put him with Clive Cussler: let him write forever, as long as I don't have to read him.

The two of us are often paired by school teachers and school librarians, however—we are two examples of that fabled creature, the "must-read" writer. School librarians love us because we move. The Vina-Bind company loves us because damn near every paperback edition of our stuff must undergo the process or fall apart. English teachers love us a little less—I'm sure there are many English teachers in this great land of ours who feel they will kill themselves if they have to read yet another book report on *Firestarter* or *Christine*. Still, they tell themselves—and they often tell me, as well—"at least they're reading." I have very little sympathy with this attitude, in fact. If the main goal is getting the kids to read anything, never mind the good stuff like *Of Mice and Men, Pride and Prejudice*, or *Macbeth*; why not hand out copies of *Soldier of Fortune* or *Cosmopolitan*, or teach grammatical construction with examples from the *Penthouse* Forum? If just "getting them to read" is the goal, those materials might serve even better than *Bridges of Madison County* or *The Horse Whisperer*, a book about which I may paraphrase Oscar Wilde and say it is impossible to finish without weeping copious tears of laughter.

In a few cars further along this same train of thought is the idea that reading Stephen King is somehow going to encourage kids who have never read before to try a little George Eliot or William Faulkner. Please. Give me a break. I just can't imagine a kid who has enjoyed *The Running Man* or *The Long Walk* moving eagerly along to *The Merchant of Venice* or *The Mill on the Floss*. No more could I imagine someone saying, "If I liked the meatloaf, I will undoubtedly enjoy the stewed rutabagas." Just because a group of kids may be slower at reading than their peers doesn't mean they're dumb.

Nor am I comfortable with the idea of being a poster-boy for the pleasures of reading, or the carnival barker outside the big tent telling people to hurry-hurry-hurry: if they like what they read on the outside, they're going to love what they read on the inside. I do what I do as well as I can, and if my work has led some new readers to the work of others, or launched them on lives where the TV stays off for whole nights at a stretch, I'm very pleased.

But I don't want to be the ramp that kids tromp over from the dirty docklands of Nancy Drew and the Hardy Boys to the great ship of literature where the Dorothy Parkers and Norman Mailers are holding court in first class. I just want to be me, and to tell you the truth, I feel happiest when I see some kid reading one of my books not in the classroom but on a schoolbus headed for an away soccer game, or flopped out on a beach somewhere during summer vacation. I dutifully glance at the term papers on my work that kids sometimes send me, but the stories I really like are the ones about people who strike up friendships or even fall in love because they shared an interest in Stuart Redman or Dolores Claiborne or Stuttering Bill Denbrough. I think that books can survive in a classroom environment for a while, but if they're kept there and only there for too long, they end up as dead as the fetal pigs in Biology Two.

Nor do I want to be a poster-boy for fighting censorship in the schools, or be pals with the groups who see it as an issue of overriding importance. I saw Judy Blume first espoused by such groups, then co-opted by them, and at last all but eaten alive by them. I'm not making a point about censorship here, but about Judy Blume. Her job isn't trying to convince people who can't be convinced that children should be allowed to read at the level of their comprehension; her job is to go on writing books like *Are You There, God? It's Me, Margaret* that kids love and treasure. Remember, each writer is a one-of-a-kind creature, and sooner or later we all fall off the shelf and break, like the vase you liked so much and cried over because not all the King's horses and all the King's men could put that puppy back together again. To ask a Judy Blume or Stephen King or even an R. L. Stine or Clive Cussler to spend his or her thirty or forty years of creative life not only writing books but defending them is unfair, impractical, and, it seems to me, a little absurd.

Don't get me wrong—I have little or no use for censorship. I've done public service announcements on TV defending the fundamental right to read, I've given money to defeat referenda aimed at restricting the free flow of information, and you'll put a V-chip in my TV remote only when you pry it from my cold, dead fingers. I have a problem with people who want to take *The Catcher in the Rye* or *Bastard Out of Carolina* out of the high schools and keep the shotguns in Wal-Mart, just as I have a problem with legislators who, at the same time, want to outlaw abortions and federal assistance programs aimed at helping single mothers. The attitude seems to be that it's wrong to vacuum 'em or drown 'em in saline, but perfectly okay to starve them once they're out, named, and properly baptized. I have the same problem with politicians who inveigh heavily against drugs such as pot and heroin but continue to support business interests which spend millions of dollars to teach our kids what fun it is to freebase nicotine. I can't think of these things too long. It makes me crazy. I Hulk out. And the Hulk doesn't write.

People who want certain books out of schools or out of the libraries will tell you that they want to protect their children from certain ideas, certain words, and certain views of American life and the human condition. The fact that they are denying these things to all the other kids around their own . . . well, they'll say, that's just too bad; tough titty, said the kitty, but the milk's not warm. Push them a little further and they'll invoke "family values," a phrase which more and more frequently makes me feel like collapsing in a fit of projectile vomiting.

Censorship and the suppression of reading materials are rarely about family values and almost always about control—about who is snapping the whip, who is saying no, and who is saying go. Censorship's bottom line is this: if the novel *Christine* offends me, I don't want just to make sure it's kept from my kid; I want to make sure it's kept from your kid, as well, and all the kids. This bit of intellectual arrogance, undemocratic and as old as time, is best expressed this way: "If it's bad for me and my family, it's bad for everyone's family."

Yet when books are run out of school classrooms and even out of school libraries as a result of this idea, I'm never much disturbed—not as a citizen, not as a writer, not even as a schoolteacher . . . which I used to be. What I tell kids is, Don't get mad, get even. Don't spend time waving signs or carrying petitions around the neighborhood. Instead, run, don't walk, to the nearest nonschool library or to the local bookstore and get whatever it was that they banned. Read whatever they're trying to keep out of your eyes and your brain, because that's exactly what you need to know.

Schools, supported by tax dollars and charged with caring for increasingly diverse student bodies in increasingly difficult and argumentative times, have a difficult responsibility when it comes to the issue of what books to teach in the classroom and what books to keep out. Parents have an equally difficult but less frequently articulated responsibility, which sometimes comes down to a decision to sit down and shut up. Easy to say but often difficult—terribly difficult—to do. Sometimes it's best just to let the kids read the book and trust them to evaluate it sensibly. In other words, trust those fabled "family values" . . . the real, working article instead of the vague concept invoked by the politicians.

When people feel they *must* speak out against a book that's being taught or kept in the school library, there should be a review procedure that can be used in a sane fashion. I believe that those who object to certain books should be given a fair hearing, but that they should have to work just as hard to explain what's wrong with a novel or story as a teacher does to explain, in the classroom, what's right with it. No fair coming in with twenty-three curse words and one sex scene highlighted in yellow. Objecting parents or citizens ought to be able to explain, in some rational way, why they feel the book has no redeeming social or intellectual merit. If they can, then fine. If they can't, which is usually the case in my experience, they should have a choice: either give the kid the book to read and also discuss it at home, giving their own perspective, or yank the kid the hell out and go the home-schooling route. But appeals should always come from parents—under no circumstances do I think that pressure groups like the Moral Majority should be allowed to clog up the teaching process with a lot of their tiresome agendas. Most of these folks should rapidly be consigned to Jim and Tammy Faye Bakker's gold-plated doghouse.

The rule of law which covers all this—disliked by all too many Americans, and hated by some—goes like this: "Congress shall make no law respecting an establishment of religion, or prohibiting the free exercise thereof; or abridging the freedom of speech, or of the press, or the right of the people peaceably to assemble, and to petition the government for redress of grievances." In other words, get your damned hands off what I'm reading, my friend, and keep your family values in your own family.

I'd like as many of my books as possible to find their places in school libraries—if nothing else, they pass the time in boring study halls and activity periods. But as long as they're available in the town library, or in paperback at the same Wal-Mart where they do sell shotguns and don't sell the new Sheryl Crow album, I'm reasonably happy. The best thing for me, and the most dismaying thing for would-be censors, is that kids have minds of their own and are engaged in learning how to use them. If you tell them Stephen King is good, they'll read me. If you tell them I'm bad for them, that I'll warp their little minds, they'll stampede to read me. As long as the stuff is there. As long as we don't reach the point where folks are piling so-called subversive books in the street, dousing them with gasoline and setting them on fire. Family values in Berlin, you understand. Circa 1938. And, I think, radical right and religious militants notwithstanding, we are a long way from that.

For literature references, please see "Reference List of Literary Works."

King and Controversy in Classrooms

▼

A Conversation between Teachers and Students

KELLY CHANDLER, JOHN D'ANIERI,
MATT KING, SIERRA KNIGHT, JEFF POULIN,
BRENDA M. POWER & JEFFREY D. WILHELM

Two highlights of the Reading Stephen King Conference were provided by students from Noble High School in Berwick, Maine. On Friday evening, eight students and their teacher, John D'Anieri, presented "Students Study Censorship: A Panel Discussion." Twelve other Noble students, all of them enrolled in a performance seminar taught by D'Anieri and Greg Bither, scripted and presented a roleplay as part of the Saturday morning plenary session. Their participation was so thoughtful that we wanted to include their perspectives on issues of censorship, student choice, and horror fiction. Three months after the conference, we talked with teacher John D'Anieri and students Matt King, Sierra Knight, and Jeff Poulin to see what learning endures from "Reading Stephen King" in the Noble community.

Kelly Chandler: John, would you begin with a thumbnail sketch of how you turned the conference into curriculum for your students?

John D'Anieri: The call for proposals said "Reading Stephen King: Censorship, Student Choice, and the Role of Popular Literature in the Canon." I took those three subtitles and made them the areas of focus in which the required junior research paper could be done, with the carrot that if these papers were done extraordinarily well, there might be an opportunity to present them at the conference the next fall. I also assigned each student to choose from a list of banned books, so they were writing a paper about either censorship, student choice, or popular literature at the same time as they were reading a book that had been banned at some time in history for one reason or another. I gave four choices of books I would provide: *Catcher in the Rye, Drowning of Stephan Jones, I Know Why the Caged Bird Sings,* and *The Color Purple.* They could also go out and find their own if they wanted to.

It was a six- or seven-week unit, consisting of two segments. For half of each class, we would work on our research papers, with students in the library doing what they did and me trying to coach them through topic selection. The other half of the class was a series of Socratic seminars in which the students presented answers to a series of questions such as "Why has this book been banned?" and "Should it be banned?" We applied the same four questions to half a dozen different books in a series of conversations. *The Drowning of Stephen Jones* would be discussed by one group during the first week, and then that book would come up again with a different group of kids in the fifth or sixth week.

Brenda Power: It's fairly rare to have teenagers presenting at an academic conference, and the response to your presentation—and the roleplay, too—was overwhelmingly positive. Can you students talk a little bit about what you did, and why you did it?

Jeff Poulin: I did a piece on censorship with homosexuality in schools and how books are banned from being in schools because they deal with issues like that.

Brenda Power: And what's your take on that? What should teachers know or think about if they're going to use books that deal with controversial issues like homosexuality? What would be your advice to teachers about that?

Jeff Poulin: The more that people know about it, the less ignorant they're going to be. I just think it should be part of education. A lot of great people from the past were homosexuals. It should be something that's seen as enriching our culture or something, and it's not. It's like a faux pas.

Brenda Power: What would be your advice to a teacher who opens up her classroom to some of those issues—readings about them, and discussions—and finds she's challenged in the community?

Jeff Poulin: I think the teacher should stay firm in their belief. I chose to do the book that I did, and other people chose other books, and that's how I got into my subject.

Brenda Power: It sounds to me like you're saying in some ways the teacher is on firmer ground when it's the student's choice. Would you agree with that?

Jeff Poulin: Yeah. The teacher suggested the book to me, and I was excited to do something the rest of the class wasn't doing, to get a little bit more insight myself.

Sierra Knight: I wrote a speech about the book *Catcher in the Rye*. I read that for my junior English class. After researching a little bit, I found out that it was a banned book. I just didn't understand why it would be. In my speech I basically said, "Why would this be a banned book?" There's no issues in it that I could find, that I could object to or anybody else would object to.

Brenda Power: So why do you think that happens? Why do you think a book like that ends up being banned? Can you put yourself in a parent or teacher's shoes and see why they might ban it, when you yourself see nothing offensive in it?

Sierra Knight: I guess it's because of the language he [Holden Caulfield] uses, and he doesn't believe in school. Parents don't want their kids not believing in school because then they're not going to *go* to school, or they're going to be disrespectful because of the way he talks.

Brenda Power: Why do you think it's OK for you to read something like that?

Sierra Knight: To get a different point of view on the world and different issues, to see everybody's point of view, whether you agree with it or not.

Brenda Power: I was wondering how attending the conference, and the work you did at the conference, fits in with the goals of your high school curriculum?

Matt King: Basically the conference is kind of like an idea the school's trying to carry out. It's trying to expand learning—instead of just going to lectures and classes—it's trying to get student input, trying to include students' experiences. And I think the Reading Stephen King Conference was a very neat learning experience for students to enjoy.

Brenda Power: Can you talk a little bit more about the response of participants to your presentation? Did folks come up to you after it or the next day and give you anything to think about?

Jeff Poulin: I started my speech in an unorthodox way, I guess. I got up in front of everyone, and everyone was looking. Instead of just going into my speech—"Hi, my name is Jeff"—I decided to say "Faggot" really loud. Some people nodded, other people turned pale, jaws dropped. I think it was a pretty good response, pretty provocative. After the entire reading was done, an English teacher came up to me and wanted to thank me, basically to commend me on what I did. And the next day a couple other people saw me and said, "Hey, I really liked what you had to say." It made me feel really good because people were listening. That's why I wanted to do it.

Kelly Chandler: Do you remember any of the questions that were asked you afterwards by the audience?

John D'Anieri: I remember one question. A bunch of the kids' speeches had to do with being able to choose what they read, either whatever they wanted or sometimes from a list of six or eight books. That was a theme in almost all of the speeches, so one of the questions was "What makes your school like that? What's different about your school?" The most interesting answer from most of the kids was a version of this: "The relationship between us and our teachers. Our teachers respect us, and we respect our teachers, and it seems like a lot of our friends go to schools where that's not the case, where it's more like an adversarial relationship." That's just one question I remember that brought the same kind of answer from all the kids.

Brenda Power: Anyone else with responses to your presentations?

Matt King: I don't quite remember the exact responses, but I know lots of people came up, mostly to talk about why we were there, I think. All the students there helped to open the eyes of the adults, because students have a very different view than our parents have and our teachers have. I think it's refreshing, and it opens them up to see the way we think.

For instance, I'm an avid reader. I love to read, but I never would have learned to love reading if it had just been through school. I find whenever a teacher assigns a book—doesn't matter if it's a good book, bad book—I won't like it. It becomes a chore. I'm not sure exactly why, but it becomes that way.

Brenda Power: Can you think specifically, Matt, of what you learned at the conference that you carried away or that stays with you months later?

Matt King: I never really understood the subtleties of the issues of censorship—like Stephen King and his view on it. I never would have thought of his view; he doesn't really care one way or the other. Like he said, if they didn't censor his books, kids would read his books. If they did censor his books, kids would come and read them in droves because parents told them not to.

Jeff Wilhelm: I remember the roleplay very well, how your fellow students looked at different issues that were addressed by provocative books, and how they said in each case, "But it could help me." I'm wondering if any of you could address why you think provocative books can help you? What's the power of a story, anyway, to help you? Why do you think some adults might disagree? What is it they fear about these books, and what would you say to them?

Matt King: What I feel most adults fear is giving kids an open mind, letting them choose for themselves. Because lots of times—especially older people—when they were growing up, they were taught to conform, that there was a certain way to go. And now people are opening up, and I think controversial books are actually the most valuable books, because they make you think. They make you think about life, they make you think about values, whether your values are right. Whether you agree or disagree with a book, it helps you understand things.

   If you're going through hard times—like if you got molested—it helps you understand the experience. You read a book about somebody who went through the same experience and it makes you feel like you're less alone. It makes you a more worldly person without actually having to go through the experience. If you're a person who likes to learn, for example, it can help you to understand people who hate school, who don't want to go to school.

   I think that's what so valuable about all these controversial books that people seem to want to ban. It seems to me that they're just trying to ban kids having open minds. They're just trying to close them down. And I think that's just because of fear, fear of what will come out of a kid that does understand these things, who makes up his own mind.

Jeff Wilhelm: Does anybody want to add about that question?

Sierra Knight: I agree with Matt. I think they just don't want to see those different kinds of issues. Those issues are not supposed to be talked about out in the open. They're supposed to be kept right behind closed doors. They don't want to talk about homosexuality out in public. They don't want to talk about people getting abused.

Jeff Wilhelm: Again, why are they afraid of that, and why are books a good way of exploring those issues?

Sierra Knight: If you read a book about it, that gives you the chance to see that stuff like this is real. You don't have to talk about it with anybody else. It's for your own knowledge. I think they should have those kinds of books, so if you want to explore some kind of issues that maybe your parents don't want to talk about or teachers don't want you to know about—then you can go to the library and pick up a book about it. You'll be able to know.

Matt King: I think reading is a more valuable medium to spread information than movies or television because you can sit and passively watch a movie and have absolutely nothing sink in. You can just mindlessly look at it and enjoy the overall plot and never really get into the real issues of it. But in a book, you're using your mind. You're thinking constantly. It makes things stick in. It makes you think whether you want to or not.

And, as I said before, maybe that's what scares some people. I think you'll find teachers—the new breed of teachers that aren't just stuck on lecturing and want to make a full, well-rounded student—will encourage this kind of reading, while teachers of the older kind, the ones who want to lecture, want to keep their students more close-minded. They almost want them to have a partial picture.

Jeff Wilhelm: Do you think there are immoral books that shouldn't be read by teenagers in school?

Matt King: I think the only time books can become dangerous is when someone is not knowledgeable. I think if you are a knowledgeable person, books generally make you become more worldly. You can decide for yourself. When you watch a movie and you see somebody get murdered, or you see somebody killing people indiscriminately or acting viciously, you're not going to go out and do that for yourself. You make that judgment because you know better. And the same thing will happen with books, if they're "immoral." People will either quit reading the book because they don't like it, or they'll read the book to understand it.

Jeff Wilhelm: Just to push this a little more, I'm wondering what you all would say—maybe Jeff especially—about a book that's racist or homophobic? Is that OK to read?

Matt King: I think that's great to read. It may help you if you are homophobic and you read a homophobic book. It can make you re-evaluate. You might think, "This guy is such a bigot. Do I want to be like that? Are other people seeing me the way I'm seeing this character?" If you're not homophobic, it might help you see the other side, see why other people feel this way. Lots of people are homophobic because of fear. It helps expand the mind.

Jeff Wilhelm: I hear what you're saying, and I like what you're saying. But what if a reader is not as open-minded as you? What if this is just adding fuel to their fire, making them more homophobic? What then?

Jeff Poulin: That's a character flaw, I think.

Jeff Wilhelm: We've talked about the private experience of reading, and how it's very important that students resist some of what they read—that they're critical about it and they think about it. What if a student's not able to do that with a homophobic or racist book? Is there a role for group reading or the teacher?

Matt King: Group reading is a great thing to help evaluate and help kids on the way to understanding these books. As you said, it might bolster somebody, but if they read it and talk about it in a group, they might ask, "What am I doing?" or change their minds.

Brenda Power: I'd like to shift the conversation a little bit. In the book we're going to have the full text of Stephen King's speech, where he talks about a lot of his experiences as a reader. I was wondering if we could hear your reactions to King's speech. Anything you remember out of it or anything that surprised you during it?

John D'Anieri: I want to jump in here because I think King is one of the best talkers about writing. He does it in a way that almost anyone who's ever written or thought about writing can understand, which is what made our kids really like him. They felt he humanized the writing process and talked about it like something someone does, as opposed to something someone studies.

Brenda Power: Would you say the same was true of his discussion of the reading process, too, John? I got the sense as I listened that he was such a passionate reader himself.

John D'Anieri: Yes, he stripped it of all of its pretense, which was very nice. He made it seem—both reading and writing—as something that was almost on the level of all of our other urges, and not necessarily something to be put in a special place. And that's also how he explained how he wrote for others, almost like a need or a hunger or something like that, as opposed to being a great work of art.

Brenda Power: John, I'd like to hear more of your perspective on the whole conference, what you saw students taking away from it, what you took away from it as a teacher. Could you take a few minutes to riff on that?

John D'Anieri: I knew this was going to be an academic conference dealing with censorship and student choice, which are issues of passionate interest to me. I knew there would be a bunch of academics gathering, and I thought it would be cool to bring some kids up, to get them involved. And that really worked. I learned so much from these eight kids writing these things and presenting them, and also from the kids who did the skit. I learned a lot more from having kids talk about my area of expertise, as opposed to talking about it myself. It was clear when we were up there that the audience was pretty mesmerized by the authenticity of these students' voices, that something seemed so genuine about them. If you get kids out there talking about the things that are of interest to them, they will do as good a job as the so-called experts will.

Brenda Power: I didn't see the presentation that these students did, but of course I saw the roleplay. And I was just amazed again at how much we underestimate what students can do if we just give them meaningful tasks.

John D'Anieri: We pulled the roleplay together about three weeks before the conference. We told the performance seminar what the framework was going to be, and those twelve kids, juniors and seniors, conceived of it with the constraint that we were going to have five minutes, and it had to be done quickly. They had a list of banned books from Sierra that she had gotten off the Internet for a project the previous year. They actually did a little research and had a little academic thing happening, too. They directed themselves, but I guess Greg [the other teacher] and I directed them, too.

Brenda Power: John, you're a fairly new teacher, right? How long have you been teaching?

John D'Anieri: I've been teaching for six years, and this is my second year at Noble.

Brenda Power: I think some teachers would wonder about some of the risks you take in terms of doing a unit on censorship where students read banned books. What would you say to teachers who say, "Oh, I could never do the things that he does in my school" or "I couldn't deal with the controversy"?

John D'Anieri: What would I say? I take a pretty extreme view on that, which is to say that I'd probably prefer to be fired than keep a kid from reading a book he or she wanted to read. Whenever I supervise a kid reading, I know I can make an argument— as literature, as individual growth—for why that's a good thing for the kid to be reading. And I know I can make that argument in front of a school board, in front of a court—whoever is going to question me. I don't have them read things which I don't think I can justify, but I think I can justify just about everything. Is that answering your question?

Brenda Power: Yes, I think it is, because on the one hand, you say you wouldn't fear being fired for a student reading a book, but on the other hand, it sounds like you really have a thoughtful, reflective rationale—or you develop one—for any book that seems to come to that edge of possibly being critiqued.

John D'Anieri: Actually I can give you a little anecdote that illustrates about how far as I'm willing to push this. In my introduction at the conference, I explained this unit in which I took the kids to the bookstore with curriculum money. I said they could buy anything in the bookstore, as long as it met their definition of literature. We had spent four weeks defining literature, and each individual kid had their own definition of literature. Kids picked all different kinds of things. We ended up with forty titles in all. One group of three girls picked a Joyce Carol Oates book that was sort of from inside the mind of a serial killer—

Jeff Poulin: Zombie.

John D'Anieri: Yeah, *Zombie.*

Jeff Poulin: That was great.

John D'Anieri: They picked this book *Zombie*, and they showed it to me. They showed me all the books they were buying. I read the back of it, and I thought, This book sounds like it's really on the edge. "What do you guys think?" I asked, and they said, "Oh, my parents let me read anything. It's no big deal." So I asked, "How does this fit your definition of literature?" And they went through how it deals with a society gone wrong. They came up with a decent definition, and I let them do it because it was Joyce Carol Oates.

When they finished this book, they came back, and they were aghast: "This book is trash." They were really offended by it. And afterward I asked, "Should I have not let you buy it?" And they said, "Oh, no, no, no. You should have let us buy it. We had to buy it and read it for ourselves to find out." This showed me the kind of book that was probably at the edge of what a tenth-grade mind could handle. Jeff, would you agree with that?

Jeff Poulin: It dealt with a lot of issues. One of my friends suggested it to me because she thought that Joyce Carol Oates was the best writer ever. And I read it. It was strange, you know, but I enjoyed it. But I think you have to have a certain maturity, a level of understanding, so you can go through this realizing that some people think these thoughts.

Jeff Wilhelm: I would like to build on that. I had a very similar experience with a seventh grader who read a book called *Blood Lust*. He came in and said, "This is trash." And I think that since Stephen King writes horror, and a lot of the conference had to do with horror, I'd like to ask you if and how you would justify the reading of horror as a genre.

Matt King: I think horror is kind of like enjoyment reading. Horror brings you to another world. People read horror books to scare themselves. Some people enjoy that. It gives them a rush without actually going anywhere or doing anything. It kind of enlivens the mind. Personally, I detest horror because I don't like that. If I'm going to scare myself, I'd rather do it in real life. Something about reading horror books really gives me goose bumps, which is the point of the book, but I don't really need a book to do that to me. But with horror you get a reaction, and lots of readers like to get this reaction. They like to be scared, like to get goose bumps. Like fantasy, for another one—the main use for that is to connect to your imagination, to let your imagination run wild. I think all books have a use; some are to stretch your mind, some are to get certain reactions.

Brenda Power: What about you, Sierra? What's your perspective on horror?

Sierra Knight: I've read some of Stephen King's stuff, but I'm not going to get any weird ideas from it. I just see it as entertainment, something different. It's not going to inform me in any certain way.

Jeff Wilhelm: I hear people saying that there's kind of this trash horror, and it's just for entertainment, but there's also this kind of substantive horror. Am I hearing you correctly, and is there anything more you'd say about that?

Matt King: That's very true, especially when you get into the kind of scientific fiction/horror that kind of brings in ideas from the future—like computers taking over the world or cloning. That just struck me real hard. I guess that's what *Pet Sematary*'s about: the kid dies, and they try to bring him back to life. That's just exactly what they're doing with the lamb thing. I'm a little scared of cloning. It really makes you wonder about humans. I know this age likes to fix things, but Stephen King illustrates in an exaggerated mode that humans have a tendency to keep on pushing and keep on pushing. It's really scary to think about how far we will actually go that we will try to bring somebody back from the dead. We won't know the consequences or the repercussions, and we won't really even care.

Jeff Wilhelm: There was a big news article recently about a school district in South Dakota that completely banned R. L. Stine, and I'm wondering whether you would, based on what you've said here, be less upset by the banning of this kind of "trash horror" or entertainment horror, versus this kind of more substantive horror that deals with important ideas?

Jeff Poulin: Banning a book at *all* from a school is morally wrong. R. L. Stine is entertainment, but R. L. Stine is also for young teenagers, young adults, and that's mostly who goes to school. . . .

John D'Anieri: I guess I'd say that R. L. Stine is sort of the McDonald's of literature but I wouldn't tell people they couldn't eat something they wanted to eat. I'd just try to get them on to more nutritious stuff.

Sierra Knight: I have to agree with Jeff. I'd be upset if they banned any book. It doesn't matter what kind of book it is. It's not right to ban any kind of literature. If you want to read it, you should be able to. That's why it's out there.

For literature reference, please see "Reference List of Literary Works."

Choice

4

Of Cornflakes, Hot Dogs, Cabbages, and King

JEFFREY D. WILHELM

Among the very greatest questions of both life and literature remains Hamlet's famous line, "To be, or not to be." Participants at the Stephen King conference put their own spin on that one, and added a few related questions to it: To be, or not to be (a person who selects and manipulates the materials available to students)? To read, or not to read (Stephen King, that is)? And ultimately, at the snack tables, banquet, and baseball lunch: To eat, or not to eat (and if so, which stuff and how much)? Part of the vitality of the conference was that all of our lives are certainly tied up in these weighty existential choices on an almost daily basis!

One highlight of the conference focused quite particularly on just these kinds of questions and choices. It occurred during the plenary session on Saturday morning, which I had the pleasure of emceeing. After partaking of muffins and coffee, the participants filed into Corbett lecture hall. There, a group of educators and two groups of students dramatized scenarios exploring the classroom reading of Stephen King.

The first role play was performed by professors from the University of Maine. The scene began with a parent reading a graphic passage from King's *Rose Madder* to a meeting at a local high school (see chapter 16 this volume, by Anne Pooler and Constance Perry). She then demanded that the book be removed from the library. The teachers were offended by this demand and argued against it. The principal tried to weave her way between the parent and teachers by refusing to remove the book, but offering to black out offensive passages. This brought on intense rejoinders from both factions.

This was followed by a second role play by U-Maine undergraduate students. Their performance involved a very organized parents group attempting to shape curriculum and book-selection policies.

The final role play was written and dramatized by students from Noble High School in Berwick, Maine. Through a series of quick vignettes, they created a kind of dramatic "slide show." In the different snapshots, students' life needs and desire for personal relevance were denied by various forms of censorship. When the text in question was taken from a student at the end of each short scene, the actor turned to the audience and pleaded, "But this book could help me!"

At the conclusion of each dramatic presentation, an expert panel fielded questions that the role plays had raised for the audience. Not too far into the session, one participant stood up and asked, "What role is the teacher supposed to play in allowing [choice] versus guiding the reading choices of students—I'm particularly worried about when the reading material might seem poorly written, unchallenging, or even gratuitously graphic and violent?"

All of our panelists simultaneously leaned forward and cleared their throats, eager to address this compelling question. One panelist began to argue that an important role of art was to help the audience confront their innermost desires and fears. Only through this confrontation can one define oneself and make more meaningful choices about how to live. This panelist stated that "you have to really face yourself if you want to grow!" Other panelists raised their voices. Another argument for allowing choice was that children intuitively know what they need to face in order to outgrow their current selves and should therefore be given control over doing so. Examples were given of children controlling the TV or video remote, running their own literature circles, and taking over daily curriculum planning.

Carol Avery, then President-Elect of the National Council of Teachers of English, broke in to challenge this line of thinking. "What if your children only wanted to eat hot dogs or macaroni at every meal? Would you give them control over that too? Or as teachers and parents, do we know things that students don't know? Do we know things about nutrition, for example, that we have to help our kids to know? Are there times when we have to guide and challenge kids to do things they wouldn't do on their own so that they can adopt insights and behaviors they wouldn't achieve without our help?"

The parrying then commenced. Some defended the choices of children and argued for very subtle kinds of guidance. One panelist argued that adults need to negotiate with children but to always treat their desires and choices seriously. In keeping with the food analogies, Carol responded with something like "Baloney!" and argued that sometimes adults must intervene more overtly to lend the learner their more expert consciousness. Carol and her camp alluded to the need for focused kinds of choices that would lead to challenge, cognitive conflict, wider awareness, and the scaffolding of student growth; others argued for a weaving metaphor in which the child's personal knowledge, needs, and choices were always affirmed, addressed, and given at least equal priority.

This provocative exchange certainly got me thinking. Was choice always good? I began to wonder if there is ever any kind of meaning or freedom without limitations and asked: so what *is* the relationship between constraints, learning, and creativity? Did I eat too much macaroni as a child and did this adversely affect my basketball playing? I began to consider the kind of choices available in my own classroom and the conditions under which choice had seemed to work best for myself and my own students. This took me to another line of questioning: What kind of animal organs are ground up into hot dogs anyway and would this knowledge affect my choice to eat them? (This last question insistently impinged itself on my consciousness during the Stephen King baseball luncheon when red hot dogs were served.)

These thoughts reminded me of my senior year of high school English in the early 1970s. The place was Marion L. Steele in Amherst, Ohio. My teacher was Bill Strohm. It was a lively class with lots of reading, writing, smart dialogue, and challenging ideas. But what I remember most are the books Bill Strohm gave me to read. He gave me Hesse's *Narcissus and Goldmund,* which spoke to me of my intense relationships with my best friend Peter and several, too short-term girlfriends. The book helped me think about different relationships and ways of knowing about the world, of knowing God, of being good. Later, Strohm shared three books he thought I would like, and from this selection I chose to read *The Centaur. The Centaur* settled itself into the very marrow of my bones. It helped to turn around my relationship with my father at a time when my mother was dying of cancer. My father and our mutual struggle began to take on mythic proportions that led to more humane understandings than I had previously achieved.

In the spring, my teacher lent me his copy of *Zorba the Greek.* This was a real barnburner for me. And oh, did I have an intense time locked in my room late at night reading and rereading the wisdom of Zorba. It shook me up and gutted me. I felt like a feather pillow with my insides fluttering about the room. I later read that it had nearly destroyed Kazantzakis to write the book. I didn't wonder why.

Each of these books shredded the sails of my soul and sewed them back together again under a new banner. Excerpts of each still live with me today, and there are situations when I conjure up Narcissus, Chiron the Centaur, or Zorba—and they speak to me.

One scene from Zorba always springs to mind when issues of choice come up. Zorba is speaking to his boss about enslavement to things. Whenever he feels the stirrings of an inner demon that have some kind of power over him, Zorba urges his boss to face it head on. In my own mind's version of this scene Zorba says, "There will be no avoiding it!" He says that whenever he is haunted by a desire, he chooses to stuff himself on the thing, swimming in it, gorging himself on it until he is sick and tired of his addiction. Then he is free! Then he can go on to more wholesome and high-minded pursuits. The boss wants to know if this technique always works. "It has for me," says the big Z, with a twinkle in his eye, "for everything but women!"

But is ruthlessly following our inclinations really exercising choice? This has led me to consider what you need to know and to do to actually make meaningful and fruitful choices. When has choice worked for me as a student, person, adult book-club participant, and as a teacher? What kind of "work" can choice do, and what can't it do?

I think Bill Strohm *was* giving me choices, but limited ones, based on his knowledge of literature, of kids, and of me. The choices were focused and therefore meaningful to me. I chose from what he offered because I could see how these books could be personally relevant and socially significant. I also preferred to choose (unlike Melville's Bartleby) because I wanted to do something for myself in my adolescent extremity, because I wanted help to address my needs and longings, and because I had real-world problems to work out. I also wanted to talk with Bill about the books and to write stories that would well up in me whenever I wanted to reply to a stirring reading experience or a great-hearted author.

These books fed me and continue to feed me to this day, and I have to thank Bill for setting the table. Now I know that reading is not eating, and that good reading is a productive and not a consumptive activity. Still, both the right foods and books can nurture us; therefore, I have to believe that a steady diet of the wrong foods and books can also keep us from growing. And we need our students and children to become independent eaters and readers who can make wise choices that will sustain them when schoolteachers are nothing but a fond memory and a signed picture in the yearbook.

My point is that choice is a most excellent thing because it moves our students towards independence, towards agency, towards exercising their will, finding and loving their own questions, interests, answers, and pathways. But in providing too much choice we renege on our adult responsibility to lend children our expertise and to assist students in ever more competent performances and widely considered experience. In schools, and maybe in life in general, choice is presented as too much of a bipolar, either/or issue. What we need is an intelligent balance and negotiation between shared and independent reading, a constant dialectic between guidance, preparation, and opportunities to fly on one's own.

Tharp and Gallimore (1988) describe all learning as beginning when a teacher or other more expert person provides assisted performance to a learner, so that learners can do and know what they are not yet capable of doing on their own. The trajectory of learning continues as peers move on to assist each other in their learning performances and is completed when the learner can assist herself. Janet

Allen (1995; please also see this volume, Allen, chapter 15; Campbell, chapter 5) demonstrates how this kind of assistance can be provided to students as she modeled reading, put particular books in front of students, and eventually asked students to help each other and themselves to make reading choices. In my own story of helping reluctant readers, *You Gotta BE the Book* (Wilhelm, 1997), I attempted to teach my students how to read in particular ways by guiding them through sequences of readings and response activities. These carefully sequenced activities were designed to assist them in adding new understandings and strategies to their reading repertoire. I call this kind of teaching a movement "from order to adventure" and argue that when students have been helped to find books that help them outgrow who they are as people and readers, they come to use what they have learned as they choose and read books on their own.

There are lots of reasons to be pro-choice. Choice helps curricula to become more student-centered, and more driven by kids' needs, interests, and questions. With more choice, there are more opportunities for students to teach each other, to share resources and ideas, and to get to know each other. Choice helps build community and leads to more dialogue with others and with the self, leading to multiple perspectives on various issues. Choice leads to and is an integral part of inquiry. Finally, choice captures what real adult readers do when they read. Of course, choice does require a rethinking of the content-oriented curriculum, traditionally seen as a means for transmitting a set body of information, or as the Romans defined it— a "racecourse of ideas." To accommodate choice we need a new metaphor of a pathway that allows opportunities for exploration, detours, and the construction of new knowledge, directions, and understandings.

What kinds of choice help create these kinds of opportunities to construct meaning? Arthur Applebee's review (1993) certainly indicates that there is very little choice offered to students in today's schools. And most of the discussion about choice seems limited to the actual texts students will read. But clearly there are other powerful kinds of choices that can encourage a stimulating learning environment. For example, students can choose a theme of study, or a research question to drive their own inquiry. They can choose how to pursue such study to meet curricular objectives (see Beane, 1990). Students can have choice about when and where to do things, such as when they pursue student-designed learning projects or when various learning stations are available. Students can choose what emphases they want in a learning product and based on this, create their own critical standards, benchmarks, and scoring rubrics (see Wilhelm and Friedemann, forthcoming).

For example, in a recent unit on civil rights and social justice, thirty-two different groups of my students chose to study various topics such as breaking the color barrier in baseball, the history of the Ku Klux Klan, and harassment in our own school hallways. Each group then refined a research question that intrigued them and would interest their classmates. Using professional- and student-produced models, they defined the purposes of a documentary and articulated their own critical standards of what made a good documentary. These student standards were formalized into a rubric. As students pursued their research, many other choices were made, such as what medium they should use to teach the rest of the class about their findings. Some students created museum displays; others created sophisticated hyperstacks or video documentaries. As these products were created and refined, students revised and remade their work so that their essential findings would be highlighted for their audience of classmates and parents. We constantly asked: How can we best represent what we have learned? What purposes are we trying to achieve with what we have learned? And then we asked: How can we help our audience to best know these things too? The answers to these questions required us all to make informed choices. Finally, students chose how and when to share their work publicly.

My own seventh graders were eager and able to choose from various alternatives when they were engaged in significant learnings that would help them to do work in the real world. And they were very careful to make the kinds of choices that would serve their ends. They learned what they had the opportunity to learn, and the role of choice offered many important opportunities. One particular group learned about the variety of traditional and electronic resources providing information on the Negro Leagues and Major League baseball. Not only did they then learn of the great resistance of white ballplayers to Jackie Robinson's entry to the major leagues, but as they made their video they also learned how to use tableaux drama to quickly summarize important information, and how to use a video-editing machine.

A lot of what these students learned accrued as they independently pursued their reading and their projects. I think it's true that many students will internalize general strategies of reading as they read, and general strategies of learning as they learn. But I also think that there are many students who will not learn to read or improve their reading without actual guidance, and this is particularly true when they are working with specific tasks and genres that require specific kinds of knowledge (see Smagorinsky and Smith, 1992, for a full discussion of this issue). There are many things that even very good adolescent readers are not going to learn how to do without the intervention and support of the teacher. This is a central insight of Vygotskian psychology: students need to be assisted in their performances to outgrow their current capacities. People can always learn with others what they are incapable of learning on their own. And I would argue that there are many things people will never learn without the expert guidance of others.

I know many intelligent adults, for example, who do not know how to judge unreliable narrators, and they totally misconstrue ironic texts. For example, after watching a video of *That Championship Season*, my friend Leon told me, "Wow, the friendships you make in high school sports really see you through your toughest time"—not realizing that the irony of the movie was that the main characters' championship basketball season had helped to cause all of their current ethical, personal, and professional problems. Their coach had encouraged them to cheat as athletes, and now they all encouraged each other to cheat in life—on their wives, on their clients, on each other. Leon did not understand that none of the main characters could be trusted and missed the clues that they were hiding the truth, and hiding from it.

Some workshop-style teachers would argue that it was not for me to disabuse my friend of his interpretation. I would argue that it was not only my right, but my responsibility. When I highlighted the clues he had missed, Leon became convinced of the film's irony and was excited to explore new interpretations with me. "How did I miss that stuff?" he asked me. "You were never taught how to see it," I told him.

Michael Smith (1989, 1992; also see chapter 9, this volume) has demonstrated that reading is a highly conventional activity, and that many sophisticated conventions of literature (and other texts) cannot be learned by just reading. In his most recent work (Rabinowitz and Smith, in press), he argues that genres ought to be understood as texts that invite the application of similar strategies. So although there are some generalized strategies of reading, the application of these varies across genre. Also, new and very particular strategies must be applied when reading particular genres. What this means is that students must be helped to develop genre-specific strategies. Smith argues that these little-known strategies are best learned when experienced readers share their expertise (see Smith, 1989; 1991).

Shared experience helps readers to know and to do more as they add new strategies and moves to their reading repertoire. In Smith's scheme, the teacher actually teaches, i.e., helps students to elaborate on existing conceptual and procedural structures, and to develop new ones, all in the process and contexts of authentic reading experiences.

In too many response-centered classrooms, I think, every response is separate and equal. As a result, student responses are accepted instead of being used as a subject and springboard for rigorous instruction. Bleich (1975) argues that this acceptance is necessary because it is the subjective response that leads to cognitive understanding. Holland (1975) likewise argues that reading is the reformulation of subconscious experience and the expression of personal identity. Therefore, personal responses must be encouraged and honored (see Atwell, 1987). But I would argue that the goal of reading goes beyond this: it is to understand the author and to take on and personally converse with various perspectives. If the goal of reading is simply responding, then students might very well end up looking in the mirror over and over again, unable to move beyond their current world view and not enabled to expand their repertoire and application of reading strategies.

Of course, when we teach something, we are constraining choice. We might need to choose texts that help us to teach, and we might need to create experiences that serve our ends. However, I want to point out that this kind of direct instruction can occur in a context of wider choice, and that this instruction actually allows for and serves wider choice. Students can subsequently choose from a wider array of materials, purposes, and tools as they pursue their independent inquiries. For example, when I am teaching my students to understand main ideas, we look at texts that demonstrate various ways of directly stating, developing, or implying main ideas. I choose the initial cartoons, poems, and short selections that I think will be interesting and accessible to them and that will help them to develop the appropriate problem-solving strategies for main idea construction. Once these strategies are in place and students can articulate them, they are asked to begin exercising this knowledge in their free-choice reading.

Many teachers have the view that "reading is reading" (Smagorinsky and Smith, 1992) and that lots of reading is sufficient to improvement in reading. This view just doesn't hold up if we recognize that particular genres and conventions make particular demands on the reader and require very particular kinds of reading "moves." A program to teach the use of these kinds of strategies means that the teacher and students care about *ways of reading* that help them to achieve "authorial readings," i.e., ways of reading that help them to understand the author's meanings (Rabinowitz and Smith, in press) and therefore to learn from these. This should not be misconstrued as the traditional emphasis on *caring solely about a particular reading*. It is a different, more empowering kind of caring that enables us to dialogue with others and exercise more choice.

For instance, in my discussion of *That Championship Season* with my friend Leon, I wasn't insisting that he share my interpretation that involvement in sports can erode our character because of the emphasis on winning. I was, however, asking him to consider textual codes and conventions he had missed that would allow for different and more varied readings, and that would allow him to understand and critique the author of this piece in new ways.

As Rabinowitz and Smith persuasively argue, reading to understand the author is necessary to actually learn from our reading. This highlights another shortcoming of always allowing student choice. They argue that a shared authorial-oriented reading promotes democratic discourse because it engages students together in a common project and because it encourages multi-perspectived ethical and political critiques of authors in ways other kinds of reading do not. This is vitally important in and of itself, but also because sharing and comparing our ways of reading, our ideas, and our critiques help to build a community of readers.

My experience tells me that our students will become readers in school and throughout their lives if they are helped to read well and to do so for authentic purposes. In the 1920s, Dewey stressed that knowledge is the *means* rather than the end product of education. Yet many teachers assume that education consists solely in providing information, allowing choice, or directing students to resources. These various approaches all fail to cultivate what Heathcote (1982) calls "authenticity." She proposes an "enabling teacher" who works alongside students but is careful to choose when to intervene and when not to, so that at different moments she will allow, guide, shape, or challenge responses as students learn together. This rarely happens in American schools. Tharp and Gallimore state this in the strongest possible terms: "In American classrooms, now and throughout the 20th century, teachers generally act as if students are supposed to learn on their own. Teachers are not taught to teach, and most often do not teach. . . . All participants in the educational enterprise have shared an inadequate vision of schooling" (Tharp & Gallimore, 1988, pp. 3–4).

Edelsky (1986), like Heathcote, also distinguishes between "authentic" and "simulated" reading. When students are made to read "out of another person's intentions, *without adopting them as their own*, the purpose of compliance interferes with the accomplishment of those other purposes owned by the person who gave the assignment" (p. 174). So this is where we must be careful. How can we teach in a way that the intentions of such instruction will be adopted by students, informing and helping them to work toward their own purposes? This will certainly require a balancing of teacher and student choices, a delicate, negotiated dance that will create new possibilities and understandings.

As I consider authentic reading, I think about the powerful human purposes that reading serves. First off, if done competently, reading is the most accessible and affordable form of learning and entertainment known to the human race. We want our students to become great readers because of the many possibilities reading will afford them—as a unique and powerful way of knowing the self and the world. After all, we read to be excited, for self-awareness, to understand others, to see possibilities, and to cope. We read to inform our choices, to help ourselves to do things, and to know things as deeply as we possibly can.

So when does choice work best to help students read better and more enthusiastically, to stretch themselves in the context of their own purposes? I put this question to former and present students and to myself. There were different answers. Choice works when a teacher knows a student and can match that person to books that connect with current interests, needs, studies, and questions. Choice works when groups are able to choose to read together in the context of joint productive activity, when kids have a commitment to read together in situations such as group inquiry and literature circles. Sometimes choice works when it is focused and limited; sometimes kids need the freedom to "graze." But the consensus seemed to be that knowing the student was necessary and would lead to different kinds of teaching decisions. The guidance of a knowledgeable adult can help match students to books that help them to become something new.

At a basketball game last weekend, I was sitting with some of my former seventh-grade students. I asked them about the role of choice in our classroom. "You made us think we had choices," said Eric, "but you were always putting things in front of us." Sean came to my defense. "He put stuff in front of us that would help us with the projects we wanted to do, like our civil rights video." Josh argued that limited choice was still choice. "Hey, when you go to a restaurant, you can choose a dessert, but only from the desserts they have." Sarah joined in with "Yeah, if you could choose any dessert in the whole wide world you might never make up your mind, like my sister choosing her wedding announcements. I told my dad he should have only showed her two or three kinds. Then she could have decided, and she would have been happy, but without all the hassle. After all, she has other stuff on her mind, too." Hmmm.

So who do I think is right—Carol Avery and the camp of limited choice or the other panelists and their argument for honoring all student choices? I'll waffle here (food pun intended!): I think they are both right. There are times when we must scaffold new learning situations for students and directly instruct them. And there are times when our students possess or have developed interests and competence, when we should deal with them as equals and weave new meanings with them. Then we should ask them to make their own choices and create their own meanings. We should move our students from Order to Adventure and Independence.

If students don't eventually exercise their own choices, they will inherit our own limitations, those of our education, and those of the culture. Instead, we should want them to transcend these limitations to become more independent learners and democratic workers. Choice in materials, themes, grouping, and responses will help us develop a richer source of books and ways of being in this complex world of ours as we pursue our joint and individual odysseys. With choice there will be more chance that the students will be sucked into the powerful Charybdis of engaged reading. There will be more chance of finding that first utterly delicious book, the lotus flower that will take us to other lands.

To steal from the genre of Stephen King, we need books that kids can eat alive, that will get inside them, still raw and red and pulsing, that will haunt them and gnaw into their bones and their internal gyroscope. As King himself said during his conference keynote: "I want to be Typhoid Stevie . . . your constant nightmare . . . I want to keep you awake at night, reading with a flashlight under the pillow."

To conclude, I'd like to tell a story of my Grandma Price, bless her soul. During the Depression, the neighbor boy refused to eat anything but Wheaties for breakfast. Back then, Wheaties were an expensive cereal and this caused his family a hardship. My grandmother, fed up, invited the boy to breakfast for a "new kind of Wheaties." The boy poured himself a bowl, noted the different color and texture, and ate it up with gusto. Then my grandmother revealed that she had filled the Wheaties box with cornflakes. The boy was astonished and decided that cornflakes were now his favorite cereal.

"That dadgum boy didn't know how to choose or what he was choosing from," Grandma mused, "and that ain't no kind of choice at all. It took someone like me to help him out."

Grandma, as you can tell, was a teacher.

Works Cited

Allen, J. (1995). *It's never too late: Leading adolescents to lifelong literacy.* Portsmouth, NH: Heinemann.

Applebee, A. (1993). *Literature in the secondary school: Studies of curriculum and instruction in the United States.* Urbana, IL: National Council of Teachers of English.

Atwell, N. (1987). *In the middle: Writing, reading, and learning with adolescents.* Portsmouth, NH: Heinemann.

Beane, J. (1990). *A middle school curriculum: From rhetoric to reality.* Columbus, OH: National Middle School Association.

Bleich, D. (1975). *Readings and feelings: An introduction to subjective criticism.* Urbana, IL: National Council of Teachers of English.

Dewey, J. (1964). The nature of aims. In R. D. Archambault (Ed.), *John Dewey on education; selected writings* (pp. 70–80). New York: Modern Library.

Edelsky, C. (1986). Writing in a bilingual program: habia una vez. Norwood, NJ: Ablex.

Heathcote, D. (1982). In T. Goode (Ed.), *Heathcote at the National: Drama teacher—facilitator or manipulator?* Banbury, Oxon: Kemble Press.

Heathcote, D. (1984). *Dorothy Heathcote: Collected writings on education and drama.* Johnson, L., & O'Neill, C. (Eds.). London: Hutchinson.

Holland, N. (1975). *5 readers reading.* New Haven, CT: Yale University Press.

Rabinowitz, P., & Smith, M. (in press). *Resistance and respect in the teaching of literature.* New York: Teachers College Press.

Smagorinsky, P., & Smith, M. (1992). The nature of knowledge in composition and literary understanding: The question of specificity. *Review of Educational Research, 62*(3), 279–305.

Smith, M. (1992). Submission versus control in literary transactions. In J. Many & C. Cox (Eds.), *Reader stance and literary understanding: Exploring the theories, research, and practice* (pp. 143–161). Norwood, NJ: Ablex.

Smith, M. (1991). *Understanding unreliable narrators: Reading between the lines in the literature classroom.* Urbana, IL: National Council of Teachers of English.

Smith, M. (1989). Teaching the interpretation of irony in poetry. *Research in the Teaching of English, 23* (3), 254–272.

Smith, M., & Hillocks, G., Jr. (1988). Sensible sequencing: Developing knowledge about literature text by text. *English Journal, 77* (6), 44–49.

Tharp, R., & Gallimore, R. (1988). *Rousing minds to life.* Cambridge, England: Cambridge University Press.

Wilhelm, J. (1997). *"You gotta BE the book": Teaching engaged and reflective reading with adolescents.* New York: Teachers College Press.

Wilhelm, J., & Friedemann, P. (in press). *Hyperlearning: Teaching with technology.* York, ME: Stenhouse.

———————

For literature references, please see "Reference List of Literary Works."

The "Wanna Read" Workshop

▼

Reading for Love

KIMBERLY HILL CAMPBELL

CREEPY CUISINE LITERARY BUFFET

A SALUTE TO STEPHEN KING'S WRITING

ARE YOU A KING LITERARY CHAMP OR CHUMP? TAKE OUR
QUIZ AND BE THE JUDGE. THE NUMBERED MENU ITEMS ARE
LINKED IN OBVIOUS OR OBSCURE WAYS TO WRITING BY STEPHEN
KING. TAKE YOUR BEST GUESS AT EACH FOOD REFERENCE.
ANSWERS AND SCORING GUIDE ARE ON THE REVERSE OF THIS
MENU.

1. HOT NADINE CROSS BUNS_____
HINT: THEY ARE (WHEAT) GERM FREE. . .

2. *YOU GOTTA EAT, YOU WANNA EAT* YOUR GREEN BEANS_____
HINT: EVERYTHING'S TASTIER WHEN IT'S YOUR CHOICE. . .

3. A NEW YORKER FIELD OF GREENS SALAD_____
HINT: THE TRUE BOYS OF SUMMER. . . .

4. ANNIE WILKES'S CHICKEN FRICASSEE_____
HINT: IN THIS RECIPE, THE FIRST THING YOU DO IS TO BREAK THE
CHICKEN'S LEGS. . .

SALEM'S LOTSA PASTA (VEGETARIAN WITH A BLOOD-RED SAUCE)

5. ROADKILL RATATOUILLE_____
HINT: IT'S NOT A GOOD IDEA TO GET TOO ATTACHED TO YOUR PET IF
YOU LIVE ON A BUSY HIGHWAY NEAR A CREATIVE CATERER. . .

I remember the day I handed out the new literature anthology to my Junior English class. It was hard-covered, three inches thick, and beautifully illustrated with real art work. I watched to see each student carefully open the cover and inhale the new-book smell as they explored the literary treasures found within. We had carefully selected this text because of its emphasis on good literature and real art. I relished the new book smell as well as the inclusion of many of my favorite authors (Emily Dickinson and James Thurber, to name just two). But not one student opened the cover of the book. They sat passively waiting for me to tell them what to do. As the weeks went on, I attempted to select the "best" pieces of literature from the anthology; they yawned, and tolerated my excitement, with no engagement on their part. I told them why they should love reading. They told me why their reading homework wasn't done. The battle was on.

As we struggled on, I began to let go of being the only one with decision-making power and asked for some student input on the literature choices. Students helped select the stories from the anthology. I asked them to skim through the poetry sections and read a poem that struck them. Of course, with some students I had to refine this slightly and tell them that if no poem struck them, they would have to read a poem that "almost-struck" them. It was not always dismal; we certainly had moments where students connected with literature. Emily Dickinson's poems touched students; her angst within the structure of poetry made sense. Walt Whitman's free verse opened students up to their own poetic voices. A favorite assignment was a rewrite of the first section of "Song of Myself." Thoreau's passion for the outdoors and transcendentalism attracted most students; they were ready to find a cabin and march to the beat of their own drummer. Roald Dahl's ironic short stories were usually appreciated. But I did not sense that a personal passion for reading was being fostered. Students saw reading as one more thing school required.

In reflecting on what was not working, I went back to my own history as a reader. What made me a lover of literature? I was one of those kids who read away Sunday afternoons. I was president of the Tab book club in sixth grade just so I could earn free books. I needed to create for students my Sunday afternoon experience—my passion for reading. I needed to provide time for non-anthology reading—reading that would go beyond study, discussion, and questions. Reading that would be cherished—for the captivating story, the compelling characters, and the sheer joy of graceful sentences.

Choice of what was read and time to read became a part of my classroom. I looked to Nancie Atwell's work, *In the Middle* (1987) and adapted her Reading Workshop format. Every Wednesday I would read aloud from a favorite book and then give students time to read a book of their choice. My expectations were that they bring a book, they read, and that they finish books.

And, they did read, but it was still a struggle (more of a skirmish than a battle), and I still saw no real joy for reading. I selected read-alouds that would enrich their choices: *Death Be Not Proud, Catcher in the Rye, Of Mice and Men*. I read my own self-selected books while my students read, modeling for them my own enthusiasm for reading. My choices were of high literary value: Barbara Kingsolver, Alice Walker, Margaret Atwood, Pat Conroy. I responded to students' reading journals, encouraging them, sharing my own insights, recommending books. I gave students time to meet in small groups and share their "good" reads. We worked together to compile lists of book recommendations. Each Wednesday I relished the time I had for my own reading and for the students to read, but their enthusiasm often waned. The battle continued.

Over many a weekend I scoured bookstores and colleagues' personal libraries in search of more "good reads" to share with students. I operated as if there were a magic book for each student that would strike enthusiasm in his or her heart. The burden of finding such books was on my shoulders.

Bathtub Breakthrough

One rainy, winter afternoon I sprawled in the tub pondering the meaning of my life as a high school English teacher. Finding no satisfaction in such wondering, I reached for my tub book, the latest by Danielle Steel (a best-selling author of romance novels). As I escaped into the world of wealthy homes and impassioned characters, an "Aha!" moment bloomed—then exploded in my head! In all my efforts to get students to read, I had neglected to share with them my *real* story as a reader. That I, the English major, lover of classic literature, curled up in the tub with romance novels. That I was a fan of popular fiction. That best-sellers graced the shelves of my home library.

The next Wednesday morning I greeted my students with a table full of books and my usual talk-show-host enthusiasm for the time we would spend reading. They slipped quietly into their desks with a book they had grabbed from my shelf of mostly classics. I opened with my story. "Folks, I want to share a discovery I made about my own reading. On the weekends, when I escape to the bathtub, I read

Danielle Steel." I held up the book. In the back of the room, a few students, mostly girls, sat up and took notice. I went on to share the reading habits of my husband. I held up his treasured copy of Stephen King's *Skeleton Crew*. More students were starting to show real interest, rather than just polite listening. Eyes were open, focused on me, students were leaning forward to see what else I had to offer. I cracked open *Skeleton Crew* and read aloud the story "Here There Be Tygers." Students listened, with rapt attention. After the story, I explained to students that reading during Wednesday workshop should be about joy. If they found themselves watching the clock rather than being so absorbed in the reading they lost all track of time, they needed a different book. I pointed to the books on the table. "These books bring me joy. Your job is to find a book that brings you joy."

As soon as I was finished talking, students came forward (I was going to write "rushed to the table," but realism matters, they were still cynical juniors) to peruse these new choices. One borrowed the King short-story collection, another my copy of Danielle Steel. Others dug through the stack of my "Sunday reads" (and my husband's favorites, which he generously donated): more Steel, more King, some murder mysteries, a collection of humorous short stories, and other popular fiction. Enthusiasm filled the room as students settled in to read.

Over time, I spent less energy on Wednesdays strolling the room looking for students pretending to read but really doing homework, students staring at pages, students sleeping. Instead, I began to observe students coming early to class to select from the classroom library, which now included more popular fiction. I heard book recommendations being volunteered by students as they stood at the shelves. "Have you read this one (holding a copy of *Eva*)? It's awesome."

Reading journals and self-evaluations reflected a change in students' reading habits. In his third quarter self-evaluation, Alexander wrote about his learning in "Wanna Read" Workshop, "I learned that even if I do pick a long book, like *Needful Things*, if it is good I have no problem getting it finished in time, and I also learned that sometimes I can read at home without anybody forcing me to."

Stephen King explored this gulf of "Wanna Reads" and "Gotta Reads" in an article he wrote for *Seventeen* magazine. King wonders, "First, why high school kids almost invariably hate the books they are assigned to read by their English teachers, and second, why English teachers almost invariably hate the books their students read in their spare time" (King, 1990, p. 240). He goes on to talk about loving the "stuff" he picked to read: "My stuff was what I read for love. It was more current, more vivid, and spoke with greater urgency about the world around me, a world that simultaneously intrigued and frightened me." Isn't this love of reading what we want for our students? If they can discover it through King, Steel, Anne Rice, Dean Koontz, or John Grisham, isn't that a good thing?

As I continued to encourage choices for students during what came to be known as "Wanna Read" Workshop, some colleagues I shared my story with began to question my methods. One commented, "Really, Kim, we cannot consider this type of reading time well spent. We must have standards." I even was criticized for "allowing" students to read during class time. Think about that one for a minute. An English teacher being criticized because her students are reading. Is there a science teacher out there doing science labs? Stop it! And, all that time solving math problems in math class must be stopped as well.

We wonder why students are not readers—look at the mixed messages we send them! Do not waste your class time reading. Or, Reading Workshop is free time. I railed against this attitude and will continue to do so. If we want readers we better give them time to read. We better help them discover reading that connects with their personal interests. We better not apologize for joining with them in their discoveries of reading while sharing our own.

And what standards did I lower? We still explored the classic literature of the anthology. At times students even made connections between the self-selected reading they did on Wednesday and the literature we studied in "Literature Workshop."

Recently a freshman student posed the question, "Did Stephen King use *Flowers for Algernon* as a model for the "Lawnmower Man"? Darcy, a junior, delightedly pointed out how her character's inner thought monologue was just like the "run-on sentence guy" (referring to Faulkner).

In addition, students began to respect me as a reader. I was no longer just an English teacher, I was Ms. C, Reader. Students began to recommend books to me. Students who had come to know my husband's reading habits sent books home for him to read. I am fortunate to share my life with a man who enjoys King, Koontz, and other authors who scare me to death. He joined me in a three-way conversation with the readers in my classroom. Students saw my willingness to embrace their world of written material. They gave me credit for the risks I took as a reader—skimming Anne Rice (I did not finish), reading *The Things They Carried, Winterkill*, and some Louis Lamour. We became a community of readers in which all of us were students and all were teachers. As Jeanne Henry (1995) discovered in her college reading workshop, "By reading what my students read, I become a part of the community that forms within the class. I am in on things" (p. 53).

Rules, Nudges, and Rebukes: Practical Tips for a "Wanna Read" Workshop

My expectations increased rather than decreased by formalizing our Wednesday "Wanna Read" Workshop. When the high school went to a ninety-minute block schedule, the students often read for more than an hour. The requirements for the "Wanna Read" Workshop were clear:

1. You must have a book to read.
2. You must read.
3. You must avoid interfering with anyone else's right to read (we once had a student laughing so hard while reading Patrick McManus that he had to go read in the hall).
4. You can leave your desks and sit on the floor to read but cannot touch other students.
5. If you fall asleep and start to drool, we have permission to humiliate you.

I do not grade students based on the number of pages they read or the number of books they finish. I do ask them to log their reading, to set goals for themselves as readers, and to finish books—but not every book they start (I don't finish every book I start). Students earn good faith participation points for their Wednesday reading. I base these points on the observations I make while they read and the self-evaluations they are asked to write. In addition, students share their reading discoveries by meeting in literature circles and creating projects to show their reading to the class. We have heard book talks, seen student-designed covers for books, developed games based on books, enjoyed literary theme parties, and written letters to authors.

Often I am asked how I hold students accountable for the content of what they read. Given that in the course of a year over 200 different titles will be read, I cannot begin to read everything they read. I rely on students to be experts for each other; I use colleagues and my husband as resources, and I trust. I observe students reading during "Wanna Read" Workshop, and I celebrate the connections they make with what they read.

There are times, however, when teachers do need to constrain choice, or even make choices for students, as Jeff Wilhelm and Michael Smith note in this volume (Wilhelm, chapter 4; Smith, chapter 9).

When I see students falling into stale reading patterns, I nudge. Sometimes I even shove. I use their current reading interest as a bridge to a book they might not know that would challenge them. If I observe students stalled with a book, I step in. Students log the title of each book they read, as well as the number of pages read. If I see just one author or not much progress based on pages read, I conference with the student. Some just need permission to abandon the book and move on. Angie, on the other hand, was caught up in young adolescent romance novels. I knew she was capable of more as a reader. I suggested *Wuthering Heights,* which she tried but politely rejected. But *Emma* captured her attention; she went on to read *Pride and Prejudice* and *The French Lieutenant's Woman.* I do not want them wasting their time when there are so many "good reads" waiting to be discovered. I often rely on students who have discovered delicious books to share their appetites with peers. Students also make recommendations of books to read aloud and/or purchase for the classroom library. Some even donate copies of their favorite books. And we solicit parent and community donations as well.

How have parents reacted to all this freedom in reading? In general, parents have been very supportive. I send a letter home at the beginning of each new semester outlining the workshop structure of the class: two days of Writing Workshop, one day of "Wanna Read" Workshop, and two days of Literature Workshop. I emphasize that the goal of the class is to immerse students in the real work of reading and writing.

I have had my share of angry phone calls that usually begin with the question, "Why are you letting my child read this stuff?" I always listen to parents' objections, and then explain that if we are to achieve the goal of creating lifelong readers, then children must love what they read. I encourage parents to talk with their child about the book he or she is reading. (In most cases the parent has not read the book in question.) I let parents and students know that parents have the right and the obligation to allow into the house only those books they feel comfortable with. I honor parents' rights to censor their child's reading, but I do not honor their right to censor another child's reading.

More frequently than anger, however, I encounter support. One mother even called to assure me that she had done everything right at home (read to her son as a child, reads herself) and she wanted me to know that she valued the reading we were doing in class even though she knew her son complained about it. We went on to form a friendship around our shared love of reading and shared frustration that her son was not yet a passionate reader, although he did make some progress.

I have also had my values about student-choice tested. One student asked to borrow my copy of Toni Morrison's *Beloved*. This book haunted me for months after I read it. As she made her request, the thought ran through my mind, " I am tenured but I could lose my job over this one." I shared my "haunted" reading experience with her and gave her the book—with an agreement that she meet with me throughout her reading of it and check in with her parents about her choice to read this book. We had a powerful time talking about the issues this book raises.

Reading for Love

Reading is a lifelong skill. It is affordable, available, and invaluable. Having watched my high school students explore choices and have time to read, I am convinced that they are all readers. My students were non- "readers," not "nonreaders" (Henry, 1995, p. 69). They had developed the habit of rejecting reading that came out of school expectations—English-teacher good intentions. They embraced reading that came out of their purposes and pleasures. "[A]ll readers are good readers, when they have the right book" (Henry, 1995, p. 73). In a recent "Wanna Read" Workshop survey, one sophomore listed her favorite authors as Stephen King, Edgar Allan Poe, and Emily Dickinson. I celebrate her choices!

"Thinking is one thing, love is another; both are important; they do not always exist together" (King, 1990, p. 241). My desire is to create a classroom where students think and love. I work to provide time to write, time to discover, explore, and connect with literature, and time to read for love. To embrace the time to read for love, I had to rediscover—or admit to—the part of me that reads for love. In fact, when I am done writing this chapter I am reaching for Joan Hess's book *Miracles in Maggody* (one in her series about Arly Hanks, female chief of police in Maggody, Arkansas). Her writing appeals to my head and my heart. As King (1990) writes,

> Read what you have to read for love. Do more than enjoy it; swim in that heady brew, fly in that intoxicating ether. Why not? The heart has its own mind, and its business is joy. For me, those two things—joy and reading—have always gone together, and another of my life's great pleasures was discovering that sometimes they mature together. When that happens, all the final exams are held in the happiest of all places: one's own heart. (p. 241)

Works Cited

Atwell, N. (1987). *In the middle: Writing, reading, and learning with adolescents.* Portsmouth, NH: Boynton/Cook.

Henry, J. (1995). *If not now: Developmental readers in the college classroom.* Portsmouth, NH: Heinemann.

King, S. (1990, April). What Stephen King does for love. *Seventeen, 49,* 240–241.

———————

For literature references, please see "Reference List of Literary Works."

When *IT* Comes to the Classroom

RUTH SHAGOURY HUBBARD

*Fear of corrupting the mind
of the younger generation
is the loftiest form of
cowardice.*

—Holbrook Jackson

62

*What he saw then was terrible enough to make his
worst imaginings of the thing in the cellar look like
sweet dreams; what he saw destroyed his sanity in
one clawing stroke. . . . IT held him in its thick and
wormy grip, IT pulled him toward the terrible
darkness where the water rushed and roared and
bellowed . . .*

Stephen King, *It*

*I*t is one of the most frightening novels that Stephen King
penned—the title character a leering, evil force that comes in
the guise of a smiling clown. But IT is also a fitting metaphor for
the view of popular culture that many educators take. IT—that frightening horror that fashions many a teacher's worst nightmares, holding our students in its wormy grip, threatening to pull them into the
terrible darkness of ignorance. Popular culture permeates all aspects
of our students'—and our own—lives. It won't simply disappear because we try to ignore it in our classrooms.

But what happens when teachers *do* open the doors to let IT in
through providing choice in the reading curriculum? What kinds of
popular reading materials do adolescents choose? When the genres
of romance, horror, and "Teen Zines" become part of the literature
read in class, what are the benefits? And what problems do teachers
need to solve? What issues need to be examined with the students?

Too often, when educators explore questions of pedagogy that
affect the everyday classroom life of students, we ruminate and speculate without turning to our real informants, the students themselves.
These adolescents have a lot to teach us about how popular literature
helps them develop lifelong reading habits, consider new angles on
issues of social justice, and find places for themselves in reading communities. In this article, I invite you to listen to the voices and words
of several students as they write, read, and discuss the books that
they choose to read when they are allowed to bring their reading
interests and passions into the classroom.

Choice in the Classroom: Letting Them "Graze at Will"

Ask most literature teachers what their goal is for their students, and they'll likely tell you they want kids who are transported by great literature, who are critical thinkers, who understand literary conventions. If you continue the conversation, you'll find that these teachers also care about their students discovering the joys of reading and writing. Advocating student choice in the curriculum doesn't mean throwing these worthy goals out the window. Instead, many educators believe this can be a successful alternate route to achieving them. Teachers like Nancie Atwell (1987), Linda Rief (1992), Maureen Barbieri (1995), and Curt Dudley-Marling & Dennis Searle (1995), are showing that if we want to help our students become lifelong passionate readers—and isn't this our top priority?—we need to open up our classrooms and invite students to interact with books the way real readers do. And that begins with choice. Author Barbara Kingsolver (1995) comments on the freedom to read as follows:

> It's well known that when humans reach a certain age, they identify precisely what it is their parents want for them and bolt in the opposite direction like lemmings for the cliff. [As a teen,] if I was going to find a path to adult reading, I had to do it my own way. I had to read things I imagined my parents didn't want me looking into. Trash, like *Gone with the Wind*. (I think now that my mother had no real problem with *Gone with the Wind*, but wisely didn't let on.)
>
> Now that I am a parent myself, I'm sympathetic to the longing for some control over what children read, or watch, or do. Our protectiveness is a deeply loving and a deeply misguided effort to keep our kids inside the bounds of what we know is safe and sure. Sure, I want to train my child to goodness. But unless I can invoke amnesia to blot out my own past, I have to see it's impossible to keep her inside the world I came up in. The world rolls on, and you can't step in the same river twice (p. 50).

It's one thing to decide to create an atmosphere for "real readers," but when we put it into practice, what happens? That's when we find IT rearing its head and invading our classrooms. What does it look like? What kinds of books do kids choose—and how do they interact with those texts?

A few years ago, I was fortunate to be a researcher in Chip Nelson's and Donna Lee's sixth-grade classroom in Stratham, New Hampshire, when they began a readers' workshop. Besides keeping a reading log and having small-group reading discussions on the books they were reading, the students, on completing a book, also wrote letters to Chip or Donna. One of the students, Joe, read books by authors from Jack London to Gary Paulsen to Alan Dean Foster. But it was in the books that reflect his current interests, such as *Star Trek Log One*, that he demonstrates his understanding of more complex literary concepts, as the following letter shows:

> Dear Mr. Nelson and Ms. Lee,
>
> I have finished *Star Trek Log One* by Alan Dean Foster. My favorite part is during Yesteryear when Spock goes back thirty years in Vulcan history and meets himself as a seven-year-old.
>
> I have decided to read another Star Trek book after this— *Trek to Madworld.*
>
> I enjoy the constant bickering between Spock and McCoy. Sometimes when a particularly suspenseful or pressing situation is going on the arguing can break the mood.
>
> Spock should show more emotion, such as a slight smile or a low chuckle.
>
> Captain Kirk appears to be a referee of sorts between Spock and McCoy. Frequent "That's enough, gentlemen" come between the two science officers. Although they bicker, there is a true bond of friendship between them.
>
> Joe

In this entry, Joe demonstrates a sophisticated understanding of the role of comic relief in the story, as well as the development of the different characters and their relationship to each other. Some of Joe's classmates brought popular culture into the classroom in a different guise—the syrupy predictable young romance stories that take place in the Sweet Valley High books. Kerri Anne wrote to Ms. Lee about the role these books play in her reading life:

> Dear Ms. Lee,
>
> I just finished Sweet Valley Twins #2 *Teacher's Pet* and #7 *Three's a Crowd*. This series is created by Francine Pascal but written by Jamie Suzanne. I think that's kind of neat how one person thinks of the idea and the other writes it. Maybe it's because Francine Pascal isn't very good at writing and Jamie Suzanne can't think of topics. I don't know why, but I like these books. Elizabeth and Jessica (the twins) are so nice. They're pretty, kind, nice. After reading these books, I kind of wish I had a twin. It seems neat. These books are good for just reading and reading because I can finish the books in around two hours if I just read. So the next book I am going to choose is going to be more challenging. Maybe I'll read a challenging book and a Sweet Valley Twin book at the same time.
>
> Kerri Anne

Author Jane Smiley (1996) tells about her own misgivings with her daughters reading Sweet Valley books, when she overhears them quizzing each other on the titles in the series. "True scholars of schlock," she writes, "both my daughters knew all one hundred and some titles, including variations." This was a subject that had surfaced before, when her older daughter was nine. "At the time, she'd been reading *Dangerous Love*, in which Elizabeth falls off the back of a motorcycle and into a coma. I said, 'I don't want you reading about such trauma!' She said, 'Mom! It's not trauma—it's drama!' I took this as a sophisticated understanding of literary theory. I closed my eyes and let them feed themselves, sort of on the model of those eating habit advisors who suggest that you let them graze at will because somehow, they will crave the good" (p. 13).

And they do go on to "crave the good," mixing it with the pure fun reading as we all do as "real readers." Like Kerri Anne reading a challenging book at the same time she reads a Sweet Valley book, Jane Smiley's older daughter now reads: "Neruda, Louise Gluck, *The Picture of Dorian Gray*, Ray Bradbury, Roddy Doyle. She considers herself something of an expert on contemporary Irish novels, and for Christmas, asked for Seamus Heaney's collected poems. From time to time, she condescends to my literary tastes—I like a good murder mystery now and then. But then, she likes a good Danielle Steel now and then, and considers Sidney Sheldon a great underrated novelist" (Smiley, 1996; p. 13).

The range of authors and styles enjoyed by Jane Smiley's daughter is reflected in a list of recommended books by high school students. Last year, these juniors from Cleveland High School in Portland, Oregon, compiled a collection entitled "You've Got to Read This!": Book Recommendations from Comp/Lit Juniors 1995–1996 (see Figure 1). You'll notice a range of books is represented here— Stephen King more than once, mixed in with Raymond Carver, Amy Tan, Dean Koontz, John Steinbeck, Barbara Kingsolver, and Danielle Steel. And their reasons for recommending these books show they are committed, involved readers.

Some teachers might characterize several books these kids read as "junk" and a waste of time but their teacher Kent Siebold and his intern teacher Rusty Simms argue that the students' responses show the importance of their reading experiences. In their reading workshop class, the students are expected to read widely from books of their own choice and to keep reading journals in which they write their responses, musings, and insights. Classrooms like this have adopted a "reader-response" approach to literature, establishing a climate that encourages readers to actively engage with the text, drawing on their background experiences in order to construct meaning (Rosenblatt, 1982; Purves et al., 1995). From this perspective, a reading that sparks an all-night marathon, sophisticated connections to

TABLE OF CONTENTS
BOOK TITLE, AUTHOR

PAGE
(page numbers omitted here)

The Alchemist. Paulo Coelho
Anne of the Island. L. M. Montgomery
The Bad Place. Dean R. Koontz
The Bean Trees. Barbara Kingsolver
The Big Sleep. Raymond Chandler
The Book of Guys. Garrison Keillor
Cannery Row. John Steinbeck
The Catcher in the Rye. J. D. Salinger
A Clockwork Orange. Anthony Burgess
Cold Sassy Tree. Olive Ann Burns
The Collector. John Fowles
Death Be Not Proud. John Gunther
The Diamond Age. Neal Stephenson
East of Eden. John Steinbeck
Einstein's Dreams. Alan Lightman
Ender's Game Trilogy. Orson Scott Card
The Firebrand. Marion Zimmer Bradley
Firestarter. Stephen King
Fried Green Tomatoes at the Whistle Stop Cafe. Fannie Flagg
Go Ask Alice. Anonymous
Gone with the Wind. Margaret Mitchell
The Grapes of Wrath. John Steinbeck
Griffin and Sabine Trilogy. Nick Bantock
The Hitchhiker's Guide to the Galaxy. Douglas Adams
Hot Money. Dick Francis
I Know Why the Caged Bird Sings. Maya Angelou
The Illuminatus Trilogy. R. Wilson and R. Shea
Illusions. Richard Bach
In the Eye of the Storm. Max Lucado
The Joy Luck Club. Amy Tan
Kaleidoscope. Danielle Steel
The Kitchen God's Wife. Amy Tan
The Learning Tree. Gordon Parks
Les Misérables. Victor Hugo
Like Water for Chocolate. Laura Esquivel
The Long Dark Tea-Time of the Soul. Douglas Adams
The Martian Chronicles. Ray Bradbury
Misery. Stephen King
The Mists of Avalon. Marion Zimmer Bradley
The Monkey Wrench Gang. Edward Abbey
My Ántonia. Willa Cather
Naked Lunch. William S. Burroughs
Not a Penny More, Not a Penny Less. Jeffrey Archer
Of Mice and Men. John Steinbeck
The Pearl. John Steinbeck
The Phantom of the Opera. Gaston Leroux
Pride and Prejudice. Jane Austen
The Return of Merlin. Deepak Chopra
A Separate Peace. John Knowles
Siddhartha. Hermann Hesse
Slapstick. Kurt Vonnegut
Slaughterhouse Five. Kurt Vonnegut
Starving for Attention. Cherry Boone O'Neill
Tales of the City. Armistead Maupin
We the Living. Ayn Rand
Wizard's First Rule. Terry Goodkind

Figure 1. "You've Got to Read This!": Book Recommendations from Comp/Lit Juniors, 1995–1996, Cleveland High School, Portland

popular culture, or explorations of affective response is actually a complex, valuable, and *quality* reading experience.

In his personal reaction to *The Bad Place* by Dean R. Koontz, for example, sixteen-year-old Pete's insights into plot structure and its connection to *Seinfeld* make a fascinating literary comparison:

> *Personal Reaction*: This is the kind of book that I couldn't stop reading. I had to read it twice so that I knew exactly what was going on with every detail. I liked the chases that the bad thing had with its prey. It was all telepathically done. That was always cool because they would be in one scene, and at the last moment before they were about to die, they would telepathically transport themselves into another country halfway around the globe. It kept me on the edge of my seat. There would be a bunch of plots all coming together at the end. Kind of like *Seinfeld*. Each chapter was devoted to one of the five main characters. It would come from their point of view. This book was very good because you always knew both sides of the hunt.

Dana was another student who recommended a book—*Misery*—because she was drawn into the story in a personal way, empathizing with the main character:

> As I read, I found myself rooting for Paul (the trapped author) to escape from the grasps of his obsessive fan. I couldn't wait to find out what she was going to do next. My family had to plead with me to put it down for just a few minutes. *Misery* is extremely emotionally provocative and graphically descriptive. There were a couple passages where I found myself actually feeling the pain Paul was going through in the book. It's great any time an author can achieve this kind of effect.

Thu Truong was also drawn into the world of her science fiction thriller, *Ender's Game*. She describes how reading the first book hooked her on other books by Orson Scott Card:

> When I was recommended to read *Ender's Game*, the first book, it was so good that when I was done, I went and bought the second book. Then when I was done with the second book, I went and bought the third and last book of the trilogy. I remember staying up all night reading because I just couldn't lay down the book. Whenever I told myself I need to stop, something exciting would happen and again I was glued to it. I read it so intently that my boyfriend got jealous because I was paying more attention to the book than to him.

As you can see from the list, the students didn't just choose science fiction or romance. Michael recommended *Einstein's Dreams*, which he classifies as the genre "Serious Deep Stuff" :

> Picking up the book, I was relieved that it seemed to be in short chapters; I could skim through a couple of the things and

bore myself enough to fall asleep. By the time I realized I'd
been fooled, that the book had drawn me in, it was too late. I
had just flipped the last page over, and my eyes were long ac-
customed to the dim glow of my bedside lamp. . . . In the next
week, the book passed enthusiastically through the hands of
several of my friends, each time gilded by a strong recommendation. I found my own dreams pondering other strange per-
mutations of time and a few waking moments spent wondering how concrete our own concept of time really is. The novel
also served to inspire my own writing, with its simple nature,
reminiscent of Edgar Allan Poe's belief in the nobility of a few
words. Whether or not the real Albert Einstein had dreams so
engaging is beside the point; I'm sure he would have loved the
book.

In these excerpts, the voices of real readers emerge with honest con-
viction. Their books are passed from friend to friend. They write of
staying up too late to read by the dim light of their bedlamps, of boy-
friends jealous of their attention to books, of their deep involvement
with characters, and of ideas that invade their thoughts when they're
not reading.

Profile of a Serious Stephen King Fan

We know that students do develop as readers when they are able to
make choices and analyze those choices in a community of readers.
But what happens if a student wants to read only one author? And
what if that author is Stephen King? Kent and Rusty directed me to
just such a student, Sarah.

When I interviewed her about her reading, she floored me with
her insights into Stephen King's work. I was surprised to discover,
for example, that one important reason she likes his work is that she
considers him a feminist author: "The last book by Stephen King that
I read in *The Gunslinger Series*—the main character was a female—
in fact he got it all in she was black, legless, schizophrenic, in a wheel-
chair. . . . But that's not the point—He doesn't, like, make stereotypes. If there's a chauvinist pig in it, he's a bad guy—you can tell he
doesn't like that character."

Looking through excerpts from her reading journal, you can
see other ways her in-depth study of King's works allows her to enter
into the author's mind, and how her writing helps her think through
characters, plot developments, and motivations, and even to make
comparisons between King's work and other writers:

Book	Excerpt from Reading Journal
Thinner	I would have liked to talk to Talduz Lemke, or one of the Gypsies to see what their whole view of this

incident was. Their whole lives were basically destroyed after Billy hit Talduz's daughter, just because they wanted justice. Personally, I think that in a way, Talduz's actions were justified. He was a very wise man. When Billy, who was very fat, was cursed by Talduz to become thinner until his heart gave out or he wasted away. I think that was poetic justice in a way.

It   Stephen King doesn't seem to care for clowns. Is he perhaps, bozophobic?

Insomnia   Another point to be made. What does Stephen King have against bald people? Why do they always seem to be the demons or the life takers? Is Mr. King afraid of going bald? Does it have something to do with age, like when old men die, they are very possibly bald, so these bald men are identifying with old men and their deaths? Or is it some sexist thing, like most women never go bald so it's kind of a male bonding thing. "Yeah, men, go bald—women don't so it's one thing men have that women don't. Let's bond brothers!" (Okay, maybe not.)

The Tommyknockers
A really confusing thing about this book is that there really is no main character. You get a first-hand view from many different characters but you never really go back to one. Hmmm . . . maybe the Tommyknockers are the main characters, because you get the firsthand view of people infested with the alien. So, if people's minds are taken over by the Tommyknockers, then what the people are thinking is what the Tommyknockers are thinking. Oh! Now I see!

I have noticed another interesting trait of Stephen King books: He likes to put little excerpts from other books or songs, poems, etc., into his novels. One I noticed was a quote from CCR, and it was pretty much the first noticeable group he quoted from *The Tommyknockers*. I instantly drew a comparison to *Macbeth*. It seems that Shakespeare stole quotes from another guy's story to put into his witches scenes!! Wow! I have achieved a link between Stephen King and William Shakespeare! Millions of kids across America will thank me (or have a death wish towards me) when they get to read a fun Stephen King book as a comparison to Macbeth! Happy days are coming!

Despite Sarah's preoccupation with Stephen King, she is continuing to grow as a reader and thinker, making connections to other works as well as challenging concepts presented in the works. But this isn't always the case. What can we as teachers do when we see that the choices our students make are keeping them from growing, cutting them off, keeping them from being exposed to new things as readers? This was the case for Chip Nelson, when Nathan, one of his very capable sixth-grade students continued to immerse himself in superficial stories that glorified and simplified war. Rather than banning Nathan's choices, Chip augmented Nathan's reading by asking him to read Audie Murphy's *To Hell and Back*. Nathan's two-page response shows that Chip helped him begin to explore the experience of fighting in a war from a more realistic perspective, as this excerpt shows:

> Early in the book, I get the picture that war isn't so great when a truckload of purplehearts passes him . . . . And Germans aren't the only thing to worry about. After being treated for malaria in a hospital he goes up to the front lines where he hears his good friend Novak was hit by a direct hit from an 88 . . . . I also get the feeling of how hard it is: "without ever looking back I walk down the road through the forest. If the Germans want to shoot me let them. I am too weak from fear and exhaustion to care."

This entry opened up a written dialogue between Chip and Nathan in which they continued to explore issues such as what war does to a person's humanity, what gets in the way of more peaceful settlements, and how often wars are fought over things that shouldn't cost human life. Rather than simply telling Nathan to "stop reading that junk," Chip used his knowledge of Nathan's reading habits as a springboard for new learning.

Other teachers have banned "Teen Zines," such as *Sassy* or *Seventeen* because of the image of women and emphasis on beauty. But we can have more of an effect if we see what they truly are reading and open up a social critique—rather than simply banning a particular piece of writing and having it go underground.

Curt Dudley-Marling (1995) reminds us that ownership isn't something we can *give* to our students; "however, even if we can't give it, we can create conditions that permit (or deny) students opportunity for decisions affecting their learning. Other teachers may discover, as I did, that encouraging student ownership requires striking a careful balance between student control and teacher support and direction. Too much teacher support risks taking control of the learning away from the students. Too little teacher direction denies students access to the voices that support their intellectual growth and development and their ability to take responsibility for their learning. But, teachers who create conditions that encourage student control over their work are not doing students a favor. Ownership is not a gift—it is an entitlement."

If we can't give ownership of learning to students, we must admit we can't take away their attachment to popular culture, either. In considering the reading of adolescents whose work I've shared, when you finally turn on the light at the creaky cellar stairs, or shine the flashlight under their beds, you won't see IT—a wormy, slimy monster threatening to devour. What you will see in these students' lives is a pile of well-read and well-loved books.

Works Cited

Atwell, N. (1987). *In the middle: Writing, reading, and learning with adolescents.* Portsmouth, NH: Boynton/Cook.

Barbieri, M. (1995). *Sounds from the heart: Learning to listen to girls.* Portsmouth, NH: Heinemann.

Dudley-Marling, C., & Searle, D. (Eds.). (1995). *Who owns learning?: Questions of autonomy, choice, and control.* Portsmouth, NH: Heinemann.

Kingsolver, B. (1995). *High tide in Tucson: Essays from now or never.* NY: HarperCollins.

Purves, A.C., Rogers, T., & Soter, A. (1995). *How porcupines make love III: Readers, texts, cultures in the response-based literature classroom.* White Plains, NY: Longman.

Rief, L. (1992). *Seeking diversity: Language arts with adolescents.* Portsmouth, NH: Heinemann.

Rosenblatt, L. M. (1982). The literary transaction: Evocation and response. *Theory into Practice, 21* (4): 268–277.

Smiley, J. (1996). Okay, go ahead. *The Hungry Mind Review, 37,* 13.

For literature references, please see "Reference List of Literary Works."

7

If Students *Own* Their Learning, What Do Teachers Do?

CURT DUDLEY-MARLING

Alittle over a year ago my 14-year-old daughter, Anne, my wife, and I met with a teacher from the Toronto Waldorf School to see if Waldorf would be a good place for Anne. Up to this point my daughter had not found school to be a very happy place. My wife and I asked our questions and the Waldorf teacher asked her questions of us. Anne had only two questions: she wanted to know where students ate their lunches (at her previous school students ate their lunches on the gym floor, a practice Anne found insulting) and she wanted to know if Waldorf teachers let their students read R. L. Stine or Stephen King. What's interesting about this is that—to the best of my knowledge—Anne has never read R. L. Stine and has read only one Stephen King book.

I think Anne was gauging the Waldorf staff's respect for their students by testing this teacher's willingness to censor students' reading selections. In Anne's experience teachers hadn't been particularly respectful of the needs and interests of their students. Underpinning Anne's question was her belief that teachers' willingness to censor—or not censor—students' reading choices was emblematic of their overall respect for students. If Anne is right, then there is abundant evidence that many teachers, administrators, school trustees, parents, and politicians have little respect for the judgment, intelligence, and interpretive abilities of our youth.

The practice of banning or restricting access to controversial books, for example, is a continuing problem in the United States, and books by Stephen King are among the most frequently challenged. Although most of the public's attention has been drawn to formal challenges of books that offend one group or another, there is a worrisome trend toward self-censorship by publishers and educators in which people voluntarily avoid books and materials that might possibly offend some group. While anti-censorship forces generally win the individual battles, they may be losing the war (Traw, 1996).

Censorship is a good place to begin a discussion of student ownership. Censorship, because it limits students' control over decisions affecting their reading, dramatically raises issues of ownership and, because it is never a black-and-white issue, censorship begins to reveal the complications, ambiguities, and uncertainties of the concept of student ownership. The issue of censorship isn't so simple that it can be resolved simply by saying, "I will not censor" because this isn't true. Each of us has a point at which we will say, "I will not allow my children or my students to read that material." The boundaries of censorship, like the more general concept of ownership, are clear only in theory. In the messy reality of life in classrooms, censorship—and ownership more generally—are slippery concepts.

In this chapter I want to complicate popular notions of what it means for students to *own* their work. In general, I will argue that there is a complicated relationship between students' need to exercise some control over various decisions affecting their reading and writing (what they read and write, for example) and teachers' responsibility to challenge students to expand the purposes for which students read and write, the genres they read and write, the authors they read, the audiences for whom they write, and how they think and talk about what they've read and written—which I take to be the purpose of literacy instruction.

Ownership and the Legacy of Progressive Education

Implicit in some versions of progressive education is a romanticized notion of childhood in which learning is viewed as the natural occupation of children. Children learn because they are children and that's what children do. All children need is things to learn about. Here the role of the teacher is to provide a safe, supportive, and enriching environment for students to learn in, including stimulating toys, beautiful picture books, field trips to museums, other children to talk to, challenging games, and so on. From this perspective student ownership equates with a kind of laissez-faire pedagogy in which teachers endeavor to keep children safe, happy, and fed, but generally seek to avoid *interfering* with children's natural development as learners (Walkerdine, 1986).

Although most of us have been influenced by progressive education, the term *ownership* seems to emerge from the writing-process movement, particularly the work of Don Graves. This research indicates a relationship between student ownership and the quality of students' writing. In particular, students are more likely to edit and revise their work and discover their voice as writers if they control the topics of their writing (Graves, 1983). As Graves puts it: "When people own a place, they look after it. When it belongs to someone else, they couldn't care less" (in Calkins, 1986, p. 23). Students' willingness to read is also affected by the degree of choice they have over their reading selections. This may be especially true of adolescent readers, whose reading choices are linked to questions of emerging identity.

The concept of student ownership isn't limited to reading and writing. Pappas, Kiefer, and Levstik (1990), for example, point out that "during the preschool years, children choose activities that interest them. Their purposes sustain their attention in projects and guide their motivation to understand. By having ownership in what they do, by following their own questions about topics, they are able to create new concepts and make new connections in their schemas" (p. 44). The need to exercise control of learning "across the curriculum" is just as important for older learners.

There is, however, more to ownership than good pedagogy. Theoretically, offering students some control over their reading acknowledges the role students have in constructing their own sense of what they read (Rosenblatt, 1978). From this perspective there is no reason to expect that students will make the same sense of a Stephen King novel, for instance, as would an adult. Politically, the concept of student ownership responds to anti-democratic, authoritarian tendencies in our schools that seek to prepare good workers by developing docile, compliant students. Within the generally authoritarian context of schooling it is possible to see Stephen King's books as unofficial—even anti-official—oppositional texts that create space for students' voices by challenging adult values about sex and violence, for example. A case can also be made that progressive practices like literature discussion groups and writing workshops provide democratic spaces where students can safely try out their voices and ideas (see Lensmire, 1994).

Language arts educators can rightfully argue that student ownership should be a guiding principle in reading and writing instruction. Reading and writing instruction cannot, however, mean just putting out the books, the paper, and the pencils and waiting for students' natural inclination to learn to take over (Walkerdine, 1986). Left to their own designs students tend not to discover how to read critically racist or sexist texts, for example (see Albright and Hammett, chapter 8, this volume). Therefore, laissez-faireism in the name of student ownership is, in my opinion, simply *bad teaching*.

An examination of student ownership isn't about defining ownership as much as exploring the complicated relationship between the needs of students to exercise some control over decisions affecting their learning and the responsibility of teachers to support students' intentions while simultaneously taking account of students' needs and challenging what and how students read and write. Too much teacher support has the effect of taking control of learning away from students, giving students no personal reasons for learning beyond pleasing their teachers and parents. Too little teacher support leaves learners without social supports critical to meaningful learning (Vygotsky, 1978). And what counts as too much or too little support will depend on the context of learning.

During the 1991–92 academic year I took a leave from my duties at York University to teach third grade. Offering students some measure of control over their learning was an explicit goal although this wasn't always as straightforward as I imagined (see Dudley-Marling, 1997). Below I consider two examples from my own teaching experience to illustrate the complicated nature of *ownership*.

Two Examples of Student Ownership

The first example is a teacher-led discussion that I had hoped would teach my students something about the role of setting in narratives.

> *Teacher:* Before I start reading more from *The Great Brain Reforms* [Fitzgerald, 1973] does anyone remember the name of the town where they lived?
>
> *Paul:* Adenville?
>
> *Teacher:* It's called Adenville. What do we know about Adenville?
>
> *Jeffrey:* There aren't a lot of people.
>
> *Teacher:* There aren't a lot of people in Adenville. Why do you think that?
>
> *Jeffrey:* It sounds like there are only a little bunch of people there.
>
> *Teacher:* What else do we know about Adenville?
>
> *Hugh:* There's not much money going around?
>
> *Teacher:* What makes you think so?
>
> *Hugh:* The houses and everything. If they had lots of money they could spark the place up.
>
> *Teacher:* OK . . . What else do we know?
>
> *Roya:* It's a small town . . .
>
> *Teacher:* You guys all seem to agree that it was a small town. Is that important to the story?
>
> *Students:* Yeah.
>
> *Teacher:* Why? Would the story have been the same in a big city?
>
> *Hugh:* There'd be more stuff going on.
>
> *Teacher:* How else would the story have been different if it happened in a bigger town?
>
> *Scott:* There'd be more people.
>
> *Teacher:* How would this change the story?

This "discussion" followed the all-too-familiar pattern of Initiation-Response-Evaluation that restricts students' opportunities to talk and subverts their intentions (Cazden, 1988). Apparently, I was so anxious to impose my own agenda (i.e., *teach* students how the setting affected the story) that I gave students little room to share their personal responses to a story they really enjoyed. I also seemed to have forgotten my own belief that large-group discussions are never congenial to student ownership (Dudley-Marling & Searle, D. 1991). It's doubtful this lesson taught my students anything beyond how to participate in a circumscribed discussion; that is, how to *do* school.

The discussion about *The Great Brain Reforms* stands in sharp contrast to the following small-group discussion in which I challenged students working at the science center to explain the "layered water problem." (I had prepared a cup in which there were two layers of water. The bottom layer was salt water to which I had added blue food coloring. The top layer was ordinary tap water to which I had added red food coloring.) When the discussion begins Scott sticks his finger in the water to find a physical explanation for the layers of water.

> *Teacher:* Stick your finger in and feel all the way to the bottom. [*He does.*] Do you agree that it's water?
>
> *Hugh:* Maybe there's a little air in there.
>
> *Scott:* Like maybe they put in the red and bubbles go all the way around the top and then the holes aren't big enough to let the water through.
>
> *Hugh:* Yeah but the water, if you added a tray full of balls and you dumped the water on it, it would just, the bubbles would pop . . .
>
> *Roya:* I think you put food coloring in.
>
> *Teacher:* You're right. I did put food coloring in there. . . . If I mix these together [showing students a container with red water and another with blue water] what's going to happen?
>
> *Hugh:* It's going to go purple.
>
> *Peter:* It's going to stay at the top.
>
> [*After asking a couple of other students to make their prediction the teacher mixes the solutions together and the water turns purple. The teacher leaves after a little more discussion.*]
>
> *Scott:* The water's cold. There has to be one way this happens.
>
> *Hugh:* Maybe he put ice . . . the top starts forming ice, then the bottom, then it goes from the top to the bottom . . . then he put a shape back in here . . .

Razika: There's got to be something else in it.

Peter: Warm and hot water don't mix. He probably put food coloring in warm water and hot water in it.

Peter: The bottom should be cool and the top should be hot.

Hugh: Yeah, so it doesn't mix. I'm going to try that ice idea and see if that works. . . . I'm gonna put it in the freezer downstairs right now and then see if the top freezes . . .

[*The teacher returns and asks about their hypotheses.*]

Hugh: You took it down to the freezer and then you froze it. . . you just froze the top and then you poured in all the blue.

Scott: But by the time it got here that red would already be melted . . .

The layered water problem produced lively, animated talk full of hypothesis testing, problem solving, and collaborative meaning making, and unlike the earlier literature discussion, it is my students' thinking that is central to this discussion. I ask general questions, but I do not control the content or the direction of this conversation. Still, it could be argued that the quality of talk here depended on my presence to initiate this discussion although the students continued to engage in rich conversation after I left. Perhaps if I hadn't been there to ask the right sort of questions my students wouldn't have focused on the problem at hand. I believe that it wasn't my mere presence that made the difference, however. After all, in the previous example my presence interfered with the quality of students' talk. And it wasn't merely the presentation of an interesting problem. Other potentially interesting science activities did not produce much discussion (Dudley-Marling, 1997).

The difference here is that I carefully prepared the activity, introduced my students to the activity in both whole-class and small-group settings, and helped my students get the discussion started. I also limited my involvement in the discussion to supporting students' intentions to solve this problem. In other words, I wasn't so intent on teaching as I was on helping students explore a series of (their) hypotheses. I have come to believe that too much teacher control will constrain children's marvelous ability to learn. However, students' ability to take control of their learning will be a function of teachers' willingness and ability to provide needed support and direction to the novice readers, writers, mathematicians, scientists, historians, and geographers in their classrooms. From a Vygotskian perspective (1978) at least, learning depends on social relationships. In the absence of social relationships, apprentice learners are deprived of the guidance of skilled mentors.

So What Does Ownership Mean for Reading Stephen King?

The meaning of ownership isn't so clear, but—whatever its meaning—it is doubtful that student ownership has a stable meaning. The meaning of ownership will vary according to the social, political, and cultural context of our schools and classrooms, which means that the meaning of ownership will be a function of *what* we teach, *where* we teach, *how* we teach, and *whom* we teach. Issues around the race, class, and gender of students and teachers complicate the meaning of ownership even further. The willingness of high school and college students to assume a large measure of responsibility for constructing knowledge in the classroom, for example, may be influenced by the power dynamics implicit in the race and gender of their teachers. (My female and black colleagues at the university tell me that their students are more likely to resist their efforts to offer students some control over the content and form of their learning and learning experiences. White male professors apparently do not encounter this resistance to progressive pedagogical practices.)

Ultimately, the meaning of ownership must emerge from an ongoing conversation in which teachers and students (and, perhaps, the community) negotiate, for example, what students read, how they read, when they read, where they read, and the purposes of reading and reading instruction. Of course, the degree to which teachers are able to offer students some measure of control over the decisions affecting their reading may be a function of the control they themselves have (see Five, 1995). Teachers who operate within the context of highly prescriptive curricula, for example, will find it difficult to make a place for student choice. But merely giving students choices or making popular books part of the official curriculum does not guarantee a democratic space in which students and teachers negotiate meanings. Student ownership depends on teachers who take the stance that the meanings students make of texts—meanings influenced by the backgrounds and experiences of students—must be taken seriously.

When Anne asked the Waldorf teacher if Waldorf students were "allowed" to read R. L. Stine or Stephen King the teacher said something to the effect: "We do not prefer that our students read these books, but we will respect the choices our students make." This response was, in my opinion, just right. If learning builds on what students know, as I believe it does, then both teachers and students themselves must believe that students bring valuable knowledge and experiences to the classroom. If our students find something worthwhile in R. L. Stine or Stephen King, we have to believe that there is something of value to be found there. To malign what students read is to denigrate what our students know and, ultimately, who they are. Teaching has to begin with respect for those we teach.

Finally, although I believe that students' knowledge and intentions must occupy a central place in our classrooms, ownership cannot mean that teachers abdicate their responsibilities to challenge students to grow as readers by expanding what and how they read. Assigned readings and writings may still have a place—although I'd recommend caution here—as long as we give students the space to stake a personal claim on classroom learning. If students "learn" only because it leads to higher grades or parent or teacher approval, they won't see how classroom learning can make a difference in how they see the world and live their lives. Laissez-faireism is always bad teaching, but authoritarian models of teaching and learning popular with neoconservatives betray a lack of respect for the rights of individuals to live independent, fulfilled, and self-actualized lives and, worse, make them vulnerable to the forces of authoritarianism. Limiting students' control over the form, content, and meaning of their reading also fails to prepare students for the possibility that other people, influenced by different backgrounds and experiences, might interpret texts differently from them and that different is not deviant. (In other words, if we control the reading of our children, we should not be too surprised if they are ready to control the reading of others. Authoritarianism begets authoritarianism.) Ultimately, a community that seeks to control what and how its citizens read will never be able to sustain a free, just, and democratic society.

Works Cited

Calkins, L. M. (1986). *The art of teaching writing.* (1st ed.). Portsmouth, NH: Heinemann.

Cazden, C. B. (1988). *Classroom discourse: The language of teaching and learning.* Portsmouth, NH: Heinemann.

Dudley-Marling, C., & Searle, D. (1991). *When students have time to talk: Creating contexts for learning language.* Portsmouth, NH: Heinemann.

Dudley-Marling, C. (1997). *Living with uncertainty: The messy reality of classroom practice.* Portsmouth, NH: Heinemann.

Five, C. L. (1995). Ownership for the special needs child: Individual and educational dilemmas. In C. Dudley-Marling & D. Searle (Eds.), *Who owns learning?: Questions of autonomy, choice, and control.* Portsmouth, NH: Heinemann.

Graves, D. H. (1983). *Writing: Teachers and children at work.* Portsmouth, NH: Heinemann.

Lensmire, T. J. (1994). Writing workshop as carnival: Reflections on an alternative learning environment. *Harvard Educational Review, 64* (4), 371–391.

Pappas, C. C., Kiefer, B. Z., & Levstik, L. S. (1990). *An integrated language perspective in the elementary school: Theory into action.* White Plains, NY: Longman.

Rosenblatt, L. (1978). *The reader, the text, the poem: The transactional theory of the literary work.* Carbondale, IL: Southern Illinois University Press.

Traw, R. (1996). Beware! Here there be beasties: Responding to fundamentalist censors. *New Advocate, 9* (1), 35–56.

Vygotsky, L. S. (1978). *Mind in society: The development of higher psychological processes.* Cole, M. *et al*, (Eds.).Cambridge, MA: Harvard University Press.

Walkerdine, V. (1986, September/October). Progressive pedagogy and political struggle. *Screen, 27* (5), 54–60.

For literature references, please see "Reference List of Literary Works."

Disrupting Stephen King

▼

Engaging in Alternative Reading Practices

JAMES ALBRIGHT
& ROBERTA F. HAMMETT

▼

Everyone knows I have

the heart of a young boy.

I keep it in a jar

on my desk.

—Stephen King, in response to an allegation
from Katie Couric on *The Today Show* in March 1996
that his writing may be harmful to youths

[*We gratefully acknowledge the invaluable advice and generous editing assistance of Dr. Patrick Shannon, our mentor and friend.*]

Let us begin by admitting that we English teachers are not avid readers or viewers of Stephen King's books or films. We recognize that this admission places us within an apparent minority among the North American reading public. We are, however, advocates of choice in school reading programs, and we do see important spaces for popular culture (that elitist term) in our classrooms. Books, films, TV shows, games, toys, songs, and advertisements which are popular, but which have not withstood the test of time, bring contemporary life into our work with teenagers in ways that traditional or canonical curricula cannot. And with that life come all the joys and troubles we face in and out of school, a life which we often fail to address in ways that engage students' imaginations.

What follows are our experiences and hopes for *all* texts in our English language arts programs, not only King's works. When students choose to read texts such as those by Stephen King at school, they resist our canon of better books. When they use King to understand their worlds and themselves, they assume responsibility for constructing their own identities. But if they *accept* King or any other text as given, they fail to practice reading in ways that we hope to foster reading practices that will extend beyond content analysis and affective and aesthetic response. Within the short space of this article, we will attempt to provide illustrations of these alternative or resistant reading practices.

While we are delighted to host Stephen King in our classrooms, we hope that he realizes that he will not leave unchallenged. We should not forget that texts are not a reflection of reality. They are constructed out of assumptions that readers can contest. Equally, they have gaps and silences that can be filled in different ways to produce different readings. How texts are put together and how they are read matters because they take up different values and beliefs which ultimately have social consequences for people. Further, texts are conflicted, having competing meanings, and readers don't have to accept the dominant reading of any text. Response is typically mediated in some way or other. In classrooms, we tend to promote unconscious or not very conscious ways of reading, which result in limited readings of the text. We feel that assisting students in understanding the constructed nature of texts means disrupting reading and resisting the text to initiate a more critical reading practice.

In this chapter, we will outline with examples from some of King's novels how alternative practices might be accomplished. We begin by describing our individual past experiences and concerns with them now, and then present the three levels of practice we collectively developed.

Practices of Pleasure and Choice: Jim's Perspective

On a corner bulletin board in my reading/writing workshop, students were invited to post reviews and recommendations of the books they chose to read. This activity was popular, eliciting much discussion that often carried over into student journals and into extended conversations that went out into the halls and carried on for several days.

Chris, a grade eight student, surveyed the five classes that were reading and writing in the workshop to create a database of the most read and popular books. His inspiration had been the published lists of popular adolescent fiction that I had posted. These came from various libraries and literacy associations, but one was a reprint of the student-created list that appears in the appendix of Nancie Atwell's (1987) book, *In the Middle: Writing, Reading, and Learning with Adolescents*. For a couple of weeks that term Chris surveyed the classes, constructed criteria for the inclusion of authors and their books on his list of those most read, then created and published his document. As you might guess, the result was a hit with his peers.

Since the creation of Chris's list, I am aware of another list, which appeared in *Seeking Diversity* (Rief, 1992). All three lists— two from New England and one from suburban Halifax, Nova Scotia— share interesting similarities and show remarkably eclectic tastes and a wide range of sophistication. The lists include titles that range from Alice Walker's *The Color Purple* to Francine Pascal's *My First Love and Other Disasters*. Stephen King appears on all three. In fact, a large number of the same authors appear on all three lists, which in certain respects may indicate the quality of these writers or the effectiveness of the growth of adolescent fiction as a marketable genre since the Second World War.

Along with the romance, teen-problem stories, and adventure books, all three lists include horror fiction. The names are familiar to teachers and can be found in book club lists passed out in schools, on the shelves of supermarket bookracks, and in the young adult sections of Coles or Barnes and Noble. They include such authors as

R. L. Stine, Christopher Pike, Dean Koontz, Jay Bennett, Lois Duncan, V. C. Andrews, Judith St. George, and Joan Lowry Nixon. And of course, Stephen King. I do not regret that my former students read Stephen King and others like him. They may still be avid readers of King's work. They may have moved on to other authors and become lifelong readers. If I have any regret, it is that I did not take the opportunity provided by their reading of horror fiction to move beyond the goals of fluency, appreciation, and comprehension. A new and more explicit reading practice might have brought into question their reading of this genre of writing. If I had taken up a more interventionist role in promoting a critical reading practice in my classroom, I may have been able to assist my students in resisting how texts establish identities for both text participants (what other practices call characters) and for readers.

In her study of middle-class pre-teen girls' reading practices at home and in school, Meredith Rogers Cherland (1994) illustrates how literacy practices work in the construction of subjectivities. Other studies, too, have shown that the literacy practices of girls and boys inform their sense of female and male agency (Fine, 1991; Gilbert & Taylor, 1991; Christian-Smith, 1993). These students' reading helps them participate in and possibly resist the way in which they see gender enacted in other texts and in the everyday world around them. Cherland's study pointed to instances where the girls formed a discourse community in which they took pleasure in imagining themselves in adult roles. Moreover, they were able to imagine choices and alternative ways of encountering the world. They admired text participants that exercised agency in the books, films, and videos that they were engaged with.

In her study, Cherland was surprised by the instances of horror as entertainment in her field notes. She saw this as a "counter-move against the girls' resistant desires for agency" (p. 179). She found that horror formed a kind of continuum of reading from children's texts through that of pre-teens, young adults, and adults in print and other forms—from Nancy Drew mysteries to stalker films. Each new text built on the prior knowledge, creating a practice that interpreted its readers and readers that interpreted the texts.

Running counter, then, to the girls' sense of resistance and agency in these texts is a continuum of narratives of the powerful preying on the powerless, the association of the sexual with the violent, and the construction of the child as victim. Boys are all the more likely to see themselves confirmed as agents, especially in the public world outside the home. These narratives construct male subjectivities that are equally troubling.

In my reading/writing workshop, I was pleased when my students consumed books, talked about them with interest and made connections with other texts and their lives. However, on their own, my students were unable to develop a form of literacy that could move beyond traditional notions of reader response. The contexts of the school, their gender, their families, their social groups had positioned them to read, write, view, listen, speak, and value in an uncritical manner.

I am no longer as comfortable with the kind of naturalized and naturalizing literacy practice that was enacted in my workshop. Beyond encouraging Chris's technical competency to survey and report on the best-liked books in the classroom and eliciting a sharing and discussion of the merits of particular authors and novels, I failed to help these students open up Stephen King texts and other texts to interrogation. We needed a reading practice that allowed us explicitly to talk back to the texts. We failed to ask: What does the text say about the world? What other texts relate to these presuppositions? How does this affect others? What alternate ways are there of rewriting this text?

Practices for Reading Popular Culture: Bobbi's Perspective

Like Jim's, my students read Stephen King novels. As a part of independent studies, one student compared King's work to genre definitions of historic horror or gothic novels. Another read a novel and wrote several research investigations of ideas from the novel about which he had little personal experience: insurance claims, inheritance law, autopsies, and embalming. In retrospect, I see the limitations of these student-proposed projects and my responses to them. These readings were not critical or in any way resistant of the values and perspectives in King's novels. They were independent studies, which precluded socially constructed and socially examined interpretations for both the texts and students' identities in relation to them. Specifically, neither I nor they questioned the pleasures of the text, although we took advantage of the fact that these texts are more appealing to students than many of the texts offered in schools. As Willinsky and Hunniford (1993) suggest: "We must decide if the publishers have bettered us in opening the pleasures of the text for the students. If what they have opened continues to disturb us, how are we to balance without closing that pleasure down?" (p. 91). My answer is the same as Jim's: we want our students to engage in more critical kinds of reading practices.

The horror genre, and King's stories in particular, have a very visual orientation. Perhaps this is the reason they transmediate so readily to film and are so popular with the TV generation. Many young people seem to prefer movies with lots of visual stimulation—action, special visual effects—to talk movies (those which are often called women's movies or, less tactfully, "chick flicks"). These young moviegoers seem to crave what might be constructed as a masculine style of cinematography that eschews emotion for action on screen. Rather than watch text participants cope emotionally with incidents and their consequences, they exhibit a preference for events—action-packed, cataclysmic, cathartic—that call for action-oriented response, not reflection, mediation, and re-mediation. These desires characterize the reading preferences of many adolescents and adults.

This desire for action is often accompanied by an appetite for violence and the emotions of fear, disgust, and fascination that are aroused in the viewer. Gerbner (1994) argues that students can examine critically both the popular media and their own tastes and habits of consumption, albeit in the context of a society that celebrates violence:

> The facts of violence are both celebrated and concealed in the cult of violence that surrounds us. Never was a culture so filled with full-color images of violence as ours is now. Of course, there is blood in fairy tales, gore in mythology, murder in Shakespeare, lurid crimes in the tabloids, and battles and wars in textbooks. Such representations of violence are legitimate cultural expressions, even necessary to balance tragic consequences against deadly compulsions. But the historically defined, individually crafted, and selectively used symbolic violence of heroism, cruelty, or authentic tragedy has been replaced by violence with happy endings produced on the dramatic assembly line. (p. 134)

From a fairly young age, boys in particular watch videos and brag about their effect, or lack thereof, on their emotions. Gitlin (1991) claims, "To be hip is to be inured, and more—to require a steadily increasing boost in the size of the dose required" (p. 247).

While not denying the personal agency inherent in this response, I do, however, want students to consider consciously their relation to the violence they consume in horror fiction, and perhaps its historical predecessors in fiction and historical events. I want them to look at the possible influence of horror genre on the self- and social-construction of themselves as "hip" viewers and/or readers of violence. For example, I engaged my students in investigations of violence by comparing Shakespeare's *Macbeth* and Roman Polanski's film version of the play (1971). Discussions were always lively, focusing on what makes violence gratuitous and on Polanski's ideas about the cathartic effect of viewing violence. I hope these discussions led to a more conscious and critical reading of violence in other films my students see.

Alternative Practices: Promoting Resistant Reading

"'Improper texts,' like horror and series novels, become the symbol of [student] readers' lack of control over one aspect of their schooling as well as a means of achieving some control" (Christian-Smith, p. 4). This is part of the pleasure of texts. Yet, resistance to what has been considered appropriate reading for the young is taken up within what we have argued are unexamined and questionable literacy practices. These practices are associated with a continuum of texts, of all kinds, of which Stephen King's novels are only one remarkably successful example. We have argued that embedded within these practices are issues that should be opened up for students to interrogate. We will try to sketch some descriptions of alternative reading practices at three levels—genre, narrative structures, and language choices—that might validate student resistance and, then, inform it with a critical stance that will empower the student. We realize these three levels leak into one another, as will perhaps be apparent as we present examples.

First, as a genre, King's work could be made an object for analysis. As Gilbert and Taylor (1991) argue, "the process of making an alternative text becomes a richer re-fashioning activity if students have acquired some understanding of the roots of the generic conventions they work with, and some understanding of the way in which such roots are ideologically constructed" (p. 143). As Bobbi suggests, students could investigate the continuum of horror from Nancy Drew to stalker films, adding analyses changes in text participants' agency from one degree to the next, up the continuum, in dealing with whatever is out there in the dark. They can monitor and confront their own acceptance of different forms and degrees of fear and violence.

Further, students can investigate historically the development of the genre, noting its changes, influences, and ideological importance over time. It would be interesting to test various works using Fox's (1994) ideas about right-wing and left-wing horror. According to Fox, in right-wing horror, the threat is external. The text participants resolve this horror by destroying an outside enemy. In left-wing horror, the threat is internal, within a person, a community, one's home, etc. This kind of conflict must be resolved by addressing sources within. In *Firestarter,* King offers as the external enemy to be over-come the supernatural power within a little girl, a power created by a branch of the U.S. government through its experiments.

After much death and destruction, the girl learns to control her abnormal ability. In *Rose Madder* (1995), on the other hand, King depicts right-wing horror in the abusive, vengeful husband who is external to the main text participant's new community and self. Such analyses might lead to critical evaluations of the depictions and rep-resentations of a variety of institutions, groups, attitudes, and val-ues—the ideologies of texts. We feel it is important to state that we are not advocating a particular left (liberal) or right (conservative) reading of King or any other author. But we are suggesting that Fox's categories might be helpful in scaffolding students' reading of this ideology and of this genre, and ultimately, in enabling them to ar-ticulate their own positions in relation to such world views and genres.

Hypermedia composition can also facilitate critical, whole-text reading and intertextual analysis. Students can show in visible form on the computer screen the associations and connections they make as they read, between sections of texts and with other texts. Programs such as *StorySpace* (1994) permit composers to link lexias (portions of text, and digitized images, sounds, and videos) to demonstrate or call attention to similarities and differences between texts or parts of texts, to provide explanations, alternatives, or reflections. These might include quotations from articles or essays, the students' digitized com-mentary, songs on a similar theme, film excerpts that show similar or contrasting viewpoints, and so on, all of which relate to the text or genre under discussion (see Myers, Hammett, & McKillop, in press). Such hypermedia compositions can disrupt the reading at the genre level or at the whole-text level (the reading practice that follows) depending on the focus of the texts that are brought to bear on the primary text.

With a second level of analysis, whole-text narrative structures, students can be asked to foreground the "already said," predicting from titles, plot summaries, situations, and bits of dialogue, and un-veiling how the intertextuality constructs their reading. Alternate endings could be explored to throw light on the text's constructedness, showing how it positions readers and ensures preferred readings. Similarly, additions might be inserted into the text, or a parallel text might be created. Reviews of the text might be read to look for alter-nate interpretations and to see how they are supported. Debates and role plays where text participants are questioned could help open up the text to disrupt what seems given and natural about it.

Deconstruction, or close reading, is another example of whole-text analysis in which students can engage in new ways. Students could look at the traditionally examined aspects of novels (like point-of-view, character portrayal, language use) through the lenses of race, class, and gender, and even sexual orientation to uncover the values conveyed in them. In this sense, students become resistant to the content of the text as well as the way it positions them as readers. For example, in *Rose Madder* there are two narrative threads. One narrative is from the point-of-view of a woman who, because she is being abused, flees her cruel husband; the other expresses the thoughts of the abusive husband. Although the quotation on the book jacket praises Rose as "the most richly portrayed female King's ever created" (Detroit Free Press), Norman overwhelms the reader; his thoughts, in stream-of-consciousness style, are interspersed throughout the third-person narration of Rose's story. As the novel progresses, these interruptions increase in frequency and length. They include comments about "niggers" and "jigs," hate scenes about male prostitutes and other women, and, frequently, highly-sexualized mutilation murders of both women and men. One target manages the haven for battered women that provides Rose with shelter and a new start on life. There are graphic accounts of a spanking, then rape with a tennis racket, anal rapes, and numerous other cruel sexual acts.

These are undeniably the acts, ideas, and values of an evil person, and therefore presumably not admirable or tempting to the reader to imitate or agree with, but they are not overtly challenged or contradicted in the novel. The persons so labeled by Norman are murdered by him in terrible ways (graphically described in the novel), and their deaths are not mourned by either text or reader participants. King creates no space for sympathy.

Discussions between text participants in the novel are often problematic to me, such as a conversation about Mapplethorpe and his photography and death with AIDS—referred to here as the "broomhandle disease" (p. 115). Descriptions of text participants by the narrator, often women associated with the home for women, tend to be negative (p. 110). At one point, the unchallenged statement "men are beasts" (p. 272) is made. I have some negative feeling because the women's shelter is financed and set up by one wealthy woman rather than a community-supported project, although there is a community fund-raising event that figures prominently in the plot. Another problem I have is with the resolution of the conflict. Rose is in the end freed from Norman (although he does not seem to be dead), but it is through supernatural means, not human agency or societal justice.

Students would not produce the same reading/analysis as we have. They would bring their own experiences, subjectivities, and biases to bear on the text they chose to read. Nevertheless, challenged to determine/describe how race, class, gender, and sexuality are portrayed in the text, the students would be equipped to read these in their world. This kind of critical reading examines not only what is assumed and omitted in relation to the conventions of reading, but also what is omitted in relation to values, voices, and viewpoints available or unavailable in the text. Texts are not innocent in relation to these issues, either.

Examining the language of specific passages, the third level of analysis, could involve rewriting by swapping bits of roles, dialogues, and times, unsettling the text's stability of meaning by focusing on linguistic choices. Certain words, paragraphs, descriptions of text participants, settings, and outcomes could be deleted and/or inserted to create gaps in the texts, to expose a range of readings, and to challenge the values associated with them.

For example, students reading King's *Needful Things*, might be invited to inspect those passages where Leland Gaunt's customers are first attracted to the objects of their desire. Students might compare them to those related passages that tell of Gaunt's customers possessing and being possessed by these objects. Clearly, King's text participants embody a wide range of desires involving nostalgia, romance, aesthetics, materialism, elitism, status, and self-worth, to name a few. Rather than accepting the given sense in the text that these desires are demonic or simply psychological, students could look at how they are socially constructed, within King's text and beyond that, in the texts of their own lives.

How King describes Polly Chamber's first meeting with Leland Gaunt is illustrative (*Needful Things*, p. 44). At this level of the text, students may see how violence and sex are conflated at the level of King's use of very commonplace language—"hurting like a bastard," "falling at this man's feet," "pop in here for a quick peek," and "fuel for the fire." These almost trite expressions are contrasted with King's peculiar wording elsewhere. Instead of writing that the ladies of the town will go "raving home" about the charming new proprietor of Needful Things, King writes, "ravening home." This represent a linguistic choice on the author's part. Students can be asked to explore what are the implications of such a choice. How are the women in this novel being positioned by this word? Is it more than a question of style, of King's ability as a wordsmith?

These three different levels of teaching practice challenge texts and acknowledge that students need teachers' assistance to resist the transparency and seeming naturalness of the text. We as teachers have a complex and critical role in this process. The popular texts of our students' existing literacy practices—horror and romance are only two—are significant places to begin reconstructing our teaching toward more productive ends for our students and ourselves. Reading practices that do little more than celebrate students' participation in "improper texts" ultimately are no better than those that restrict their reading to "proper" ones.

Works Cited

Atwell, N. (1987). *In the middle: Writing, reading, and learning with adolescents*. Portsmouth, NH: Boynton/Cook.

Cherland, M. R. (1994). *Private practices: Girls reading fiction and constructing identity*. London; Bristol, PA: Taylor & Francis.

Christian-Smith, L. K. (Ed.). (1993). *Texts of desire: Essays on fiction, femininity, and schooling*. London; Washington, DC: Falmer.

Fine, M. (1991). *Framing dropouts: Notes on the politics of an urban public high school*. Albany, NY: State University of New York Press.

Fox, R. (Ed.). (1994). *Images in language, media, and mind*. Urbana, IL: National Council of Teachers of English.

Gerbner, G. (1994). Instant history, image history: Lessons from the Persian Gulf War. In R. Fox (Ed.), *Images in language, media, and mind*, (pp. 123–140). Urbana, IL: National Council of Teachers of English.

Gilbert, P., & Taylor, S. (1991). *Fashioning the feminine: Girls, popular culture, and schooling*. North Sidney, NSW, Australia: Allen & Unwin.

Gitlin, T. (1991, Spring). On thrills and kills: Sadomasochism in the movies, *Dissent, 38* (2), 245–248.

Myers, J., Hammett, R., & McKillop, A. M. (in press). Opportunities for critical literacy/pedagogy in student constructed hypermedia. In D. Reinking, M. McKenna, & L. Labbo (Eds.), *Literacy for the 21st century: Technological transformations in a post-typographic world*.

Myers, J., Hammett, R., & McKillop, A. M. (in press). Connecting, exploring, and exposing self in hypermedia projects. In M. Gallego & S. Hollingsworth (Eds.), *Challenging a single strand: Perspectives in multiple literacies*.

O'Neill, M. (1990). Molesting the text: Promoting resistant readings. In M. Hayhoe & S. Parker (Eds.), *Reading and response*, (pp. 84–93). Milton Keynes [England]; Philadelphia: Open University Press.

Polanski, R., (Director). (1971). [Film]. *Macbeth*. Playboy Enterprises.

Rief, L. (1992). *Seeking diversity: Language arts with adolescents*. Portsmouth, NH: Heinemann.

StorySpace. (1994). Watertown, MA: Eastgate Systems, Inc.

Thomson, J. (Ed.). (1992). *Reconstructing literature teaching: New essays on the teaching of literature*. Norwood, South Australia: Australian Association for the Teaching of English.

Willinsky, J., & Hunniford, R. M. (1993). Reading the romance younger: The mirrors and fears of preparatory literature. In L. K. Christian-Smith (Ed.), *Texts of desire: Essays on fiction, femininity and schooling* (pp. 87–105). London; Washington, DC: Falmer.

––––––––––

For literature references, please see "Reference List of Literary Works."

9

Because Stories Matter

▼

Authorial Reading and the Threat of Censorship

MICHAEL W. SMITH

> We need to stop pretending that students who are
> force-fed the entire Modern Library will choose to
> read those classics as adults. If students don't read
> for pleasure by the time they graduate, the only
> choice they'll make is which new release to rent at the
> local Blockbuster.
>
> —Kelly Chandler, op-ed piece, *Bangor Daily News*,
> September 23, 1996

> Teaching is about stretching students; challenging
> them to reach, ponder and contemplate great ideas
> beyond the everyday pap of the mass market and
> relate those ideas to their lives. . . . True educators
> don't dumb down the curriculum, they reach the
> students and pull them up.
>
> —Mary Bliss Haskell, letter to the editor in response to Kelly
> Chandler's op-ed piece, *Bangor Daily News*, October 2, 1996

n the 1995 *Banned Book Resource Guide*, Robert Doyle lists the books banned or challenged in 1994–1995. It's a long list, one in which Stephen King's name appears frequently. (Nine of his books were banned or challenged in 1994–1995.) So it makes sense that any book about Stephen King and the place of popular literature in the classroom has to address the issue of censorship. But I'm afraid that those of us who love literature too often simply dismiss the objections of censors, ridiculing them by publicizing what seem to be their silliest and most extreme arguments. (For example, a sample press release in the *Banned Book Resource Guide* highlights attacks on Jane Smiley's Pulitzer Prize-winning *A Thousand Acres* for having "no literary value" and Hans Christian Anderson's *The Little Mermaid* for being "pornographic.")

Such facile dismissals seem to me to ignore the fact that would-be censors and teachers of literature are likely to share a fundamental belief about literature: *Stories matter.* In this chapter, I'll argue that if we accept the premise that stories have the capacity to change readers, then we have to ground our response to censors in a literary theory that allows us to critique readers' misuse of moral stories and to resist authors of immoral ones. I'll argue further that a theory of authorial reading allows that critique and resistance in a way that reader-response theories do not.

Don't Tell Your Mother

When I think about why I became what I became, I think about stories. I think about the formation of my social conscience and how when I was in eighth grade my dad gave me Claude Brown's *Manchild in the Promised Land*, saying, "Read this. It's something you should know about. Don't tell your mother I gave it to you." I think about how Parson Adams from Henry Fielding's *Joseph Andrews* taught me that trusting people is okay even if you might get fooled once in a while and how much that has meant to the way I've worked with students. And on and on.

Of course, my experience is not unique. In *The Call of Stories* (1989) Robert Coles provides a moving testimony to the potential that stories have to affect readers' lives. He quotes one of his students:

> When I have some big moral issue, some question to tackle, I think I try to remember what my folks have said, or I imagine them in my situation—or even more these days I think of [characters in books I've read]. Those folks, they're people for me . . .

they really speak to me—there's a lot of me in them, or vice
versa. I don't know how to put it, but they're voices, and they
help me make choices. I hope when I decide "the big ones"
they'll be in there pitching. (p. 203)

I suspect that many of us became English teachers because we've
had similar experiences.

But I'm afraid sometimes we forget the power that literature
has had in our lives or at least we pretend it doesn't exist when we
respond to censors. In *The Company We Keep*, Wayne Booth explains
how "academic norms of objectivity" (1988, p. 3) keep teachers from
treating seriously the contention that a literary work can be so dangerous that it should not be taught.

However, if we acknowledge the impact that literature has had
on our lives, we are at the same time acknowledging the principle on
which most censorship attempts are grounded: Literature has the
capacity to affect readers' lives. Such an acknowledgment requires
teachers to take seriously attempts to censor what students read. It
also requires teachers to construct a pedagogy that will help students
experience unique and powerful ways of knowing what literature
provides, while at the same time minimizing the potential dangers of
certain texts. Such a pedagogy, I believe, has to be grounded in a
recognition of the importance of authorial reading.

Getting to the Other Side

The notion of authorial reading is based on the recognition that authors have to imagine their audiences in order to do their work (see
Wilhelm, chapter 4, this volume). As literary theorist Peter Rabinowitz
has argued, although the characteristics of every individual reader
are different from those of any other reader, writers have to base their
rhetorical decision not on those differences but rather on what readers have in common (Rabinowitz, 1987, Rabinowitz & Smith, in press).

Let me illustrate Rabinowitz's idea with what may seem to be a
trivial example. My six-year-old daughter currently delights in telling jokes. Or a joke anyway. The beginning is always the same: "Why
did the chicken cross the road?" I say, "I don't know." And she responds with some silly statement like "Because his hair was on fire."
Catherine's joke depends on my familiarity with the form and my
expectation that "To get to the other side," is the response that other
joke-tellers have offered.

When Catherine tells the joke, I play along, as any parent would,
and pretend to be surprised and entertained at her revision of the
punch line. Playing the authorial audience of a literary text is much
the same. It's playing along with the author by provisionally trying

on the values, experiences, habits, familiarity with genres and artistic conventions, and so on that the author seems to be counting on.

This approach is fundamentally different both from what is commonly called reader-response theory and from the New Criticism, the theory whose influence in schools reader-response theory seeks to supplant. Although I don't want to oversimplify, I think that the difference in these three theories can be illustrated by posing the central question of each. The New Criticism would have readers ask: "What does this mean?" Reader-response theory would substitute "What does this mean to me?" The theory of authorial reading, on the other hand, calls upon readers to ask "What would this mean for the audience the author was writing for and how do I feel about that?" This may seem a small difference, but I believe its pedagogical implications are significant.

Alex!

In the first place, a pedagogy built on authorial reading allows teachers to offer a corrective to students who are misusing moral texts so that they may be harmed rather than helped by them. In *A Clockwork Orange,* for example, Alex describes his experience reading the Gospels in his own unique slang, noting that he reads "all about the scourging and the crowning with thorns and then the cross veshch" in order to imagine "helping in and even taking charge of the tolchocking and the nailing in" (Burgess, 1988, p. 92; thanks to Peter Rabinowitz for the example).

The example may be extreme but I don't see how reader-response theory allows any corrective even in this extreme case. Radical subjectivists such as David Bleich argue that "the role of personality in response is the most fundamental fact of criticism" (1975, p. 4). To be fair, Bleich would, I think, use such a response to try to get Alex to face up to his violence. However, his theory would not allow him to go back to the text with Alex and work with him to read it in a different way. After all, Alex is clearly following Bleich's dictum by bringing his personality into his reading.

Even much more moderate voices seem to me to fail in this regard. Rosenblatt (1985) has worked to articulate a balance between "notions of the passive reader acted upon by the text, or the passive text acted upon by the reader" (p. 40). She put it this way in *The Reader, the Text, the Poem: The Transactional Theory of the Literary Work* (1978):

> First, the text is a stimulus, activating elements of the reader's
> past experience—his experience both with literature and with

life. Second, the text serves as a blueprint, a guide for the selecting, rejecting, and ordering of what is being called forth;
the text regulates what should be held in the forefront of the
reader's attention. (p. 11)

The Gospels *are* about scourging and crowning with thorns, so Alex's
mention of them certainly falls within the "blueprint" the text provides. However, if a reader, or more powerfully, a class of readers,
asks, "What would this mean for the audience the author was writing
for and how do I feel about that?" the text can challenge Alex's violence. Alex would have to answer that the authorial audience is expected to be horrified at the violence and moved by Jesus' willingness to endure it. At least for a moment, he'd have to treat that response
seriously. And he'd have to recognize how much his response differs
from that of the authorial audience. I'm not saying that a text, no
matter how powerful, is likely to transform a reader like Alex. I am
saying unless he reads authorially no text has a chance to transform
him.

 Not long after my dad gave me *Manchild in the Promised Land*,
he overheard my telling a friend about "a dirty part." "I'm disappointed in you," he said. I felt terrible because I had violated a covenant. My argument here is that I violated a covenant not only with
my dad but also with the author. Claude Brown didn't expect me to
read about the sexual experiences he had at a young age in order to
be titillated. Rather he expected me, I think, to see them as evidence
of his living in a world that made him grow up much too fast. Authorial reading is what allows me to argue that his book is moral.

Get It?

Not every text is moral, however. Authorial reading also provides a
theory that allows resistance to texts that are immoral. Asking "What
would this mean for the audience the author was writing for and
how do I feel about that?" encourages readers to identify the knowledge, beliefs, behaviors, and so on that authors count on when pro-
ducing their texts. With that identification comes the possibility of
resistance.

 Once again, jokes provide a case in point. In our forthcoming
book, Peter Rabinowitz provides an example by contrasting three
versions of the same joke:

You're sitting at lunch with a colleague who says, "Hey! I just
heard a good one. Why won't a barracuda eat an IRS agent?"
You reply, "I don't know. Why?" Your friend chuckles: "Professional courtesy!" Now imagine the same scenario, but sub-

stituting the word "librarian" for "IRS agent." Now imagine a
third version, substituting the word "Jew."

Rabinowitz argues that this example establishes how authors pre-
sume genre knowledge. Anyone expecting a serious biological answer to the question will surely be disappointed. Moreover, the example establishes how authors are constrained by their audiences.
Even though the second version of the joke is formally correct, it
doesn't work because it presumes an audience that doesn't exist in
this culture, one that presumes that librarians are an especially vicious class of people.

What's most important for my discussion here, however, is
Rabinowitz's analysis of the third version of the joke. He puts it this
way:

> Most interesting: the strongest way to deal seriously with the
> immorality of the third version is to recognize, to begin with,
> the values that it presupposes in its audience. That is, only
> after we understand the audience experience presumed by the
> joke, only after we confront what sort of person would in fact
> have that experience, and only after we recognize such people
> really do have a significant presence in our culture can we
> come to terms with the key difference between the second and
> third versions: the problem with the third is not simply that it
> expresses a personal animosity, but that it taps into a larger
> culture of anti-Semitism. And we can learn something signifi-
> cant about that anti-Semitism and about how to resist it by
> putting ourselves, momentarily, in the position of the autho-
> rial audience. And who knows? Perhaps this experience might
> illuminate the dynamics of the first version—the "safe" one—
> and encourage those of us who laughed at it thoughtlessly to
> reconsider our reaction, and think about the political ramifica-
> tions of such a quick, anti-tax response.

As Rabinowitz explains, what allows us to speak against such
jokes is a recognition of the beliefs upon which they depend. The
same is true for literature. Some literature does employ violence or
sexual content to titillate readers. Such literature ought to be resisted.

By providing an opportunity for resistance, authorial reading
differs radically from New Criticism and from reader-response theories. On the one hand, as Scholes (1985) points out, one influence of
the New Criticism is that it conditions teachers (he includes himself)
"to see the power [to select, shape, and present human experience]
vested in the single literary work, the verbal icon." As a result "we
have been all too ready to fall down and worship such golden calves
so long as we could serve as their priests and priestesses" (p. 20). On
the other hand, reader-response theory, the theory most often offered
as a corrective to an emphasis on the text as verbal icon, casts the

reader as the maker of meaning. Why resist what you have just created? Authorial reading, however, makes resistance possible because it makes authors responsible for the beliefs that they count on in the production of their work. Moreover, authorial reading promotes resistance because it makes authors responsible for the characters they create. (See Rabinowitz & Smith, in press, for a more detailed discussion.)

Peter Rabinowitz (Rabinowitz, 1987; Rabinowitz & Smith, in press) explains that one dimension of doing an authorial reading is playing the narrative audience. He explains that virtually every story depends on readers' pretending while they are reading that the narrative is detailing actual occurrences and that the characters about whom they read are people who deserve their concern. Unless readers provisionally accept the reality of characters, no emotional effect—suspense, terror, sadness, joy—is possible. When readers do play the narrative audience, texts are not simply objects of art and authors the geniuses who created them. Authors are people who have a special kind of power over others, their characters. With that power comes the obligation to use it humanely.

Consider, for example, how one secondary school student began an essay on his favorite book:

> My favorite book that I read was *It*, by Stephen King. The main reason that I liked this book so much was not the horror but the characters of the kids. Throughout the story, I felt like I knew each and every one of the characters and they were my good friends, I even felt that I had a best friend, Stanly Uris and I also thought of Eddie as a close friend as well. I really enjoyed reading about these friends of mine and I never wanted to put the book down, and when the book ended I felt disappointed that there was no more that I could read about these people. If there was enough written I would still be reading and never get tired of it.

Playing the narrative audience as this student does places a special burden on writers of horror, for bad things happen in horror stories. If a reader has these kinds of feelings for the characters of a story, then that reader has the grounds to resist an author who treats the characters cruelly or unfairly.

My point is not that any book in which bad things happen to good people is an immoral book. My point is that asking what those bad things mean for the audience the author was writing for allows a reader to assess its morality. If the audience of a book is expected to be engrossed in the violence the way Alex would be or even to be unmoved by it, I think that there are grounds to resist that book. And it's not just Stephen King who bears a responsibility for his characters. I'd argue that the question of whether *The Adventures of Huckleberry Finn* is racist ought to rest not only on Twain's use of the word "nigger" but also on how he expects the audience to respond to the way Huck and Tom treat Jim through the course of the novel. If Twain expects his audience to ignore Jim's suffering at Tom's hands in the final portion of the book in order to appreciate Twain's comic satire of romance novels, I think there might be grounds to resist that book as well.

The reading and teaching of literature, it seems to me, are moral enterprises. I think we make a mistake when we pretend that they're not. If we recognize that there are immoral texts, then we have to base our teaching on a theory that encourages resistance to those texts. If we recognize that even moral texts can be misused, then we have to base our teaching on a theory that allows those misuses to be challenged. The notion of the importance of authorial reading is such a theory. And in providing the basis for such teaching, it also provides a powerful way to respond to censors who share our belief that stories matter.

Works Cited

Bleich, D. (1975). *Readings and feelings: An introduction to subjective criticism.* Urbana, IL: National Council of Teachers of English.

Booth, W. (1988). *The company we keep: An ethics of fiction.* Berkeley, CA: University of California Press.

Coles, R. (1989). *The call of stories: Teaching and the moral imagination.* Boston: Houghton Mifflin.

Doyle, R. (1995). *Banned books resource guide.* Chicago: American Library Association.

Rabinowitz, P. J. (1987). *Before reading: Narrative conventions and the politics of interpretation.* Ithaca, NY: Cornell University Press.

Rabinowitz, P., & Smith, M. W. (in press). *Resistance and respect in the reading of literature.* New York: Teachers College Press.

Rosenblatt, L. M. (1978). *The reader, the text, the poem: The transactional theory of the literary work.* Carbondale, IL: Southern Illinois University Press.

Rosenblatt, L .M. (1985). The transactional theory of the literary work: Implications for research. In C. R. Cooper (Ed.), *Researching response to literature and the teaching of literature: Points of departure* (pp. 33–53). Norwood, NJ: Ablex.

Scholes, R. (1985). *Textual power: Literary theory and the teaching of English.* New Haven, CT: Yale University Press.

For literature references, please see "Reference List of Literary Works."

Popular Literature

Canon Construction Ahead

KELLY CHANDLER

How many people would write a novel like King does and include all those epigraphs from literature? He's a key mediating figure between mass culture and traditional culture. That split between high and mass culture can be debilitating. We can't just have high culture. But if all we have is a media culture, then we're impoverished. He has allowed us another possibility: to get these two perspectives into dialogue.

—Burton Hatlen, quoted in "UM hails Maine's king of high cult" by Alicia Anstead, *Bangor Daily News*, October 14, 1996

▼ ▼ ▼ ▼ ▼

Walk through the entrance of Waldenbooks, and you're immediately confronted by a six-foot cardboard display containing copies of Stephen King's most recent offerings: *Desperation* and *The Regulators,* the latter written under King's *nom de plume*, Richard Bachman. Buy the two of them together, and you'll get a free book light for your bed. A demonstration model beckons from the top of the display.

But you're not here to purchase pap fiction. You want to buy a copy of Henry James's *Portrait of a Lady* so you can read it before you see the new movie version. It's always good to revisit a classic before critiquing its translation into film. You start searching for the J's in the aisle closest to the door, but there's no "James." That seems odd, until you realize that you're looking in Fiction. This must be one of those stores with a separate section for Classics. Sometimes they call it Literature.

Sure enough, there's *Portrait of a Lady,* sandwiched between titles by Washington Irving and James Joyce. Picking up a copy, you head to the register. You brush past the King display on your way out the door. You don't stop.

Some English teachers' brains seem to be divided in the same way as those chain bookstores: Classics and Fiction. One hemisphere contains teachable books, the other doesn't—and never the twain shall meet. For these teachers, a popular writer like Stephen King—a "bestsellasaurus," as King himself has put it—is so obviously unteachable as to go unnoticed during bookstore visits. (Unless, of course, the mass market promotions make it hard to walk around the store.)

English teachers aren't the only ones who make this distinction between popular fiction and literature. Politicians rail from the stump about the lowering of academic standards in our universities, professors lament the closing of the American mind, and subway travelers furtively read their Danielle Steel novels with the covers folded over. They, too, divide the literary world into two camps.

Nor is the division of fiction a new distinction. In the 1880s, Henry James dismissed the female writers whose popular fiction competed with his work by calling them "scribbling women." Although Jack London's work sold well, the critics called it "crude and uneven," terms that sound a lot like modern-day criticisms of Stephen King. As literature professor Carroll Terrell (1990) has said, the "idea that a popular writer can't be a real artist or a best seller can't be literature is a mind-set many years in the making" (p. 69).

Focusing on the underrepresentation of women and minority authors, recent debates about the literary canon have often been heated, politicized, and polarized. Because women and members of ethnic minorities were historically denied access to literacy, many of the proposed new texts are contemporary ones, raising questions for traditionalists about potential "dilution" of the canon. Book and article titles such as "Attentive Reading in the Age of Canon Clamor" (Howland, 1995), "Canon Fodder" (Burke, 1993), and *Battle of the Books: The Curriculum Debate in America* (Atlas, 1992) demonstrate the combative nature of the disputes.

Perhaps because of this shrillness, it may seem to some people like we've arrived at some sort of unprecedented crisis in intellectual history. This assumption is unfounded. As Stanford professor Herbert Lindenberger (1990) points out, tidal changes in the literary canon have occurred in various settings throughout history, often during times of political and intellectual shifting—from Greece in the third century B.C. to Germany in the mid-nineteenth century; from first-century Judea to twentieth-century America. In fact, it's this longstanding tradition of debate—both about what constitutes good literature and about what literature should be taught in schools— that I intend to address in this chapter. Contrary to conventional wisdom, the literary canon has not remained static over hundreds of years. Instead, its revision has been a constant, recurring process, with important implications for school curricula.

I believe that tracing these shifts over time can illuminate our current conversations about the place of popular literature, such as Stephen King's works in our high school classrooms. Knowing the history of the literary canon and of our own profession as English teachers can help us to think more critically about the choices we make today and the canon we shape for tomorrow.

More Arbitrary than Ordained: How Authors Find a Place in the Canon

Knowing more about the history of the canon often forces us to question long-held assumptions about certain authors. Take the case of Shakespeare, the author considered by many teachers to be the linchpin of Western literature. Yale critic Harold Bloom (1994) goes so far as to claim that "Shakespeare *is* the secular canon. . . . forerunners and legatees alike are defined by him alone for canonical purposes" (p. 24). Bloom's attitudes seem to be reflected in American secondary schools, where Shakespeare's plays are taught more frequently than the work of any author. According to a nationwide study in 1988, the most commonly required text in the country was *Romeo and Juliet*, used in 90 percent of schools, with second-place *Macbeth* required by 81 percent of the schools surveyed (Applebee, 1993, p. 71).

In fact, Shakespeare's position in our schools is so entrenched that it is hardly possible to imagine a time when his works were not taught. Yet prior to the 1870s, Shakespeare was not generally part of the school reading experiences of most Americans. When the plays were taught, they often caused controversy, as Applebee (1974) reports: "In 1828, a Boston teacher was dismissed for reading to his class from one of Shakespeare's plays, and even at the college level, Oberlin refused to allow Shakespeare to be taught in mixed classes" until the latter part of the century (p. 22).

The same charges of vulgarity recently leveled at Stephen King's work were also hurled at Shakespeare in the *New England Journal of Education* as late as 1893:

> All honor to the modest and sensible youths and maidens of the Oakland High School who revolted against studying an unexpurgated edition of *Hamlet!* The indelicacies of *Hamlet* in the complete edition are brutal. They are more than indelicacies, they are indecencies. (Applebee, 1974, p. 22)

Please do not misunderstand my purpose here. By citing these examples, I do not mean to argue against the teaching of Shakespeare, nor even to attack his canonical status. Personally, I have chosen to teach Shakespeare. Although my 10th graders have often approached his work with trepidation, very few of them have finished *Taming of the Shrew* without enjoying it and learning a great deal from it. It needs to be clear, though, that teachers who don't share my belief aren't the first people in American history to break the chain. I think we need a little healthy skepticism about the things we consider most "permanent" in our profession.

And potential permanence has often been one of the most important criteria for determining what literature will be read in schools. Many teachers reject popular fiction because they want to use literature that will pass the test of time. History shows us, however, that the literary community has not always been successful at predicting which texts will endure.

Here's a notable example: In 1929, American critics voted on the most outstanding contemporary novelists, and the results, divided into ten groups of distinction, were published in *English Journal*. Willa Cather and Edith Wharton, whose work remains widely taught in secondary schools, reigned alone in the first group. The second and third tiers included luminaries such as Theodore Dreiser, Sinclair Lewis, and Thornton Wilder, as well as some lesser names like James Branch Cabell, Glenway Wescott, and Joseph Hergesheimer. Perhaps most surprising to today's teachers, however, is the relegation of F. Scott Fitzgerald to the fifth group (Hook, 1979, p. 80).

More than a quaint story, this anecdote demonstrates the futility of basing our curricular choices on predictions about future classics. I'm not sure that English teachers even *need* to be gazing into that crystal ball. If a group of students in the 1930s had an enriching intellectual experience with Hergesheimer's *Balisand,* should we really question the wisdom of that choice, simply because the literary canon has left Hergesheimer behind?

Other examples from literary history reinforce this idea that the difference between popular fiction and the classics is not always as clear as some critics and chain bookstores suggest. Terrell (1990) has written about the "historical irony" that

> one generation's most popular writers become a future generation's classics: Sir Walter Scott, Jane Austen, and Charles Dickens were bestsellers in their days, but most Oxford and Cambridge dons frowned upon their work because they lacked what Matthew Arnold called "high seriousness." But in the twentieth century, these novelists . . . have been considered classics. (pp. 10–11)

Stephen King's decision to serialize his recent novel *The Green Mile* was condemned by many as a commercial ploy. But King is hardly the first writer of complicated, many-charactered novels to be disparaged for such a publishing decision. He's also not the first author to appeal to a wide-ranging audience in terms of education or socioeconomic status.

In England during the 1830s, Charles Dickens began a phenomenon by printing his first novel in serial form—considered by critics of the time to be a low, cheap type of publication. All of his subsequent novels appeared in the same fashion. *The Pickwick Papers* was so popular that "The poor clubbed their farthings to purchase or rent each installment, sometimes going to the house or shop of some literate person to have it read aloud; the middle class and wealthy bought the flimsily bound paper copies into their libraries, to mingle with the rich leather bindings of more respectable works less often consulted." Nineteenth-century schoolmasters would probably have been horrified at the suggestion that Dickens's work replace the study of rhetoric and grammar in schools. More than a hundred and fifty years later, Dickens is the third most-commonly read author in American public high schools, following Shakespeare and Steinbeck (Applebee, 1993, p. 66).

Two more examples of critical shifts can be drawn from anti-slavery literature in the United States. When they were published in the mid-19th century, *Narrative of the Life of Frederick Douglass* and *Uncle Tom's Cabin* by Harriet Beecher Stowe were widely read and stirred up a great deal of sentiment for abolition. Treated as popular political tracts, they were not, however, critically acclaimed. For more than a century, both works were buried in large libraries; neither was taught in schools. The civil rights movement of the 1960s and the women's movement of the 1970s sparked a great deal of revisionist literary scholarship, helping both texts to be "rediscovered." By the late 1980s, when I majored in American literature at Harvard, both books were considered to be literary classics.

All of these examples highlight the ambivalence of teachers toward popular literature in its own time. Bonnie Sunstein (1994) writes about the student whose former English teacher told him that a book cannot be considered a classic "unless it has had enough time to grow mold on the shelf," a process requiring about 150 years in that particular teacher's estimation (p. 48). Under this system, no one would teach Stephen King's work until at least 2124.

Although few of us really use such arbitrary criteria, many teachers do treat literature like fine wine that needs to age before it can be fully enjoyed. The trouble with this metaphor is that our students are not always as eager to be connoisseurs. They are more interested in the literary equivalent of Jolt Cola, vintage 1997. The other trouble is that texts, unlike wine, do not change over time. Only their critical reception and their readers do.

The History of the Canon in American Secondary Schools

Although the teaching of literature is considered by many to be the most traditional component of the secondary English curriculum, it has not always held this central place. Literacy historian Arthur Applebee (1974) reminds us of the crucial role of the university in shaping the literature curriculum:

> In 1800 formal instruction in literature was almost unknown; by 1865 it had made its way into the curriculum as a handmaiden to other studies [grammar, elocution, history, philology]; by 1900 literature was almost universally offered as an important study in its own right. College entrance requirements were the moving force. (p. 30)

In 1874, Harvard began the practice, soon widely adopted by most other colleges, of issuing a standard booklist on which entering students could expect to be tested. Previous to that, the entrance examinations had required students to do little more with literature than parse it or read it aloud. Subsequently, "any student who wanted to get into Harvard had to study these works," writes NCTE chronicler J. N. Hook (1979), "so high schools began requiring them of *all* students" (p. 8). Unfortunately, many of the colleges required different titles, which made it nearly impossible for teachers to prepare students adequately for all of the different examinations.

This confusion was cleared up in 1892–1894 by the Committee of Ten, a group chaired by Harvard president Charles Eliot and charged by the National Education Association with examining secondary school curriculum in nine subject areas. The committee's report recommended the unification of the previously splintered English program, and soon after it was filed, standard reading lists—the canon of the day—were established by the National Conference on Uniform Entrance Requirements in English. Within five years, these lists dictated curriculum in most secondary schools.

But, as Gere and her colleagues report, "Not all teachers found the Committee of Ten's work helpful, however. Some secondary teachers noted that they had been virtually excluded from the process of curriculum development; others wondered whether the texts on the Uniform Lists were appropriate for their students" (1992, p. 7). By 1911, opposition to the booklists provided the spark that led to the founding of the National Council of Teachers of English, arguably the most influential professional organization for English teachers. Then, as now, NCTE members argued for the importance of relevance and student interest in selecting curriculum material. Then, as now, they cautioned against creating a single set of expectations for all students.

Today, colleges no longer test entering freshmen on *The Vicar of Wakefield*. Texts like Burke's *Speech on Conciliation with the Colonies*, Macaulay's *Essay on Addison*, and Lowell's *Vision of Sir Launful* have long since vanished from the high school English curriculum (Applebee, 1974, p. 50). Still, many of the titles on the Uniform Lists continue to be taught in schools a century later, and some of the issues from NCTE's inaugural meeting—including the nature of the literary canon and the influence of the university on secondary curriculum—are still being discussed at conference sessions and in the pages of *English Journal*.

For me, this history is a good reminder of the constructed nature of the canon we teachers have inherited. If the Committee of Ten had not convened, our conception of appropriate literary texts might be less narrow. If NCTE had not been founded, high school curricula might be dictated more directly by colleges and universities. Each of these events, and scores of others, has contributed over time to the definition of the literary tradition we teach in schools.

Why Consider Popular Literature?

This fall at a conference I heard author Edwidge Danticat suggest, half jokingly, half seriously, that the canon might be defined by the books in the English department closet that are still bound and still in groups. Everyone in the audience chuckled at the time, including me, but the comment has stayed with me. I wonder if our choices are indeed sometimes that arbitrary.

Booklist columnist Hazel Rochman (1996) writes about a more systematic process of canon-making in her account of an advisory committee faced with the task of recommending 6,000 titles for a high school library catalog. In the committee meeting, there was considerable debate about whether to nix *Silas Marner*, a book which Rochman calls a "pious classic" (p. 114). At the end of her column, she includes a little dig about the novel being "on the edge" of exclusion: "Somebody, please, just one good push should do it" (p. 115).

Maybe Rochman is right. Maybe *Silas Marner* doesn't resonate for our students anymore, and it should stay on the shelf. I certainly didn't want to teach it to a class of 10th graders, and I never saw one of them read it as an independent choice. But there were people on the committee with Rochman who felt that this book still speaks to today's teenagers. Maybe it does.

In the long run, *Silas Marner* probably doesn't matter any more than the next 19th-century classic. I'm not arguing here for the inclusion or exclusion of any particular book—or for that matter, any particular author—from someone else's syllabus. What I am arguing for is a more critical stance toward selection and for better reasons supporting our choices than "It's a classic," or "It's in the book closet."

As far as I'm concerned, it's no more excusable to *exclude* an author thoughtlessly from our curriculum than it is to *include* one for equally arbitrary reasons. And this is exactly what many teachers seem to have done with an entire body of popular literature. It is especially true of Stephen King. The more popular he has become in the world at large, the more vigilant some teachers seem to be about keeping him out of the classroom.

Survey data from the Reading Stephen King Conference indicates that some teachers exclude King from the curriculum without having read many (or sometimes any) of his books. In fact, for several respondents, refusing to read King seemed like a point of honor, a figurative finger in the dike between popular culture and the classroom. One disdainful teacher returned the survey with the following comments, even though he did not plan to come to the conference:

> I do not like [King's] books but envy his income. . . . His command of the language is sophomoric, as is his manipulative style. His imagery is banal and his sentence 'structure' nonexistent.

This teacher had read only two books by Stephen King, one of them ten years ago and the other twenty years ago.

I think we teachers need to quit taking the literary high ground. Trying to keep out the pernicious effects of popular culture is a losing battle. This does not mean that we give up teaching the classics or that we organize our courses around what students already know and have experienced, but rather that we acknowledge that the membrane between high culture and popular culture is, in many cases, a permeable one. As Vito Perrone (1991) argues, good teachers

> don't close the curriculum to the world that their students listen to and look at every day outside school. It is helpful for teachers to know as much as they can about the neighborhoods their students come from, what they encounter on the street, what the sounds and smells are, what is watched on television and what the popular music is. (p. 16)

I would add "what the popular literature is" to Perrone's list, including popular literature by King. In an era when so many educators complain about how little students read, it seems senseless, even wasteful, to ignore an author whose work affects adolescents so strongly. Yet that is exactly what many scholars and teachers have done, rationalizing King's enormous popularity as the misguided adulation of readers who don't know any better.

Note, for example, how Applebee (1996) dismisses King's work and other pieces of popular fiction with the following:

> [When these books] are brought into the classroom, however (as they sometimes are to encourage "reluctant" readers or "motivate" uninterested students), there may be little there to sustain conversation. Instruction is then likely to deteriorate into vocabulary development and reading practice, because there is little else to do with the text. Teachers sometimes reach out to the mediocre and the second rate in the hope of responding directly to student interests, only to grow frustrated when they and their classes discover how little there may be to say about it. (p. 55)

Some teachers may indeed have experienced this frustration when teaching literature by King or other popular authors. I have not. Nor have Kim Campbell, Michael Collings, John Skretta, or Mark Fabrizi (see chapters 5, 11, 12, and 13, this volume). Contrary to Applebee's gloomy pronouncement, the teenagers with whom I have discussed

King's work have had diverse, insightful, and provocative things to say about it.

Perhaps this is true because the list of books that I consider appropriate for whole-class study with my students is a short and carefully chosen one. It includes *Different Seasons* (my personal favorite), *The Stand, Pet Sematary*, and *The Shining*. I think that's as it should be. For me, suggesting that English teachers consider popular fiction like King's an option on the curricular menu isn't the same as recommending a steady diet of it.

I don't suggest these four books for any of the reasons most commonly cited for using Stephen King's work in the classroom:

- because it's better than kids reading nothing
- because you can use it for a stepping stone to more classic texts
- because it allows discussion about contemporary issues

These reasons are probably valid for some teachers, but they're not enough for me. I offer these books as possibilities because I consider them to be literature of value. The themes are complex, the language is imaginative, and the characters are sharply defined. To use Jonathan Howland's (1995) criteria for canonical literature, these books "demand work," and the "work they demand [is] satisfying and fruitful" (p. 38). As Michael Collings puts it, they "repay the reader/critic with new insights into life, society, literature, and art. [They are] unique artifacts of the movement of American life in the final quarter of the twentieth century, chronicled by an unblinking and highly perceptive eye" (Beahm, 1995, p. 181).

I don't feel this way about everything that King has written, I will admit. But I don't feel this way about everything Charles Dickens or John Steinbeck has written, either. Although I'm well aware of the literary tradition in which I work, I'm making my choices year by year, class by class, text by text . . . no matter where the text is shelved in the nearby bookstore.

Ultimately, I believe that acknowledging the constructed, changing nature of the literary canon does not have to mean overthrowing it. It means that as teachers we need to be more thoughtful and deliberate about the books we choose to teach. It means that we need to throw out a wider net in making those choices. Most important, it means that we need to recognize that as teachers of literature we are not merely inheritors of our cultural tradition, but potential creators of it as well.

Works Cited

Applebee, A. N. (1974). *Tradition and reform in the teaching of English: A history*. Urbana, IL: National Council of Teachers of English.

Applebee, A. N. (1993). *Literature in the secondary school: Studies of curriculum and instruction in the United States*. Urbana, IL: National Council of Teachers of English.

Applebee, A. N. (1996). *Curriculum as conversation: Transforming traditions of teaching and learning*. Chicago: University of Chicago Press.

Atlas, J. (1992). *Battle of the books: The curriculum debate in America*. New York: Norton.

Beahm, G. (1995). *The Stephen King companion*. Kansas City, MO: Andrews and McMeel.

Bloom, H. (1994). *The Western canon: The books and school of the ages*. New York: Harcourt Brace.

Burke, J. (1993). Canon fodder. *English Journal, 82* (2), 56–59.

Gere, A. R., Fairbanks, C., Howes, A., Roop, L., & Schaafsma, D. (1992). *Language and reflection: An integrated approach to teaching English*. New York: Macmillan.

Hook, J. N. (1979). *A long way together: A personal view of NCTE's first sixty-seven years*. Urbana, IL: National Council of Teachers of English.

Howland, J. (1995). Attentive reading in the age of canon clamor. *English Journal, 84* (3), 35–38.

Lindenberger, H. (1990). *The history in literature: On value, genre, institutions*. New York: Columbia University Press.

Perrone, V. (1991). *A letter to teachers: Reflections on schooling and the art of teaching*. San Francisco: Jossey-Bass.

Rochman, H. (1996, September 1). YA talk: Loose canon. *The Booklist 9* (1), pp. 114–115.

Sunstein, B. S. (1994). Attempting a graceful waltz on a teeter-totter: The canon and English methods courses. *English Journal, 83* (8), 47–54.

Terrell, C. F. (1990). *Stephen King: Man and artist*. Orono, ME: Northern Lights.

For literature references, please see "Reference List of Literary Works."

11

King in the Classroom

MICHAEL R. COLLINGS

Most of the time, I think that trapped inside of King is one of the finest writers of our time. . . I think he has done an almost unthinkable thing; he has not narrowed down, but rather has expanded the definition of what he is as a writer, to the point where he can say, as no one else can, that he has tried everything and made it work in some sense.

—A. J. Budrys

One afternoon a few years ago, my then-teenage second son came home from high school chuckling. Given the difficulties he had had in high school and his near-hatred for the entire experience of high school, that chuckle in itself constituted an odd enough circumstance to merit my remembering it (even now that he is a highly successful college sophomore). But the reason for his laughter that day turned out to be even more intriguing than the fact of it, particularly as it related directly to my own efforts over the past fifteen years in writing science fiction, fantasy, and horror criticism.

His junior English class, he informed our family, was preparing to face the great unmentionable, the horror of the year—the dreaded TERM PAPER. His teacher had dutifully handed out a long list of acceptable topics, all based on American authors. The students were required to submit proposals for a paper that would discuss at least three works by a single author, or one work each by three authors, combining the students' perceptions with relevant outside sources.

During the discussion, one student noted that his favorite author, Stephen King, had not been included on the list.

No, the teacher answered solemnly, King had not been included.

Another student noted that several other contemporary popular writers were also missing from the list, and asked why.

In response the teacher said that such writers were only of interest to readers unable to handle the more sophisticated expression of the "classics."

"In other words," the second student shot back, defending himself and his friends who read King and other popular writers, "we read them because we're too stupid to understand the classics?"

"Uh, no," the teacher answered, obviously backpedaling. She continued to talk in generalities about the lack of sophistication in contemporary popular writers, noting in passing that most students hadn't even considered writing a paper on King until a few years before, when a professor from Pepperdine began publishing a flurry of books about him.

At this point, my son sat up and began paying more attention.

Then, the teacher continued, the professor made things worse by holding literary discussion groups at the local library, actually talking with groups of high school students about King and his works as if they had literary merit.

Now my son was *really* paying attention, wondering if he should raise his hand and say, "That was my father," or wait it out and see what else the teacher would say. He decided to wait it out.

By the end of the teacher's comments, my son had discovered that in spite of such distinctly peculiar behavior (fortunately isolated) in a college professor, there really wasn't enough criticism on Stephen King or other writers like him to merit including them on the list of possibilities for the TERM PAPER.

End of discussion.

The High School Literature Curriculum

When my son reported this experience—grinning the whole time and (I'm sure) wondering how I would take this implied slur on my reputation (such as it was)—I was struck again by the short-sightedness of those academic establishments that continue to exclude Stephen King, Dean R. Koontz, and others like them from the lists of "approved" materials.

While Hawthorne's *The Scarlet Letter,* Melville's *Moby Dick,* and Dickens' *A Tale of Two Cities* are certainly central literary achievements in our culture, even fascinating topics for further research and discussion by adult readers, I am even less convinced now than I was as a high school student that they are necessarily appropriate for 9th-grade students, sophomores, and juniors in high school—many of whom are barely beyond being functionally literate, many of whom lack even the barest backgrounds or historical perspectives for assessing such novels, and most of whom are explicitly more interested in Poe, Bradbury, and King than in Hawthorne, Melville, and Dickens. Yet mandated curricula force instructors to force students to read works that probably even most teachers would be unlikely to read for pleasure.

On the other hand, the alternative approach seems to be requiring texts that are themselves demonstrably less literary artifacts than pedantic exercises in political correctness, sociological conditioning, and artificially induced diversity-for-the-sake-of-diversity. Either way, established English and literature programs often simply ignore the fact that students like to read (and, with less effectiveness, to watch) stories by Stephen King.

There are, of course, strong arguments against allowing King into high school curricula, even as tangentially as letting students use his works as the basis for an out-of-class term paper. His writing is admittedly violent. It is often gross and explicit, both sexually and linguistically. It is often fantastic, but his fantasy is tinged with darkness and seriousness. It is often devastatingly critical of traditional, accepted institutions, including home, family, politics, and education.

But students *read* him. Based on my experiences leading discussion groups about his books, adolescent readers often *devour* his books, memorize his books, know more about what he has written than I do, even after a decade of reasonably intense scrutiny on my part.

Then they are told explicitly by teachers that King is too unsophisticated, too clumsy, too peripheral to what is really important in the universe, too *common* for students to waste their time on—and implicitly that his student readers are themselves too unsophisticated, too clumsy, too peripheral, too *common* to merit attention. By contrast, it would seem that teachers would welcome the opportunity to confront a writer who perhaps more than any other is molding the imaginations and minds of contemporary adolescents. After all, if so many students read him, and he is so awful, so damaging to the social fabric, so utterly without redeeming social value, what could be more important than to discover what draws young readers to him and to try to "cure" them of their obsession with his works?

To refer back to my son's experience, the teacher stated to the class that anyone who read more than two or three King novels had to be warped, perverted, or highly disturbed. At that point my son couldn't help laughing out loud. He was tempted to put the teacher even more on the spot by noting that he (my son) had read about thirty King novels and that his father had read virtually *everything* that King had published. If two or three relegated a reader to warpdom, where would thirty, forty, or fifty books put someone? Perhaps wisely, my son restrained his impulse, and the teacher was free to continue her defense of the status quo reading list.

No, King is not sufficiently elevated, not sufficiently elegant, not sufficiently a part of the teachers' own university backgrounds (implying that they might actually have to read and study his books themselves in order to lecture to classes)—and thus he is simply inappropriate as the subject for a research project.

And to prove their point, they pound the final nail into the coffin of any would-be term-paperist: *There's just not enough criticism written about him to make the effort worthwhile.* Again and again I have heard this comment and been stunned at the ignorance it betrays. Certainly for many science fiction, fantasy, and horror writers, the claim is at least partially warranted. Some of the finest writers in these genres have been ignored by traditional critics and scholars to the point that accurate bibliographies are not even available for many, if not most. This is in spite of the valiant efforts of publishers like the late Ted Dikty of Starmont House and his series editor, Roger Schlobin, who between the two of them saw to the publication of several dozen introductory monographs; or Rob Reginald at Borgo

Press, with his continuing series of definitive bibliographies. In spite of the work of dozens of scholars and critics approaching such monumental tasks as the lifeworks of Isaac Asimov, Robert Heinlein, and others, it is still too easy for teachers to issue lists of term-paper topics that ignore some of the most popular and influential writers of our times. In many cases, they are right; there is *not* sufficient secondary materials to provide students with intensive exercise in reading, assimilating, and integrating outside materials into their papers.

But to make that claim for Stephen King?

I glance at my bookshelf and see a 500-page tome that represents my work on a Stephen King bibliography, published in January 1996 by Borgo Press, after six years of concentrated work compiling, revising, and updating . . . and I wonder. Ready to be augmented by hundreds more items within a year of its publication, the book nevertheless includes over 5,000 entries, both primary and secondary, including titles of several dozen scholarly or critical books exclusively about King (a number of them from prestigious university presses), more dozens of articles in scholarly and popular journals and magazines, and hundreds of reviews ranging from the *New York Times Book Review* to localized fan presses.

But this, apparently, does not represent a sufficient body of secondary materials to allow high school students adequate exercise in the fine and ancient art of literary research.

Granted, not all of the criticism and scholarship available on King is first-class. I think of one article that discovers intricately drawn Vietnam allegories in a King story, when King himself has stated publicly that he sees (or intended) no such subtext himself. Or I recall one critic who, after publishing three very expensive specialty editions of interviews and criticism, notes condescendingly that he considers King little more than a literary hack (although presumably a source of no little income).

Nevertheless, it seems important to recognize that much of the criticism is solid and, more important yet, that horror writers are an intrinsic and essential part of late 20th-century American culture. Writers such as Stephen King, Dean R. Koontz, Robert McCammon, Dan Simmons, and others have written works that transcend narrow genre classifications. They have grappled with the fundamental social problems we face today, particularly as we approach what Koontz has repeatedly referred to as the climax of the "pre-millennial cotillion." They have explored these issues through the metaphor of the monstrous and the horrific, because AIDS, molestation, homelessness, physical and psychological abuse, racism, sexism, and other frightening -*isms* of various sorts are indeed monstrous and horrific.

These writers have described *us* in the clearest and broadest of terms—and not always pessimistically or nihilistically, curiously enough, but often with an undercurrent of true hope. On the surface, their images may be frightening, but then so is our world. The worldwide plague that wipes out most of humanity in King's *The Stand* is only a few degrees beyond the plagues—diseases, social unrest, political threats—that we presently face. The "pre-millennial cotillion" that Koontz depicts graphically in *Dragon Tears* and elsewhere is not just a figment of his imagination. The fictional disintegration of society in McCammon's *Swan Song, Mine,* or *Stinger* reflects real disintegrations we see around us. These writers' unique visions of what it is to live here, to live now, is captured in these and other novels and stories in ways that no alternate form can legitimately duplicate.

And our children read those novels and stories.

Our children see the world in terms of the visions these novels and stories create.

Our children need to understand more completely what it is that these writers are struggling to achieve.

"Classic" Texts and Contemporary Icons

This means—for me, at least—that books of this sort are not only appropriate subjects for exploration, but may in their own way outweigh the merits of a Hawthorne, or a Melville, or a Dickens—for the adolescent audience at least. Classics endure because they speak to generation after generation of new readers, stimulating new levels of thinking, presenting as new old images that have penetrated to the core of human motivation for generations, for centuries, for millennia. The ancient epic of *Gilgamesh* has as much power to transfix and entrance now as it had when it was inscribed on clay tablets; Milton's *Paradise Lost* constantly opens itself to new readers of each succeeding generation, presenting them with age-old challenges and contemporary debates.

Yet many of these works require mediation, either directly or indirectly, for the student reader. It is possible, but unlikely, that the sparse narrative of *Gilgamesh* will enthrall a student who has as yet had no contact with myth, with epic theory and history, with the principles and problems of oral transmission, with the importance of poetry in archaic civilizations. *Paradise Lost* requires footnotes for most readers, extensive notes for many, and wholesale paraphrase for some. Even in his own time, Milton was aware that he was writing for a "fit audience, though few," and the difficulties inherent in his poem have not diminished with time.

Consequently, many of the books required for literature and composition courses in high schools—and perhaps well into college—may be valuable in and of themselves, but are often so extraordinary in one form or another that students frequently resist them. Students may not understand the language, the authors' concerns, the social and cultural heritages which elicited the stories. And without those backgrounds, much of the value of the book may be overlooked, ignored, or lost.

Contemporary texts, on the other hand, are *not* classics; in some senses it is impossible for them to be considered "classic" since by definition (one definition at least) the term requires a consensus of valuation over time by society at large. We acknowledge Milton's greatness because his own contemporaries acknowledged it, for example, and because their judgment was confirmed by influential minds of succeeding generations. By that standard, it is impossible for King to be a "classic" writer—yet.

On the other hand, there is an immediacy in King's storytelling—and in Koontz's, McCammon's, and others—that is itself almost compelling as the applicability of a "classic" text. Indeed, King's concern for taking the pulse of our times occasionally leads him into weakening his storytelling for the sake of emphasizing a social or political problem, as in *Gerald's Game* and to a lesser extent in *Dolores Claiborne* or *Rose Madder*. Yet the very elements that argue against these works as great novels open them to discussions as icons of our time, our place, our world.

Works by King as Teachable Texts

Having said all of this, having defended King's works as appropriate texts in generalities, it might be useful to consider for a moment several specific works that have lent themselves well to class study. Here I must refer not to my son's experiences in his high school class or to my opportunities to assess King in high school discussion groups, but rather to my own discoveries in using King's novels in freshman-level college courses. Over the past years, several texts have emerged as highly teachable, both as source texts for ideas and as foci for literary analysis and discussion.

First, and perhaps most accessibly, *The Shining* invites students to enter into a conscious game of literary allusion, while at the same time providing a concentrated expression of character, landscape, plot, and theme. More than in any of his other major novels, King allows literature in *The Shining* to provide an important subtexture to the novel, with references to Peter Straub and Victoria Holt, to Arthur Miller and E. L. Doctorow, to Emily Dickinson, Horace Walpole, Johnson, Boswell, Frank Norris, and Martin Luther King, Jr. In each instance, unraveling the allusion leads to additional understanding of what Stephen King wants to say in *his* novel, as well as an opportunity for students to discover for themselves the relationship between current text and literary heritage, the interplay between the contemporary novelist and all that has entered into his cultural and social awareness. To this extent, *The Shining* comes closest to a universalizing expansion while still retaining the specificity that allows readers to identify with characters—to what is called in classical studies a "concrete universal."

At a different level, *The Stand* provides equal opportunities for student development, less literary in one sense, more literary in another. *The Stand*, especially in the restored version, reflects Stephen King's most accomplished, completed attempt at a modern epic (ignoring the incomplete "Dark Tower" series, which promises to become King's single most ambitious experiment in a number of genres, including epic). Sheer length certainly qualifies either version of *The Stand* as "epical," in whatever diluted sense of the word remains current. The geographical and cultural scope of the novel similarly provides an "epic" sense. But beyond these relatively debased usages of an ancient and powerful word, the novel taps into a true epic impulse, the same impulse toward telling a story—if not *the* story— that impelled epics like *The Iliad, The Odyssey, The Aeneid, The Faerie Queene,* and *Paradise Lost.*

There are differences, to be sure. Most obvious of all, King's epic is not in verse; but since the middle of the 18th century, the epic impulse has consistently—in fact, increasingly—revealed itself in prose, which may now be considered the primary mode of artistic verbal communication in the same way that poetry was the primary mode for Homer, Virgil, Spenser, and Milton. But if one grants the possibility of a prose epic, *The Stand* meets many of the traditional criteria that go back as far as classical epic: catalogues of heroes, along with an emphasis on their weaponry; epic councils; supernatural intrusions, both divine and demonic; warring nations and rival gods; and the sense of cultures in collision. In writing *The Stand*, King approaches the nearly impossible task of composing an epic on America in the final decades of the 20th century, with its clash between technology and nature, science and society, a desire for order and a sense of incipient chaos. He challenges and tests our assumptions about political democracy, about our ability to control the devices we have created, about our need for religion—whether light or dark. And in doing so, King provides a text that students can use as a springboard for serious inquiry and exploration.

A final approach that has proven valuable is simply to use King's most *recent* novel as a text. I first experimented with this approach during a summer session the year that *It* appeared. While the text is long, there was sufficient time during two-hour blocks each day to discuss backgrounds and to monitor the students' progress through the novel. The true challenge of the novel, however, came in the assignment: to write a twenty-page discussion/analysis of the novel. Since, other than a handful of reviews, no scholarly or critical articles had yet been published about the novel, students had to develop their own ideas and interpretations based primarily on their reading of the text. There was enough available information about King and his *other* works to allow for a strong research component to the assignment. In addition, since King consistently develops certain recurring themes in his novels, it was not difficult in the case of *It*—nor would it be difficult with any of his recent novels, including *The Green Mile, Desperation,* and *The Regulators*—for students to make connections between the assigned novel and critical studies of earlier novels. The result of the assignment was a series of unusually strong papers, including one that was ultimately published in *Castle Rock: The Stephen King Newsletter.*

Those of my students who have worked with King's novels have appreciated the opportunity to address a text that, quite often, they feel strongly about (negatively as well as positively). More important, however, they also appreciate the opportunity to respond to a text that impinges in important ways upon their own lives and experiences. They appreciate the immediacy of his themes, the consistency of his vision, the vigor of his imagination, the power of his images. And, in spite of the fears my son's teacher expressed years ago, none of my students (or, I think, my children) has been any the worse for the chance to engage their own world on their own terms.

Portions of this chapter originally appeared as "Of Books and Reputations: The Confusing Cases of King, Koontz, and Others" in *Demon-Driven: Stephen King and the Art of Writing* (1994), edited by George Beahm (Williamsburg VA: GB Publishing/ink).

For literature references, please see "Reference List of Literary Works."

12

King's Works and the At-Risk Student

▼

The Broad-Based Appeal of a Canon Basher

JOHN SKRETTA

I was a Stephen King snob. Yes, it's true and I am here to confess. I was a literary elitist in the grand tradition: I scoffed at popular literature and its appeal to what I deemed the ignorant masses. I sat alone, off in a corner, reading my Kierkegaard and Wallace Stevens, pitying the less enlightened. I learned to strike a moderately cool pose that looked good in college classes and coffee-shop poetry readings. But my critical posturing remained untested as a pedagogical stance in the classroom.

A few short years later, I find myself presenting at a Stephen King conference and having the opportunity to hear the author speak. I now hold a certain kind of reverence for King's works, a reverence due to the special appeal the author's works possess with the student population with whom I have worked most closely: Strugglers. At-risk readers. Kids on the institutional margins, often on the verge of dropping out. My journey from staunch defender of literary tradition to selective advocate of pop lit—and the students who have been an integral part of it—are what I would like to reflect on in this chapter.

Most English teachers are literary elitists, and those of us in the profession go through a kind of ordination during high school and teachers college. We participate in the recycling of literate histories, the handing down of privileged orthodoxies. I spent countless hours in and out of undergraduate and graduate seminars meticulously poring over line-by-line details from the likes of John Donne and T.S. Eliot. I took not one, not two, but three upper-level courses in Shakespeare. I was never alone through these endeavors: there were dozens of other undergraduate and graduate students at the same time in the same department, taking very traditional, canonically oriented classes, considering picking up their teaching certificates or already committed to going into education.

It was not by chance that I pursued the educational program I did, focusing my development as a reader primarily upon canonized works. A high school teacher who had a profound influence on me consistently encouraged me to limit my reading selections almost solely to "The Greats" because, in an adage I've often heard repeated since, "So many books, so little time." Two of the few contemporary authors she encouraged me to read seriously were John Updike and Arthur Miller. Although King was already widely published and a huge draw for millions of readers, I never heard his name uttered by my literary mentor.

I suspect that what I have just said resonates with the majority of high school English teachers. We are often, not surprisingly, former students in advanced placement, college-track high school English courses. We validate the orthodoxies of canon and curriculum because the orthodoxy always validated us as students: it reaffirmed our belief that masterful readings were the privilege of an erudite few, and the only works worth reading were musty with the scent of age, stability, and tradition.

I went through high school with no real idea that my reading history—my experiences as a reading snob—made me a statistical anomaly. I had no compelling reason to analyze the situation. In many ways, of course, my education in the canon was valuable. But it wasn't until years later that I realized most sixteen-year-old high school students are dramatically more interested in football quarterbacks Troy Aikman and Brett Favre than in Friedrich Nietzsche and Ayn Rand. And that, if we are talking about literacy development among younger, reluctant readers, Stephen King is a safer bet than Immanuel Kant any day of the week. My growth process as a teacher hardly occurred as a sudden moment of Zen enlightenment. It would be more truthful to admit that it was a gradual, long process best accentuated by a "Duhhh." My earlier opinions about the lack of literary merit in pop lit generally and King's work specifically were transformed through three teaching experiences.

1. First, students in the classes I was teaching had dramatically different life-concerns from those I possessed as a high schooler. Our lives were discontinuous, and our reading choices reflected this. I came from a background of privilege where educational attainment was a given, an unwavering expectation. Going to college was never the conversational topic; it was where to attend college.

As a fledgling teacher, I found myself immersed in culture shock. For many of my students, reading was hardly a key life-priority. My students were embattled kids from working-class families, struggling to make ends meet. They were concerned about immediate tangibles. A few specific examples leap to mind: one student was terrified that her father would kidnap her from her stepfather and mother when he was released from prison. Another student wondered aloud if the power would be on when she returned home from school. She had been living in a house without lighting for several weeks.

The point is simple: these life issues were outside my domain of experience. My students did not have the time, the privilege, or the inclination to engage in detached reflection and meditative inquiry on long-dead literary greats. Many worked thirty-plus hours weekly in addition to their high school class schedules in order to feed and clothe themselves. This is not to imply that my students had no desire to read. But for them, the attraction of books stemmed from a simple and undeniable source: they wanted riveting stories, full of compelling characters and sweeping action. They wanted ingenious plot twists that would interest and amaze them. They wanted books that would speak to their interests and life-concerns. They wanted the immediacy and urgency of Stephen King. (In this regard, please see chapter 14, Kristo and Bamford, this volume.)

2. A second defining experience I had as a teacher was something repeated with alarming frequency: I saw district identified, so-called "skills-deficient" readers reading and responding quite enthusiastically to works by Stephen King. The district I work in continues to use standardized comprehension tests to measure individual students' grade reading levels. I was bewildered to discover that many of my supposedly inept young readers were reading, enjoying, and expressing articulate statements about King's works as complex and long as *It* and *Needful Things*. Despite the observable phenomena, I was supposedly working with nonreaders and kids who couldn't really read. The inference I made wasn't brilliant so much as it was obvious: if it looks like they're reading and sounds like they're reading, they're probably reading. If the diagnostics say kids can't read, but they're avidly reading King, you're left to draw one of two conclusions: either the diagnostics are messed up and do not really measure reading competency, or there is something aberrant and twisted about King. It's been easier for English teachers to lie about the latter than admit the truth of the former.

3. A third defining experience was consistently discovering that students skeptical about the merit of so-called "serious literature" or "Literature with a capital L" would enthusiastically read and respond to works by Stephen King. It's not an airtight formula, but it is a fairly accurate one. Students who like King tend to be skeptical about the merits of so-called Serious Literature. A case in point occurred during my student-teaching experience. I was teaching at a fairly large high school of over two thousand students where many of the students were looking for some sense of sanctuary and personalization amidst the anonymity. A number of students tended to cluster in the English room during their lunch period prior to our regularly scheduled sophomore English class. Although the topics of discussion varied widely, my students often discussed literature—but almost never the literature we assigned in class. Almost invariably, students like Josh and Ro-

chelle would discuss King's *The Stand* with a level of insight and enthusiasm that exceeded the discussions and responses I facilitated over an assigned text like *When The Legends Die*. The fact that the lunchtime discussions over King always seemed more exciting and engaging than the talk about assigned, curricularized works left me scratching my head as to why. But there was undeniably something to the appeal of King.

Defining "At-Risk" Readers

As I worked with an at-risk student population in the context of an alternative school-within-a-school program by my second year at Northeast High School, I realized that *at-risk* was a very broad and profoundly vague appellation for my students. Typically, "at-risk" students are those who meet any number of a broad range of criteria indicative of potential school failure. But I quickly realized that "credit-deficient" and "skills-deficient" were not necessarily one and the same. Students who have failed school tend to have their own complex rationale explaining their lack of success. Many view the institution as adversarial and adult authorities as antagonists plotting their failure rather than collaborators who wish for them to succeed.

At-risk students defy stereotypes: One student I work with is a brilliant sketch artist who draws fabulous caricatures and reads H.P. Lovecraft avidly, claiming Lovecraft's symbolic order far surpasses the work of any contemporary horror writer, King included. I work with kids who have been labeled highly gifted since elementary school but have not succeeded on the school's terms, kids who are introspective writers with books of personal journals and spiral notebooks loaded with poems, computer-literate kids who are into video gaming and read *Electronic Gaming Monthly* religiously, and even one student who is a BMX biker with a corporate sponsorship that sends him around the country competing in races. On a case-by-case basis, generalizations always break down. But generally speaking, my struggling students are also students who happen to read and enjoy Stephen King.

As I completed interest inventories with students and became acquainted with my students as people behind the roster numbers, I discovered that their reading interests often tended toward horror generally and King particularly. A number of students who claimed to have no interest in horror as a genre were nevertheless fairly regular readers of King because of his overriding popularity and his masterful storytelling. As one student put it, "King kicks ass and scares the hell out of you simultaneously!" I began reconsidering my premature dismissal of King's works and using a few of his short stories such as "Children of the Corn" and "Word Processor of the Gods" to teach literary elements, such as imagery, symbolism, and foreshadowing.

Collegial Contradictions and Protesting Parents

Through all of the above, I consciously questioned the importance of the canon and prescribed curriculum in high school English classes. I began to wonder aloud if we weren't condemning a certain segment of our student population to failure simply because we did not provide these students with a wide array of literature choices. If the district mandates that students need to be able to make inferences or generalizations about works of American literature, is it essential that those works be entirely selected by teachers and written at least half a century or more ago? Nothing I read nor was experiencing in the classroom indicated it was. Instead of trying to force-feed students literature by the labeled masters, I began to challenge students to become more critical and keen readers of authors they were already reading. Readily embracing students' literary choices meant embracing King.

Despite the fact that most educators nominally oppose censorship and support intellectual freedom, a wide range of covert censorship strategies is used against King and other popular authors deemed controversial. When I inquired about the sparse selections available from King and Stine, one media center director in my district replied: "Well, what's the point of getting their books on the shelves, anyway? The students just steal them!" So King's works don't get ordered. Her response is indicative of a dismissive attitude taken toward King by many in our profession. It is easy to avoid assuming any accountability for ordering and making accessible an author whose works might cause some controversy or raise some objections by shifting that responsibility to anonymous, thieving students. Instead of absorbing the occasional loss of a King paperback as the inevitable price of popular demand, media centers don't allow King's books to reach the shelves.

Teachers are often reluctant to embrace King's works in the classroom because, quite simply, they would rather not deal with the potential controversy stirred up by using horror fiction which sometimes contains graphic portrayals of violence and profanity. For me, the infrequent objection is worth the increased learning outcomes. Of course, there are a number of strategies teachers can and should use to be proactive in their defense of King or any other work which might be viewed as controversial in the classroom (see chapters 15 through 17 in this volume).

Another factor teachers should keep in mind when using popular literature is that parents want and deserve reassurance. Adolescents are often reluctant to communicate with people who care about them a great deal: their parents. When parents take the time to attend parent–teacher conferences or call to check on their student's progress, I have heard them ask questions such as, "Do you think it's all right that he's reading all that King stuff? Isn't it supposed to be kinda creepy?" These parents are usually just looking for information and encouragement. They simply want to know their child is being encouraged to read works by authors other than King. I sometimes ask parents to read some King themselves, share some biographical information about King and his works, talk with them a little about how they see their child as a reader, and recommend some authors which their child might be interested in, in addition to King. (See chapter 9 by Michael Smith, this volume, for another way to provide that reassurance.) But no strategy for rationalizing or justifying the use of a controversial author like King will work all the time, as I recently discovered.

As I have become more vocal in my support of students' right to reading choices and their right to read authors such as King, I have sought public forums to convey my viewpoint. In Lincoln, a local woman attempted to have some books by Christopher Pike and R.L. Stine removed from a retail store aisle on the basis of her objection to the books' cover art. In addition, the local papers reported that she was preparing to go to the school board to confront the availability of these books in the classrooms. Our school paper typically publishes guest editorials by teachers, so I composed a quasi-response defending student choice for literature and addressing the need to confront censorship and make certain that books by Stine, Pike, and King, among others, remained accessible and available to readers who chose to read them. Other than some collegial response from within the English department, the article ran without notice—or so I thought.

A month later, when the next issue of the school paper came out, it included a letter from a parent of a student at our school. The letter to the editor in the December 1996 issue of the *Northeastern* was headlined, "Skretta offers no moral leadership." In the text of the letter, the parent accused me of lacking moral leadership, advocating a "moral free-for-all" in the classroom, and promoting the works of "moral degenerates" like King. The letter's conclusion suggested a random page-sampling formula for book censorship and decried the fact that public schools do not teach the Bible.

I was alarmed by the publication of this letter. I met with my department chair and principal several times and contemplated an appropriate course of action. I was mystified that a relatively simple guest editorial would prompt a vicious attack from a parent whose child was not even a member of any of my classes presently or in the past. I was stunned that my letter, which was in many ways simply a paraphrasing of the district's anticensorship policy as stated in curriculum guides, would warrant such a response. And I was disappointed that my own colleague, the faculty advisor for the student paper, printed such a letter—unedited and without informing me prior to its publication. In the end, I opted for a relatively mild response: I wrote the faculty advisor/journalism teacher a brief note and responded to the parent with a personal letter. A number of my students stated their interest in writing responses to the school paper.

Perhaps the above-mentioned letter-writing incident should not have come as a surprise. Far more powerful ultimately than the outright oppositional strategy employed by the parent in his letter are the quiet condemnations, the general institutional vibes of distaste, of down-turned lips and wrinkled noses, regarding Stephen King's use in schools from educators themselves. For example, I received a range of different reactions from colleagues when they discovered I was going to the Reading Stephen King Conference. I could classify them into several broad categories: Disparaging remarks about King such as, "What a freak that guy must be!" "I hear he collects severed heads in a jar!" and the inevitable, "Have you seen that guy's house? What a spooky place—they say it's haunted!" I also heard a number of questions regarding my professional credibility: "What *is it* you intend to do there?" and so on, basically implying that I was headed out to Maine for some semi-literate slumming. And finally, requests for autographs: "Do you think you could get a book signed for me if I loaned it to you?" Paradoxically and hypocritically enough, sometimes I would hear versions of all three of these remarks within the same ninety-second small-talk exchange, all from the same person.

Why the At-Risk Reader Reads King

Despite the occasional attack from a parent and the sometimes-disapproving attitude of colleagues, the works of King have enjoyed an integral place in my classroom for a while now, not because I am a voracious reader of King (my wife is the household King fanatic), but because my students revere King. They are fascinated by his storytelling capabilities and inspired by his prolific, undeniable work ethic. One student, David, said to me just last week, "Wouldn't it be amazing to be that guy and find a story in everything?"

After I started using King more directly to help facilitate students' literary development, I began to hypothesize about what factors were responsible for the undeniable attraction King's works possess for struggling students. I continue to find it amazing that students who have been labeled by the district as "skills-deficient" readers in need of remediation are sometimes thoroughly acquainted with King's works. Our use of standardized reading comprehension tests as a sole indicator of reading competency must be woefully inadequate.

I postulate three general theories at this point explaining King's popular appeal with strugglers. The first two form an ironic contrast: (1) King's works are situated on the margins of institutional acceptability, so students on the margins are naturally drawn to them. (2) King's works are written with accessibility and broad appeal in mind. And (3) video literacy and the changing nature of readership in the late twentieth century have added to King's appeal with strugglers.

King on the Margins

King is attractive precisely because he is risky. He is attractive precisely because he is frightening, graphic, and sometimes downright brutal to his readers. In this respect, King inhabits a fringe peopled with the renowned and notorious. His appeal to struggling students resonates with the appeal of recording artists like Nine Inch Nails and Marilyn Manson, sports stars like Dennis Rodman, and moviemakers like Quentin Tarantino also have for these adolescents. The gesture of limit testing is a time-honored tradition among at-risk students. The idea of inhabiting the borderlands of artistic acceptability is considered very endearing by the students I work with, and they usually express their allegiance to any artist or performer who expresses any kind of symbolic flip-off to the tired old-fart adults and authorities in charge. Thus, King enjoys great appeal with resistant readers precisely because his works are not generally used in traditional classroom environments.

King's Accessibility

King's stories are also attractive to readers who have struggled to experience classroom success because these readers perceive very early in their encounters with King's prose that it is much more accessible and inviting than most of the works they are required to read in the classroom. King is not writing his works for an elitist audience of academicians schooled in the latest post-structural French philosophies. Speaking candidly, younger readers are often bored silly by the ambiguity, interiority, and complexity of narrative devices used in the character studies which comprise such a great number of canonized works. *The Turn of the Screw* may be a literary masterpiece, but King's "Sometimes They Come Back" offers readers a ghost story of a different type: like a solid bass line in a throbbing rock song that brings even the most reluctant listeners to their feet, King's short story offers the spectacle and sense of pace that overpowers the reluctance of readers who may not possess a lot of confidence in their abilities to enjoy and appreciate literature.

For the reader who has not experienced academic success with literature, the opportunity to appreciate King in an academic context and apply academic objectives to King can be a liberating inspiration. But canonizing King would require the equivalent of a paradigm shift in the critical elite: a movement away from interior character studies to stories peopled with mostly average characters and driven by fantastic plots. The difference is one which draws at-risk readers to King, but has generally driven academicians elsewhere.

Video Literacy

King's appeal with at-risk readers is also attributable to the changing nature of literacy in the late twentieth century. One can argue that in terms of an art form that is widely, powerfully accessible to millions, motion pictures are the greatest artistic innovation of the century. King's "pop lit" prominence and the success of his stories when translated into movies have gone hand in hand. One cannot deny the popularity of the cinema, although for the most part English educators have done very little to equip students with sophisticated skills and strategies for viewing, analyzing, and interpreting visual texts. Many writers and cultural critics attack movies and the popularity of movies in America as a kind of cultural cancer which, left unchecked, will systematically destroy any literate impulses in our populace. Some authors have been reluctant to see their works translated into movies.

My students know the language of cinema and watch or rent movies regularly. Surprisingly, these credit-deficient students who supposedly have difficulty analyzing and comprehending an achievement-test reading section can quote from a huge compendium of movies at will. They toss movie lines around like nobody's business. The challenge they issue one another has become a protracted verbal game in our classroom: find an appropriate moment, just the right context, then drop a line. The game for the other students becomes identifying the movie quoted.

As I saw the aforementioned cinema-literacy trivia game developing in my classroom, my question became: If I am working with the supposedly subliterate classes all day, what does their lack of compunction for quoting movie lines imply about the nature of literacy at the end of this century? I can suggest this much: it is high time for teachers to engage in some revisionary work. We need to widen our notion of literacy to include electronic and visual texts, and we need to rethink our literacy curriculum in a manner more consistent with the interests, needs, experiences, richness, diversity, and intelligence possessed by our students. Our students are now—and have been for some time—embarking on amazing literate adventures that we have not begun to tap into as educators because some of these texts, including the movie versions of King's works, are of the nonprint variety. King's works translated to the screen have become a touchstone for me in this quest to grow as an educator in order to facilitate the literary growth of my students.

I do not know if incorporating King curricularly or advocating his canonization would actually carve out a literary sanctuary for an at-risk student population. I doubt that it would, since, as previously stated, a significant part of King's very appeal to my students stems from his marginalized status. The standardization of King in literature curricula would result in a loss of his appeal because, in my students' eyes, standardization equals mainstream predictability. King would no longer be one of "us" in the "Us and Them" adversarial dynamic so common among at-risk students.

King's works are a powerful and inspiring tool for classroom use. Teachers must make careful decisions about classroom literature and student choice, and certainly some of King's stories are more suitable for specific academic purposes than others. In my experience, King's works provide students with a highly accessible, enjoyable, and appropriately challenging means of fostering literacy and literary appreciation. For that reason, I will continue to use King selectively in the classroom and encourage students interested in his works to continue to read King. The occasional personal attack or faculty lounge frown should not discourage us from helping our students tap into their own unique literate potential.

13

Reading the Cool Stuff

▼

Students Respond to *Pet Sematary*

MARK A. FABRIZI

▼ ▼ ▼ ▼ ▼

Why not stick to the classics?" In October of 1996, a local reporter asked me this question as part of an interview about my use of Stephen King's *Pet Sematary* in a contemporary literature class at North Branford High School. The reporter wanted to know why I was teaching a popular fiction book like this one in school. My answer was this: I use popular fiction novels in my classroom because they spark student interest (more so than classic literature) which helps students learn specific, critical reading skills through practice. While emphasizing classic literature in the curriculum is important, interspersing popular novels can be a great way to foster a love of reading among students as well as help them practice the same skills they use when they read the classics. This chapter discusses how my students and I came to realize the power of popular literature like King's in the high school English classroom.[1]

"What Does This Have to Do with Our Lives?"

Located northeast of New Haven, North Branford, Connecticut, is a predominantly white, middle-class town with a population around 15,000 people. The high school has more than 650 students. The curriculum for the first three years of English at North Branford is well established: freshman year is a genre-based approach to literature, sophomore year concentrates on American literature, and the junior year is devoted to British literature. Seniors are allowed to choose their English class from a variety of electives such as Old World literature, theater arts, rhetoric, and contemporary literature—virtually all of which are half-year courses.

Last year, I taught an eleventh-grade British literature course. The curriculum was straightforward: a chronological study of major British literary texts, ranging from *Beowulf* and Shakespeare to George Orwell and Doris Lessing. From the students' perspectives (and they let me know this from day one), the course was utterly unappealing and thoroughly unrelated to their lives. A variety of students com-

---

[1] Students' names have been changed to protect their privacy.

prised the class of twenty-two. Some were academically talented, some were intelligent but bored by school, some had struggled in previous English classes, and some were contemplating dropping out of school completely.

The students were difficult to manage both in and out of class: they skipped their homework assignments, joked around in class, and neglected much of their written work. They often made comments such as, "Why do we have to learn this stuff?" and "What does this have to do with our lives?" As an English teacher, I am used to students asking such questions. Indeed, it is my job to help them find the answers for themselves, so I was not too surprised by their reactions.

I *was* surprised at the response I got when I asked one student about halfway through the year why he was particularly negligent in his work. He said, "It isn't that we [the class] don't want to do any work. We just don't like the stuff we have to read. It's boring. Can't we read books that deal with modern issues, stuff we see in our lives today?" I was struck by the depth of his question. Though I knew the subject matter was difficult, I assumed that many students were being troublesome or just plain lazy. I realized at that moment that the students were not resisting books and learning; they were just resisting the content of this particular course. They wanted to read, but they wanted to choose the books.

Though I had to stick with the curriculum, I began to allow the students greater flexibility in the choice of reading materials. We read Mary Shelley's *Frankenstein*, a difficult book but one the students requested. I noticed that the students became more interested in the course and were more apt to complete their assignments. This is not to say that all the students became scholars; many, because of poor work habits, continued to neglect their work. But overall, I received a positive response when I gave the students more choice in creating the curriculum.

The students also complained about the antiquity of the texts we read, saying that the books were outdated and no longer applied to them. They could make no connections between the texts and their lives. Throughout the year, I struggled to reconcile the students' desire to learn with the British literature curriculum. They wanted high-interest material they could relate to their lives. The problem was the subject matter. As I began teaching contemporary literature in the second semester of the year, I began to understand the value of using high-interest, modern literature in the classroom.

"Will We Be Reading *Pet Sematary* This Year?"

Since contemporary literature was my love in college, I looked forward to teaching a course on it. The reading list included novels such as Alice Walker's *The Color Purple*, Bernard Malamud's *The Natural*, Ken Kesey's *One Flew Over the Cuckoo's Nest*, and Stephen King's *Pet Sematary,* in addition to various short stories and poems.

I began the course with *Pet Sematary* and a brief look into the world of horror literature, a particular interest of mine. The students were engaged immediately. The students knew the book had been used in the course during previous years, so typically their first question upon entering the room was, "Will we be reading *Pet Sematary* this year?" I was not surprised by their enthusiasm; many other students who had seen the book on my shelf had shown a strong interest in reading it in their classes.

At first, though, I was concerned about the subject matter. The novel contained graphic depictions of violence, sex, and offensive language, and I was concerned about the possible reactions of the students' parents. I was confident I could defend both the book and the horror short stories I was using, but I did not want to force the issue.

Pet Sematary is about Louis Creed, a young doctor who moves his wife, Rachel, and his children, Gage and Ellie, to a rural town in Maine. After the family cat is hit by a truck, he discovers (through the help of his elderly friend Jud) the ancient Micmac burial ground which can bring the dead back to life. After his son dies, Louis begins a downward spiral toward insanity which leads him to resurrect his son, a decision that ultimately destroys Louis, his wife, and Jud.

To help the students focus on the issues within the text and to facilitate classroom conversation, I asked them to keep journals while they read, noting their reactions to the novel. In this way, I hoped to see what the students considered important. What did they see as they read the book? Were they offended by some aspects of the novel? Though some parents may feel that books like *Pet Sematary* should not be taught in high school, the students did not seem overly affected by the language, sex, or violence it included. When students wrote about the themes in the novel, few even mentioned them as issues of concern.

I asked students to use their journals to find a passage that seemed particularly important to understanding some issue in the book. They read these passages aloud in class and discussed the significance of the passage to the text, describing why they felt the passage was integral to understanding the book on a deeper level. This technique is called a "text rendering."[2]

Students' text renderings dealt with significant themes in *Pet Sematary*. One important issue in *Pet Sematary* concerns the way the various characters deal with death. Christy examined a passage she found (pp. 277–278), which describes a daydream Louis had about his dead son: "But Gage was not killed . . . oh, dear God, his cap is full of blood."

> This passage is key to understanding a very important issue in the novel, and that issue is coping with death. Throughout the entire book, the Creed family does not deal with death very well. . . . This passage shows just how much Louis misses his son. By Louis imagining that Gage was still alive, however, did not help him deal with his son's death. If anything, Louis realized just how much he wanted Gage to be alive again, no matter what it took. . . . A [reader] could tell that Louis feels a pain so great that no matter what sympathy or condolence he receives, he will bury Gage and bring his son back to life again to end his pain.

Christy has moved beyond a mere surface reading of the text and explored some of the deeper issues with which the novel is concerned.

Katherine also chose to write about the theme of death in the novel and the way Louis reacts at his son's funeral (pp. 238–239), but she took the discussion a level further. She connected the literature with her own life and created an interpretation directly relevant to herself.

> This vivid description of Gage's death also shows how quickly Gage was gone. We can see how he was so full of life and energy, then seconds later, dead. The more and more that Louis thinks about this, the more control he is losing over himself. He begins to realize that he is going to bury Gage [in the Micmac burial ground] and bring him back [to life]. This passage made me think of our lives today, how quickly they can be altered. We have no control over fate, and fate is what killed Gage.

Students often fail to see any connection between their lives and the lives of the characters they read about in novels. They frequently ask, "So what?" when confronted by a question about a character's dilemma or motivation in making a decision. They cannot see the value of studying literature as a way to govern their own lives and help

---

[2] Many thanks to Robert Fecho and Marsha Pincus of Simon Gratz High School in Philadelphia, who introduced me to text renderings and reading journals.

them make important decisions. In contrast, Katherine demonstrated an involvement with the text and a willingness to learn from the literature she read.

Other students elected to discuss recurrent images in the text as a way to understand the novel on a metaphorical level. Jason examined the recurring image of the spiral:

> This spiral holds more power than anything that Jud, Louis, or any of those other men had ever dealt with before. It is this unsurmounted power that eventually becomes the evil that brings Louis and Jud down. The spiral is described as a symbol of a bridge which exists between our world, and the other side. This "bridge" had never been crossed before people started messing around with the Micmac burial ground. Once Louis became involved, his life began to fall apart.

In his text rendering, Jason discussed the philosophical significance of the image of the spiral as well as its effect on Louis and Jud. He connected the image with events in the text and used the information to formulate hypotheses about the main character's motivations and actions.

In discussing *Pet Sematary*, I encouraged students to create their own interpretations about texts, but I also required them to use the text to support their assertions. Christy, Katherine, and Jason's text renderings demonstrate that they have read and understood the book thoroughly. They have used the events and actions in the novel to formulate opinions about the characters, demonstrate connections between the text and their own lives, and discuss significant images.

Another goal of mine is to encourage students to ask questions of a text. When I prepare for class by rereading a book and developing questions for discussion, I learn a great deal about the book because I am forced to read it carefully. I want the same kind of learning for my students. By having the students generate both the questions *and* the answers, I accomplished two goals at once: the students read the book thoroughly, and they used critical thinking skills to arrive at a deeper understanding of the text. These questions and answers were generated in small groups of four or five students and offered to the rest of the class through a panel presentation. In their presentations, the students first posed a question they had previously developed, then they answered their own question with a well-developed, insightful response. I encouraged students to think of "deep" questions about important aspects of the novel—open-ended questions that required interpretation and a thorough understanding of the novel. The idea was to help the rest of the class understand the novel on a more meaningful level than simply comprehending the plot.

I was often surprised at the depth of both the questions the students generated and the answers they supplied. As I listened to their preparation for their presentations, I enjoyed hearing them argue about different points in the text. Their conversations often led them into conversations concerning other books, characters, and incidents in their lives.

Here is an excerpt from a panel presentation in which the students generated some interesting questions about the characters and events in the novel:

> Q: "Why didn't Jud bury Norma in the Micmac burial grounds?"
>
> A: ". . . because I think Norma at her age was willing to accept death and Jud was willing too. He didn't bury Norma because she was no longer going to suffer. As Jud said, 'I hope she goes somewhere with no arthritis.'"
>
> Q: "Why did Jud want to bring Louis to the sacred burial ground?"
>
> A: "I think Jud didn't want Ellie to have to face the fear of losing her cat. But I think his purpose was more to let the secret out. If Jud never told anyone, the secret of these grounds would not continue on. If Jud is to hold a secret like that in, the secret would fizzle out and no one would know about the powers of the Micmac burial grounds."

English teachers like me want students to practice their reading skills as much as possible by actually reading the assigned books. Too many students are able to slip by in class simply by paying close attention to the classroom conversations about a particular book rather than having to go through the process of reading it. It is not as important to me that a student recall the plot of a novel I have assigned as it is that they practice their reading skills. They will not do this if the text seems irrelevant to them. However, if students enjoy the books they read in school, they may choose to read them and often read them more closely than if they were "forced" to by their teacher.

I see reading as a pleasurable activity like watching television or going to a movie, yet many teens view it as an unpleasant chore. If students gain an appreciation of reading from popular novels like Stephen King's, they may be more likely to spend their free time with a book. Thus, by instilling a love of reading, teachers can help students practice on their own the same critical skills they practice in school.

Shelley, one of my students, expressed her enjoyment of *Pet Sematary* eloquently:

> From the minute I opened the book I was interested, capti-
> vated, and had to read on. The only part that frightened me
> was Zelda [Rachel's spinal meningitis-afflicted sister], although
> I didn't know why. There are so many clues and premonitions
> in section one that I can almost guess what will happen deeper
> into the story. The story seems all the more real because the
> relationships between family members are so true to life.

In her discussion of the novel, Shelley displays an understanding of
the plot, an ability to infer meaning from the events, and a recognition of foreshadowing. She also sees the relationship between King's
fictional creation and real-life events, making the novel more meaningful to her.

Teaching Students, Not Books

In a skills-based curriculum, what we teach is not as important as
how we teach. My primary goal in teaching literature is to help the
students become more critical and skillful readers. For me, virtually
any text will suffice as long as it is interesting to the student. Any
book that students read will help achieve this goal. When we read,
no matter the subject, we cannot help but learn. Though some might
argue that classic literature teaches us more about life and human
nature, popular fiction makes literature accessible to a wider audience and helps students practice important reading skills.

English teachers (myself included) often discuss "teaching a
book" to their classes as in, "I will be teaching *Pet Sematary* next
semester." This verbalization leads to a common misconception concerning teaching, but the phrase is actually a kind of verbal short-
hand. What the teacher really means is, "I will be teaching my students, using *Pet Sematary* next semester." This is an important
distinction because the former places the focus on the text, not on
the students. Teachers do not teach books. They use books to teach
students. I believe one of the reasons people become so upset when
they hear about someone "teaching" an objectionable book in school
is that they believe the teacher is promoting the values of the book. In
"teaching a book," the teacher is seen as espousing the values within
the book, validating the book because it is being "taught." Instead,
teachers are guiding students toward a more thorough, educated reading of the book and detailed discussion of the issues raised by it.

Books are not an end in themselves but a means to the end of
students becoming more skillful readers. It is more important to emphasize skills acquisition and a positive attitude toward reading than
to teach a specific knowledge base (i.e., classic literature). There is
no "golden text" or "magic genre" that will transform students into

model citizens. The content of the texts covered in class is less important than helping the students improve their ability to read and interpret any text.

––––––––––

For literature references, please see "Reference List of Literary Works."

14

When Reading Horror Subliterature Isn't So Horrible

JANICE V. KRISTO & ROSEMARY A. BAMFORD

"I write because my heart demands it." What a powerful statement! Hearing that, and believing in its sincerity, rousted out the last of my indifference to Stephen King. I had never heard him speak and went somewhat reluctantly [to the conference], mostly because I was intrigued by this person, our local celebrity, who seems to command so much attention, but in whom I've never really been interested. I'd read Thinner at the insistence of a friend who is an avid Stephen King fan, and much more the reader than I will probably ever be. I recall being drawn in, feeling a sense of suspense, wanting to see what happens next, and thinking that if I ever had the time I'd probably read another of his books.

I'm also more open to the idea that there is value in the genre for children. I listened to "Why Goosebumps Is Good for Your Kids" and heard the message. As a parent, I carry my own childhood with me when I deal with my daughter. Sometimes I react against a childhood experience, and other times fall into a familiar mode. Can my willingness to let my daughter take the risks I was never able to take extend to letting her do things in which I see little value? It's a constant question, and a weighing one. Although I can't say I'm a believer, I am at least willing to let her have her Goosebumps, although I secretly pray that she doesn't ask me to read it to her!

"I can't wait 'til I get my hands on the next R. L. Stine. I already have thirty of them! I like the *Goosebumps* books because they leave me hanging at the end of every chapter. I want to find out what happens next."

"Books like *Teacher Vic Is a Vampire . . . Retired*, the *Graveyard School* books, and the *Spooksville* series are just neat. I mean they're a little scary—kinda weird but really good."

So, what do pre-teen and adolescents find so mesmerizing about all these blood-dripping, bone-chilling, gut-spilling stories? Scores of new books with gruesome titles such as *Nightmare in 3-D* (Stine, 1996) from the *Ghosts of Fear Street* series (Stine), *The Skeleton on the Skateboard* (Stone, 1994), and *Laura for Dessert* (Piasecki, 1995) flood the market, competing with each other, as well as for bookstore shelf space. There is no question that horror subliterature series have high appeal for readers of all ages. For example, R. L. Stine's phenomenal success with his *Goosebumps* (for pre-teens) and *Fear Street* (for adolescents) series has attracted other horror writers and their series to the trade book market. The *Graveyard Creeper Mystery* series (A First Stepping Stone Book) by Geoffrey Hayes, the *Spookeville* series by Christopher Pike, the *Shadow Zone* series by J. R. Black, and the *Graveyard School* series by Tom B. Stone among many others (see Children's Books in Reference List of Literary Works) are, perhaps in fact, the precursors to a future steeped in Stephen King.

However, it's not just horror or even R. L. Stine (who, as even he attests, will eventually lose appeal), it is the lure of series subliterature, fad or brand name literature, that has had a historically seductive influence on readers—books written to a formula that provided predictability, security, and identifiable characters (Carlsen, 1980; Havighurst, 1948; Runyon, 1996; Sherrill & Ley, 1994). Reading series literature is almost a rite of passage for young adolescent readers—a "must-have" experience on the road to refining and, perhaps, defining reading tastes. Most of us who are avid readers today were yesterday's readers of series books. Who among us doesn't recall being mesmerized by the adventures of Nancy Drew, the Hardy Boys, the Bobbsey Twins or Honey Bunch? And, who among us wouldn't reluctantly admit to curling up at some point with the newest release in a Harlequin romance or detective series?

Carlsen (1980) found, "That for most of us the first unconscious delight in reading comes through subliterature. This delight is fundamental to the development of appreciation of literature" (p. 54). He goes on to say, "We should not be concerned when children reach this stage, but only if they don't pass through it " (p. 55). The nonfiction market has not been excluded from the interest in horror and the macabre. The Scholastic series, *Horrible Histories* series, written by Terry Deary and others, focuses on "history with the nasty parts left in"—topics teachers usually avoid, such as the reason the Romans had a vomitorium, why the Celts liked severed heads, which king had the worst blackheads, and other details equally appealing to kids.

Not only are authors taking advantage of this avid interest in the horrible, so are the bookstores. A quick tour will find these hot sellers grouped together on shelves with displays of horror paraphernalia close by. Readers do not have to search the shelves for favorites; they are prominently displayed. The quality of the books varies; it doesn't take more than a rapid perusal to determine that the contrived and artificial plots are probably the result of a "quick write." Stine has reported that he usually completes a book in a couple of weeks (Santow & Kahn, 1994). An examination of works by other authors suggests a similar writing timeline. Even some series such as Stine's *Ghosts of Fear Street* and *Give Yourself Goosebumps*, Betsy Haynes' *Bone Chillers*, and Vincent Courtney's *Skeletal Warriors* are produced in Stratemeyer-like "fiction factories" where lead authors create the ideas and then turn them over to hack writers. In many cases, the actual authors receive no credit on the cover nor on the title page.

Although these horror titles seem to be multiplying faster than a vampire teacher sucking blood from a classroom of zombie-eyed students, this chapter will focus primarily on those authored by horror subliterature's most successful literary hero—R. L. Stine. As many parents, teachers, and librarians dread seeing yet another snappy eye-catching volume of Stine's *Goosebumps* or *Fear Street* on the bookstore rack, pre-teens are racing to cash registers with their newest purchases. Blake, an eleven-year-old avid reader, commented that, "The cover makes you want to read the next *Goosebumps* book, because it always has a scary picture on it, and the title sort of lifts off the cover. I like how they do that. And, there's always another one to read!"

High Kid-Appeal: It's What's on the Cover That Counts

Scholastic, the publisher of the *Goosebumps* and *Fear Street* series, has brilliantly marketed these books. With well over 160 million books in print and 4 million sold every month in sixteen languages including Chinese and Czech (Dugan, 1996), Scholastic is keenly aware of the purchasing potential of stimulating covers. Each cover illustration plays with the tension between glossy color, movie-set lighting, and a teaser statement daring the dark side of readers to be enticed into a tale of evil beasts and grotesque creatures who invade the rather uneventful lives of average kids. Adults, who shriek with horror over each new Stine book, may forget how many of them gravitate toward the captivating covers of Stephen King books or are lured to romance books with half-dressed women and irresistibly bronzed and muscular male bodies on the covers.

The ambitious marketing effort, of course, doesn't stop with the cover. Readers are tantalized at the end of the *Goosebumps* books by a sampling of several chapters from a forthcoming volume. Additionally, there are opportunities to join the *Goosebumps* fan club and to order other titles, advertisements for the television series and videos, *Goosebumps* trading cards, and more. Even some large chain stores are selling clothes based on the books by Stine. Dugan (1996) reports that forty-four licenses have been issued for *Goosebumps* merchandise. She further states that, "The licensed toys and TV show have confounded the children's book industry which is used to measuring success strictly by the number of books sold" (p. 174). The response of other publishers to the success of the *Goosebumps* marketing is reflected in a comment by Golden Books Children's Division President, Willa Perlman, "*Goosebumps* is a wake-up call for all of us to look at all of our books and see how we can expand them into a brand" (Dugan, 1996, p. 174).

The Inside Story: Horror or Horribly Written?

This seemingly recent addiction to series books isn't precedent setting (Nodelman, 1992). Many of us remember our own devotion to such literary luminaries as Frank and Joe Hardy, Nancy Drew and her best friends, George and Bess, the Bobbsey Twins, and Cherry Ames, Student Nurse, all creations of the Stratemeyer syndicate. Although certainly not in the horror genre, these early series books were too satisfying to stop with just one.

What's inside the cover of these books that makes them so appealing to kids and so hard for them to put down? Like earlier series books, the plethora of recently published horror titles, particularly those of Stine, might satisfy a reader's desire to escape from the inescapable problems of real life. Contemporary realistic young adult fiction abounds with stories about real life horrors—AIDS, divorce, physical abuse, and alcoholism. Perhaps reading horror books is therapeutic for kids who are witnesses to terrifying real-life circumstances, are blasted with the sensational and sadistic by the news media, and see all of life's worst moments dramatized in a myriad of ways in pop culture. The plot lines in many of the horror series are simply ridiculous and probably more worthy of a good laugh than a terrifying scream or at least a safe scare. Stine sums up his success this way:

> I think [kids] like the books because they're like a roller coaster ride . . . They're very fast. They're very exciting. You think you're going in one direction—they take you off into another direction. So they tease you. They fool you. [The books]. . . let you off safe and sound at the end, and you know—no matter how scary it is, or how thrilling, or how exciting—you know that you're safe the whole time. (Alderdice, 1995, p. 209)

Carlsen (1979) says that "[t]hrough reading subliterature, most of us for the first time encountered a story so exciting that we forgot we were reading" (p. 54). Texts that make few demands on readers in terms of such features as vocabulary, concept density, and syntax can lead young readers to develop the automaticity of strategies required, for more sophisticated reading. Further, these books are short and highly predictable, yet the cliff-hanger at the conclusion of every chapter is like a trajectory (Paton Walsh, 1980) literally pulling the reader rapidly through the book like a needle pulling a piece of silken thread through thin fabric.

Trademarks of subliterature are the economical and pedestrian use of language and literary conventions in skeletal form (Carlsen, 1979). Both are descriptive of Stine's writing, which is characterized by typically simple vocabulary, short sentences, and dialogue-laden paragraphs of one or two sentences. Young readers are elated by how quickly they can complete a Stine book and eagerly look forward to tackling the next one. Because each page has considerable white space, the reader's eyes only periodically have to move to the far right edge of the page, giving readers a sense of flying through the book. Stine offers the bare facts and not much more. Because settings are usually commonplace and ones that readers can easily imagine, they are minimally described. The predictable structure quickly introduces a problem that is highly consequential to the protagonist and then quickly jumps from climax to climax in two- to seven-page chapters. The language and writing style appear sophisticated by adolescent standards because of the inclusion of a few scantily descriptive sentences that set the scene or describe the characters in just a few words. Dialogue is primarily used as a means of relating the story events and scarcely delineates characters. While subplots are used sparingly, there is a heavy dependence on cliff-hangers that even kids see through. For example, Blake remarked that most of the chapters end with the main character being afraid that a monster is coming in the room or about to attack, only to find that it is a trusted friend or family member. Ultimately, the main character has just overreacted and seems to enjoy the fright as much as the reader relishes being scared by the book.

Bethune (1995) observes that Stine's success lies in his "intimate awareness of the psychic and social lives of his target audience—children eight to twelve . . . . Just as Stine's readers are at an age to be concerned about proving that they are not frightened, his characters constantly egg each other on to such acts as looking for a werewolf in the middle of the night" (p. 46).

Characters may be the same or similar from book to book in the series and lack any demonstration of self-growth or reflection. Readers can easily separate the good from the evil characters. They identify with these characters who are average kids and, in spite of warnings from adults, usually manage to save the day in heroic ways. Stine uses these predictable adolescent expectations of character qualities to provide readers with intriguing surprises. For example, in *Beware, the Snowman* (1997), Stine takes advantage of the reader's expectations about characters to create a twist at the end. Conrad, an adult, at the start of the story seems crazed, dangerous and, to use Stine's favorite word, "weird." However, at the end of the story, Conrad saves Jaclyn, the protagonist, from the monster snowman and admits to being her father who left the family after the mother died. In *Killer's Kiss* (1997) from Stine's *Fear Street* series, Delia appears to be the victim of Karina, an envious high school classmate. In the last four pages of the book, though, readers discover they have sympathized with the wrong character. Delia staged all the events and even murdered her own boyfriend to ensure victory over Karina. These plots are top candidates for soap opera scripts; perhaps, that's what gives them that melodramatic appeal.

Other plots are full of drama and surprises—most of which are absolutely implausible. For example, Larry Boyd in *My Hairiest Adventure* (1996), who is often chased by stray dogs, is mystified that after using some INSTAN-TAN he starts sprouting bristly hair on his hands and face. Later, just before he turns into a dog, his "parents" tell him he is part of a failed experiment to turn dogs into humans. In *Ghost Camp,* Harry and Alex, who are off for a great summer vacation, find that the other campers behave very strangely and are just plain "weird." They soon learn that the rest of the campers are ghosts needing human hosts to escape the camp. Unfortunately, Alex gets permanently possessed.

We could go on relating plot after plot, but they don't get any better. Plots should challenge and intrigue readers, as in typical suspense stories, but in Stine's books the purpose is to offer minimal structure in which evil or odd acts can occur. Reed (1994), in writing about literature for young adults, states, "The major difference between adult suspense, such as the stories of Stephen King, and young adult suspense is the age of the protagonist and the complexity of the plot" (p. 161). We would argue that another major difference is the quality of writing, i.e., a lack of well-developed plots and characters, rich description, and, particularly, exploration of thoughtful or interesting themes.

Stine also breaks other conventional rules young readers have come to expect—hopeful or uplifting endings and victory in the end for the hero or heroine. Instead, Stine uses these expectations about the conclusion to create unanticipated turns at the end. Blake commented that at the end of the book there isn't always something good that happens; sometimes it's bad. For example, in *Ghost Camp* (1996), the ghost takes over the younger hero's body and that's the way the story ends. Blake said that this kind of ending leaves you with a lot of questions, and that's not always bad! Perhaps, part of the appeal is that Stine plays mind games with readers, manipulating conventional literary elements.

Young adolescents who view their lives as being controlled by parents, teachers, and others relish seeing the adults in their books outsmarted by characters who are only ten or twelve years old—responding just like their parents and their parents' parents, who were drawn to the Nancy Drew and Hardy Boys series. The main characters seem to be in charge of their lives, making decisions and moving freely around the community. For example, Jaclyn in *Beware, the Snowman* leaves her house at 9:00 p.m. and again at 2:00 a.m. to investigate her new town. These characters ably outmaneuver and override adult interference. The few parents or caregivers who are present do little to influence their children and are seldom even identified. If adults are given any attention by the author, they are depicted as either evil or dangerous. Isn't it the secret fantasy of preteens to be in charge of the world without an adult telling them what to do next? In *Goosebumps* and other horror series, instead of being hampered by adults, adolescent readers fulfill their fantasies through identification with a protagonist who is resourceful, clever, and in most cases, a successful problem solver. Rather than creating a reasonable and authentic interplay between the world of the children and adults, authors such as Stine involve their protagonists in suspenseful situations devoid of credible adults and with problems that kids cannot plausibly solve. Thus, the improbability of it all heightens the appeal for readers, who live vicariously through these experiences.

Subliterature that Creeps and Crawls into the Classroom

So, what are teachers to do? On one hand, we may lament, weep, and shriek about the dearth of high-quality literature entering our classrooms, but on the other hand lots of kids are reading Stine books and other types of series subliterature. It's just that many of us are disappointed with the books that engage and excite our students. As teachers our philosophy is one that supports students as readers. We would love to see our students reading and enjoying high-quality, well-written literature; but the reality is that we can't have it both ways—many adult and child readers look to a variety of literature to satisfy "the series habit." In fact, Chambers (1985) recommends that we become "intergalactic," exploring the wide, expansive world of literature and not limit ourselves to "flat-earth" reading—confining ourselves to only certain kinds of books. Let's take advantage of the fact that kids are reading and explore ways we can increase their power as readers and writers—meet them where they are but be ready to guide them in exploring new reading and writing territories.

Assuming that subliterature, such as the Stine books, is not censored from the classroom, we believe that teachers have an active part to play in designing strategies that will take advantage of the series habit. According to Stephen King, "Kids have minds of their own and are engaged in learning how to use them. If you tell them Stephen King is good, they'll read me. If you tell them I'm bad for them, that I'll warp their little minds, they'll stampede to read me" (see chapter 2 by Stephen King, this volume). King's comments acknowledge reader choice and the need for the recreational reading of subliterature in our culture.

We also know that pre-teens are influenced by the books their peers and teachers recommend and that eventually reading habits change. Blake commented that having read eight titles in the *Goosebumps* series, he was more than ready to sample other kinds of books. He seems to recognize subliterature for what it is, probably because he had read and heard some really "primo" titles and had a basis for comparison. It is a predicament if teachers truly want students to read and believe in the power of choice of reading materials but close the classroom door to series subliterature. Teachers and students need to be invited to read series literature, too. Additionally, teachers need to be ready with great titles that will entice students to sample from another literary plate—perhaps, other more sophisticated scary titles, mysteries, tales of the supernatural, or maybe an entirely different genre! A starter list of these titles appears in the following section.

Capturing Vampires, Ghouls, and Other Beasties

Who hasn't heard a pre-teen remark with a great sense of bravado that he or she has never read a book ever? Subliterature can be the gateway for some students who have never discovered the joys of reading. Making one's way through a series provides many students with a sense of accomplishment and power over text.

Why not design minilessons that take advantage of the literature that seduces our students? Discuss aspects such as the marketing features that promote publishers' sales and attract even the most reluctant readership. Collaborating with peers to experiment with print size, color, graphics, and advertising, students might promote their own writing in ways that will get others interested in reading what's inside the covers of their books.

Read aloud well-written books in the horror and mystery genre. Reading aloud a text can work as an equalizer in the classroom, bringing works of literature alive for many students who might not be able to read the books independently. Here is a sample of some worthwhile titles to consider for read-alouds and as independent reading that build on students' fascination with the horror genre, yet move them beyond subliterature:

Give Yourself a Fright: Thirteen Tales of the Supernatural by Joan Aiken

The Selkie Girl by Susan Cooper

Stonewords by Pam Conrad

Stranger with My Face by Lois Duncan

The Half-a-Moon Inn by Paul Fleischman

The Bunnicula Series by James Howe

The Mermaid Summer by Mollie Hunter

A Stranger Came Ashore by Mollie Hunter

The Root Cellar by Janet Lunn

The Dark-Thirty: Southern Tales of the Supernatural by Patricia C. McKissack

The Blood-and-Thunder Adventure on Hurricane Peak by Margaret Mahy

The Haunting by Margaret Mahy

The Duplicate by William Sleator

The Ghost Comes Calling by Betty Ren Wright

Out of the Dark by Betty Ren Wright

Balyet by Patricia Wrightson

Greyling by Jane Yolen

Even novelette series by such authors as Elizabeth Levy, Zilpha Keatley Snyder, Mary Pope Osborne, and Geoffrey Hayes can be considered (see Reference List of Literary Works, this volume). Although the series are written for much younger readers, they offer some opportunities if the teacher is sensitive to the issue that these are horror stories for the "junior" set. "Buddy-reading" extends an opportunity for older students to read to much younger ones. Older readers who may perceive themselves as nonreaders may gain some power over text and some classroom prestige by "overlearning" one of the novelettes for the purpose of sharing the book aloud with a much younger reader.

Novelettes offer readers a chilly but safe ride into the horror genre with stories using the same characters and plots that develop in a logical manner and incorporate believable but captivating cliffhangers. For example, Osborne in her series transports readers to different historical time periods through the vehicle of a magic tree house. She successfully incorporates information and language about the time period into an appealing storyline. In addition, each book in the series offers readers a new clue about the identity of the original owner of the magical books found in the tree house.

Purves (1993) states: "[W]e see that in literature programs our students are not simply reading texts, they are reading writers" (p. 359). Teachers could seize the opportunity to design effective writing minilessons based on the interest of students in becoming potential horror writers. For example, students could examine the novelettes described above in terms of literary conventions and the structure of horror tales. Because the novelettes are short and unencumbered by complexities and subtleties in plot, their simplicity is perfect to discuss such aspects as building tension and creating dialogue. These same techniques could also be examined in the Stine books, as well as comparisons made to the novelettes and techniques used in more complex horror writing.

A more in-depth study of Stine's writing could involve his use of dialogue markers. For example, on page 65 in *The Beast from the East* (1996), Stine uses seven different dialogue markers—*muttered, asked, replied, answered, said, warned,* and *yelled.* This variety of ways to say "said" is typical of what readers will find in his books. Students could develop a chart of all the different dialogue markers used by their favorite horror series writer. Charts could also list other interesting uses of language, such as metaphorical expressions, adjectives, expressions that might be repetitious to readers, and so on.

Take any chapter from a *Goosebumps* book and invite students to examine it for the various techniques they see Stine using as a writer—dialogue markers, use of primarily dialogue to keep the flow of the plot with limited descriptions of scenes or actions, the extent to which Stine allows readers and/or characters in on what's happening behind the scenes, etc. Compare the ways in which Stine uses these literary conventions to more sophisticated literature. Additional opportunities to examine, explore, and thoughtfully consider horror subliterature series in the classroom might ultimately contribute to defining one's taste in books while becoming a more discriminate reader. Chambers (1973) suggests that

> [w]ide, voracious, indiscriminate reading is the base soil from which discrimination and taste eventually grow. Indeed, if those of us who are avid and committed readers examine our reading history during our childhood and look also at what we have read over the last few months, few of us will be able to say honestly that we have always lived only on the high peaks of literature. (p. 122)

Conclusions

Carlsen (1979) reminds us that, "For most of us the first unconscious delight in reading comes through subliterature. This delight is fundamental to the development of appreciation of literature" (p. 54). No one will disagree that these horribly written books about horror are popular partly due to multimillion dollar marketing pitched directly at a ready audience—eight- to twelve-year-olds. But as teachers we also need to recognize and acknowledge the power of subliterature for fostering interest in reading. On reflecting about questions on the use of *Goosebumps* books in her third-grade classroom, Joanne Hindley (1996) states that she did not choose to read these books aloud. She did not put them in the basket of well-worn books for a discussion of the qualities of good writing, nor did she spend the class's hard-earned bake-sale money on them. What she discovered was that kids who became engrossed in the Stine books, for the first time, became members of "Frank Smith's Literacy Club." Runyon (1996) confirms that, "If our goal as reading teachers is to create lifetime readers then, instead of discouraging students to read series books, we need to rejoice when they can't read just one" (pp. 24–25).

After all, most of us also sharpened our literary eye teeth on similar literature, and look at how well we all turned out! So, keep the faith, and let's be grateful that at least Stine cares about children. He says, "My thinking is that these books are entertainment. I'm very careful to keep reality out of it. The real world is much scarier than these books. So I don't do divorce, ever. I don't do drugs. I don't do child abuse. I don't do all the really serious things that would interfere with entertainment" (Alderdice, 1995, p. 209). But R. L. Stine does keep kids reading!

Works Cited

Alderdice, K. (1995, July 11). R. L. Stine: Ninety million spooky adventures. *Publishers Weekly, 242* (29), 208–209.

Bethune, B. (1995, December 11). Master of thrills and chills. *Maclean's, 108* (50), 46–48.

Carlsen, G. R. (1980). *Books and the teen-age reader: A guide for teachers, librarians, and parents.* New York: Bantam.

Chambers, A. (1973). *Introducing books to children.* London: Heinemann.

Chambers, A. (1985). *Book talk: Occasional writing on literature.* New York: Harper & Row.

Dugan, I. J. (1996, November 4). The thing that ate the kids' market. *Business Week,* 174–176.

Havighurst, R. J. (1948). *Developmental tasks and education.* Chicago: University of Chicago Press.

Hindley, J. (1996). *In the company of children.* York, ME: Stenhouse.

Nodelman, P. (1992). *The pleasures of children's literature.* White Plains, NY: Longman.

Paton Walsh, J. (1980). The lords of time. In V. Haviland (Ed.), *The openhearted audience: ten writers talk about writing for children* (pp. 177–198). Washington: Library of Congress.

Purves, A. C. (1993). Toward a reevaluation of reader response and school literature. *Language Arts, 70* (5), 348–361.

Reed, A. J. S. (1994). *Reaching adolescents: The young adult book and the school.* New York: Macmillan.

Runyon, L. (1996). Why they can't just read one. *Journal of Children's Literature, 22* (2), 23–25.

Santow D., & Kahn, T. (1994, November 14). The scarier the better: Author R. L. Stine specializes in giving kids the creeps. *People Weekly, 42,* 115–116.

Sherrill, A., & Ley, T. C. (Eds.). (1994). *Literature is . . . : Collected essays by G. Robert Carlsen.* Johnson City, TN: Sabre Printers.

For a bibliography of children's books, please see "Reference List of Literary Works."

Censorship

15

One Book Can Hurt You . . . But a Thousand Never Will

JANET S. ALLEN

> The worst, most insidious effect of
> censorship is that, in the end, it can
> deaden the imagination of people.
> Where there is no debate, it is hard
> to go on remembering, every day, that
> there is a suppressed side to every
> argument. It becomes almost impossible
> to conceive of what the suppressed
> things might be.
>
> —Salman Rushdie

What Orwell feared were those who would ban books. What Huxley feared was that there would be no reason to ban a book, for there would be no one who wanted to read one.

Neil Postman

Censorship issues are certainly prevalent in classrooms and communities across the United States. When I moved to Florida I was initially overwhelmed with the stranglehold that censors seemed to have on schools and classrooms where teachers were attempting to make student choice the foundation for their reading and literature programs. Each time I was asked to speak in schools in Florida, at least one teacher (and sometimes all of them) would ask me how I managed to teach the books I suggested to them. "We can't even teach *Tex* (Hinton, 1979) without getting in trouble and you're suggesting that *The Drowning of Stephen Jones* (Greene, 1991) would be a good book for our eleventh graders?"

It was a legitimate and understandable question, given that teachers are most often the ones who must face the initial censorship challenges—challenges which will probably increase in the future. In fact, in his article, "Censorship in the Schools: No End in Sight" (*ALAN*, 1991), Simmons predicts that we can expect an increasing number of censorship cases. In times such as these, many educators seek what they consider to be safe literature rather than introducing students to the rich and realistic contemporary literature that is available for readers. Teacher educators have a critical responsibility to help preservice and inservice teachers understand their roles in nurturing lifelong readers. This leads naturally to the necessity of exploring the dynamics of censorship as well as helping teachers plan strategies for dealing with challenges which will eventually occur. Preplanning can alleviate much of the stress that teachers experience when building classes based on student choice.

Over several months' time and in schools across the country, I made it a point to talk with middle- and secondary-school teachers about the books they chose for their classroom libraries, as well as those which they would use for whole-group reading and discussion. In my twenty years of secondary teaching, I had always chosen books for our classroom based on students' interests and the quality of literature available. When I began teaching, there were no state or district curriculum guides, so contemporary adult and young adult fiction and nonfiction became the reading foundation in all of my English classes. King's books were mainstays in our independent reading curriculum, and the reading of those books greatly influenced students' continued reading and their writing.

One of my best teaching moments came when Jason brought a three-page, single-spaced response to *The Wastelands* (King, 1992) and said, "I think I've finally written something that is good enough to revise and edit." As I read his piece, I understood what he meant. His lead immediately pulled me into the piece, "We left our heroes on the beach in book two," and continued to hold me with its vivid descriptions: ". . . the bear is in pretty good shape except for a virus that has tiny, wiggly, white worms eating away at his brain. They tickle the inside of his nose and ah-ah-ah chew—thousands of gooey parasites come out of his nose in clouds that cling to all that is near." Jason's writing was a classic example of what I had always believed— rich writing comes from wide reading of writing that is engaging and finely crafted.

Given the quality of the reading and writing that Jason and his friends were engaged in, I worried little about whether or not someone would object to a word or what some might consider inappropriate behavior. After all, what better place to talk about real-world issues than in the context of books that reflected the lives my students were living, the ones they might have lived if others had not taken risks, and the lives they might live if they could make good choices today?

In just a few months of visiting classes and interviewing teachers, I realized that although this level of student choice was available in many classrooms, it was not the norm. I was shocked and saddened to discover that for all of our talk about diversifying the curriculum and exploding the canon, the literature curriculum was amazingly similar in classrooms across the country. In spite of cultural differences and language barriers, wide ranges of reading abilities and interests, and hundreds of newly published books, most of our students were receiving amazingly similar fare. There were still very few women and minorities represented in the books most commonly taught in secondary schools (Applebee, 1989). I was saddened to discover that the statistics of this study were alive and well in the schools I was visiting.

I continued to explore this phenomenon with teachers in my workshops as well as the preservice and inservice teachers in my classes. I questioned them about their book choices based on the literature goals they had established. "If you want students to experience the prodigal son theme, why would you choose to use only *Great Expectations* rather than young adult books like *The Tiger Orchard* (Sweeney, 1994) or *Out of Nowhere* (Sebestyen, 1994)?" I asked.

I found that in some cases it was due to a lack of knowledge of contemporary literature; in many instances it was because teachers did not want to risk censorship cases. Teachers freely admitted that in spite of their belief that students should have choice in their reading, they wouldn't have books with controversial language and issues such as *Basketball Diaries* (Carroll, 1978) or *Jay's Journal* (Sparks, 1979) in their classrooms. One teacher said, "I might have fought over those books when I first started teaching, but I just don't want to get into that kind of battle today. There is so much to fight about that nothing seems worth fighting for today. Plus, most kids don't want to read anyway. Why should I risk my job for kids who don't even care about reading?"

Sadly, I had taught long enough to see both Orwell and Huxley's fears come true: We have many who would censor books, and we have a generation of young would-be readers who choose not to read because they don't have reading mentors who will help them find books which might engage them in spite of the controversial issues.

With this information from teachers, I began to understand that the work which needed to be done could start in our university classes. Students in these classes read widely and developed useful classroom resources, but that wasn't enough to sustain them in schools that could not or would not support the importance of student choice in reading. Teachers needed to know how to choose good books and how to develop rationales so they could feel confident in supporting those books. They also needed to be familiar with where to find resources if they did experience censorship problems with books they had chosen.

Knowing Why

The first issue we struggled with in our classes was related to why we should be advocates for student choice. Many students came to our state-required, adolescent literature classes at the university feeling that the books we read for class might be palatable as beach reading, but they could hardly take the place of the classics that formed the foundation in most secondary English classes. Some were willing to take a step toward bridging the two worlds by using books such as *Adolescent Literature as a Complement to the Classics* (Kaywell, 1993; 1995; 1997), but the merit in adolescent literature at that juncture was that it served as a motivation for reading the classics. While I didn't deny that function and, in fact, fostered the importance of that connection, I wanted my university students to develop an understanding that contemporary adult and young adult literature would most likely help their students make the transition from school to lifelong reading.

As a beginning step, we began to examine books that were targets for censorship. We looked at materials from Banned Books Week for the past several years and noted the cited reasons for banning many of the books graduate students might have chosen for their classroom libraries. When we compared the reasons for censorship cited in Banned Books with the reasons teachers might choose to have students read the book either independently or as a class (see Figure 1), teachers began to see that their professional judgments had value both in terms of book choices and the broader curricular decisions that have an impact on the language arts and thus on all our lives. They began to think about the importance of choosing books that connect so powerfully to their students' lives that they could change readers' world views. In our discussion, many students talked about the power of good books as the impetus for their having chosen to become English teachers. Yet, few of them were experiencing with their students the transforming power of literature that Huck talks about when she says, "Literature has the power to take us out of ourselves and return us to ourselves, a changed self" (1977, p. 369).

Reflecting on the issues and developing a rationale seemed to open the door for these teachers to look at the ways in which they had allowed others to make curricular decisions for them. The notion of teachers as decision-makers and not decision-followers was a new one for many of these teachers! Not surprisingly, most teachers had never really been asked to articulate their reasons for using any piece of literature—even the classics.

Developing Rationales

An examination of the brief purpose statements led us to examine ways that teachers could be proactive in thinking through the decisions they made about books. Turning their purpose statements into rationales for selecting books helped them develop confidence in their decisions and look critically at the books they were purchasing. When teachers had to ask themselves if a particular book really was the best one to meet their purposes, some of them decided that there were other options. One teacher laughingly said, "I can't think of a single reason why I should teach all of my students *A Tale of Two Cities*!" Conversely, many of the teachers decided that when they tried to write rationales for some of the novels they were planning to use as

Figure 1. Comparison of Censors' Complaints and Teachers' Brief Rationales for Use

Title/Author	Censors' Complaints	Teachers' Rationales
1. *I Know Why the Caged Bird Sings* (Angelou)	"pornographic . . . encourages premarital sex and homosexuality"	Teaches students to overcome obstacles, survive
2. *Go Ask Alice* (Anonymous)	"contains profanity and indecent situations"	Helps students take responsibility for their actions
3. *Crazy Lady* (Conley)	"contains 'swear words'"	Students learn about personal and community responsibility as well as trust
4. *Killing Mr. Griffin* (Duncan)	"strong language and umflattering references to God"	Students confront issues of responsibility and liability
5. *The Drowning of Stephen Jones* (Greene)	"it is about gays and lesbians"	Students confront prejudice and impact of irrational acts
6. *Tex* (Hinton)	"foul language and violence"	Readers see the importance of friends and family; survival
7. *The Giver* (Lowry)	"violent and inappropriate passages—infanticide and euthanasia"	Readers experience the opportunity to examine society from multiple perspectives
8. *Boy's Life* (McCammon)	"recurring themes of rape, masturbation, violence and degrading treatment of women"	Readers learn to value others' opinions, writing, home, and community
9. *The Great Gilly Hopkins* (Paterson)	"uses the words 'God,' 'damn,' & 'hell' offensively"	Readers understand that survival can be aided by significant and caring people
10. *Fair Game* (Tamar)	"ethics take a back seat to graphic sexual material"	Readers have to confront a social issue by looking at their own actions and reactions

whole-group selections, they couldn't defend their choices either in terms of literary value or the censorship issues they might confront. We quickly realized that while most of us would defend an individual's right to read the book as part of independent reading in our reading workshops, many of us were not ready to defend that choice as a requirement for an entire class.

We used chapter 8 of Brown and Stephens's (1995) *Teaching Young Adult Literature: Sharing the Connection* as a model for writing our rationales. Brown and Stephens recommend the following components in the rationale:

- complete bibliographic information
- summary of the important elements of the book
- identification of major controversial issues
- citation of related reviews
- articulation of a case for using the book

As several county censorship cases escalated during our semester, teachers decided to add two other components to their rationales:

- skills and standards which would be enhanced through this work of literature
- the alternate reading assignment which would be given if parents chose to have their children excluded from the reading of the text

I Know Why the Caged Bird Sings (Angelou, 1970) was one of the books under attack, so our class worked collaboratively on writing a rationale for that book (see Figure 2).

The intensity of our class discussions carried over into the classrooms where these graduate students were teaching. As these teachers shared the books they were reading for our Issues in Young Adult Literature class with their students, they began talking about censorship. One night in class, I told my students that the best reading motivation I ever did was by setting up a display of books for students with a sign that said, "Someone doesn't think you should be allowed to read these books." My high school students read more of those books and their writing was more impassioned than at any other time of the year. Many of the teachers took this strategy to heart and when our Banned Books Week materials arrived, teachers began sharing this information with students in a variety of ways. Marianne Raver, a high school teacher in Orlando, shared with us two of her strategies for helping students become more aware of censorship issues (see Figure 3).

Title: *I Know Why the Caged Bird Sings*
Citation: Maya Angelou, 1970, NY: Random House
Course: Honors English III

Summary
This book is a remarkable autobiographical account of Angelou's life from age three to sixteen. In spite of the historical setting of the 1930s, the issues raised in the book are those which many children experience today. From a rape at age eight, to years of silence, to coming into her own, Angelou's journey is a powerful example of overcoming life's tragedies. Today a well-known poet and author, Angelou's voice continues to affect millions of readers. *I Know Why the Caged Bird Sings* gives readers the background for her journey of survival. The honest situations, vocabulary, and events in this book are of a sensitive nature.

Reviews
  • Nominated for the American Book Award (1970)
  • *Contemporary Authors* states: "That [the author] chooses to recreate the past in its own sounds suggests to the reader that she accepts the past and recognizes its beauty and its ugliness, its assets and its liabilities, its strength and its weakness."

Rationale for Using This Book
This autobiographical book is a powerful model for readers today. As they encounter Angelou's inner strength, her tenacity, and her eventual accomplishments in spite of the challenges in life, readers may acknowledge that they, too, can overcome the adversity in their lives. Angelou's fame, the quality of her writing, and the engaging story that is her life contribute to our belief that this book should be read and discussed.

Skills and Standards
Some of the skills which will be enhanced and standards which will be met through the reading, discussion, and writing connected to this book follow:
  • Writing autobiographies
  • Generating interview questions and conducting research
  • Comparison/contrast writing

Alternative Assignment
It is the policy of this school that an alternative reading assignment would be given to any student whose parent or custodian chooses to exempt him/her from the reading of the class text. The alternative assignment for this book will be *O Pioneers* by Willa Cather.

Figure 2. Rationale for Inclusion of Supplementary Text

As other teachers tried these strategies, they found that students immediately were ready to fight for their right to read. When Kyle Gonzalez tried Marianne's first activity with her middle school students, she nearly had a riot. Kyle allowed students to choose their favorite books or books on tape from the classroom library. After the first two books were confiscated, students began yelling at Kyle, grabbing lots of books and tapes from the shelves, and putting books and

Banned Book Week Activity

Banned Book Week is sponsored by the American Booksellers Association, the American Booksellers Foundation for Free Expression, the American Library Association, the American Society of Journalists and Authors, the Association of American Publishers and the National Association of College Stores. It is also endorsed by the Center for the Book of the Library of Congress. The message of Banned Book Week is to draw attention to the danger that exists when restraints are imposed on the availability of information in a free society.

To bring up the subject of censorship and banning books, I do the following activities with my high school students:

1. As a homework assignment, I ask my students to bring their very favorite book to class. The day these books are due, I tell them we're just going to discuss our favorite books and share them with each other. As the first student shares his/her book (no matter what the book is), I find some excuse that it is unacceptable. I interrupt the student's description and, in an accusing voice, I go on and on detailing reasons why (made up reasons, of course) the book is unacceptable, and I take the book away, throwing it on the floor at the front of the room. The students are mostly horrified, but no one ever says anything. I call on another student. I find other reasons to censor his book and take it away too; it joins the first on the floor. By now, most of the students realize I'm not totally serious and they are eager to share just so they can see what excuse I find to take their book away. In a few minutes, we have a pile of "banned" books on the floor in the front of the room. I cordon these off with "Danger" tape (available at most home supply stores). By now, a few students are arguing with me, saying, "But, Mrs. Raver, you can't take away my book!" This leads us into a wonderful discussion of censorship.

2. I bring several children's books to class that have been listed in *Banned Books Resource Guide* (ISBN 0–8389–7791–X, available from The American Library Association, Publishing Services Order Department, 50 East Huron Street, Chicago, IL 60611; 800-545-2433, ext. 7). This year I brought Shel Silverstein's *Where the Sidewalk Ends*, William Steig's *The Amazing Bone*, Maurice Sendak's *In the Night Kitchen*, Rudyard Kipling's *The Elephant's Child*, Martin Handford's *Where's Waldo?*, and Roald Dahl's *The Enormous Crocodile*. I got mostly picture books because they are easy to work with in one class period. The students read several books and decide why they think the books have been challenged or banned. I then share with them the actual reasons for the challenging or banning of the books. They decide if they agree and think the book should be removed or if they disagree and think the book should be available to children. They then write persuasion letters to the library giving reasons for their opinions.

This activity helps my students think critically, form and support their opinions . . . plus, it's fun!

Figure 3. Banned Book Activity created by Marianne Raver (Oak Ridge High School, 6000 South Winegard Road, Orlando, Florida 32809 (MJRaver@aol.com). Reprinted with permission.

tapes in their book bags and refusing to take them out. Several books and tapes were stolen as some students were never entirely convinced that this was just a way to get into a discussion about censorship. They just weren't willing to take a chance that some of their favorite books would be taken from their classroom library. The voice and power expressed by one of the sixth graders in Kyle's Literacy Workshop served to remind us of the importance of including our students in censorship issues: "Books help people to learn and you won't let us learn if you ban the books we like." Our students today are the parents and community members of tomorrow. What an important memory for these students to take into adulthood—a memory of how carefully they guarded books once they had experienced the power of choosing their own books every day.

These activities, followed by reading books in which students confront censorship issues such as those explored in Lasky's *Memoirs of a Bookbat* (1996), can give students a forum for talking about student choice and censorship from different perspectives.

Building a Support Network

People for the American Way (PAW) cites the importance of community support in censorship cases. Anyone who has ever gone through a censorship battle knows the truth in PAW's statement: ". . . where schools enjoy the support of their communities, the censors are hard-pressed to prevail. This simple and most democratic of strategies is far and away the best safeguard against attacks on the freedom to learn." I believe that knowing how to establish and maintain this support network is a critical piece of preservice and inservice teacher education. The resources we researched in our university class fall into four categories: personal and professional knowledge; school and district-level planning; community relationships; and professional support systems.

Personal and Professional Knowledge

As an ongoing guard against censorship, teachers and administrators must become aware of the newest books, the professional journals which review books, and the ways in which people have previously defended censored books. As more diverse literature is included in the curriculum, both for independent and whole-group reading, I believe we can anticipate more censorship controversies. Literature is a reflection of life and as that reflection becomes a more accurate picture of all our lives, the literature becomes more realistic. It also becomes more offensive to those who believe that all should live as they choose to live. The intensity of these issues makes staying abreast of the literature and professional reviews an essential piece of teachers' professional development. Teachers can accomplish this by reading journals that consistently review contemporary books. NCTE's *English Journal*, *The ALAN Review*, *Voices from the Middle*, and *Language Arts*; IRA's *Journal of Adolescent and Adult Literacy*; and *The School Library Journal* all offer reviews of new books as well as articles relating to their use in the classroom.

School and District-Level Planning

Each school district should have a plan in place in the event of a censorship issue. When I have asked teachers about this plan, most have been unaware that such a plan existed. When I asked them to check with their district-level offices, they were surprised that in all cases there was a documented plan in place. Just knowing that the district had a plan was helpful for some teachers who were self-censoring "just in case." This is further evidence for me that the plan needs to be clearly written and disseminated to all teachers so that they are aware of the district-level support they can expect as well as the district's policy for selection of materials for classroom and school use. If a plan is not in place in your school district, NCTE offers a Censorship Packet which contains a collection of policy statements, what-to-do documents, and background materials. These materials can be very helpful in writing policy statements that fit your district and community.

Community Relationships

Developing and maintaining positive community relationships that center around reading help bring parents, community members, and business leaders into a discussion of literacy before there is a censorship issue. Asking businesses for their help in supplying books for classrooms and then inviting them in to share in the results of their support can create fiercely loyal supporters of independent reading choices. I recently visited a school in Anchorage, Alaska, where a local business had donated money for T-shirts. The shirts carried a great reading slogan, "I Choose to Read," which students sold at a district-level community meeting. The proceeds then went toward buying books for their classroom libraries. There are hundreds of positive ways such as this to get community members involved: book drives, book clubs, reviews written by students for the newspaper, television spots, etc. The list may be endless but the results can all be the same: we bring interested others into our discussion of the importance of creating lifelong readers.

Professional Support Systems

Professional support systems can help as you gather material both for rationales and in the event of censorship cases. Publishers and authors can give you reviews of their books as well as background information from others who may have dealt with censorship cases related to a specific title. When a parent in our district complained about *A Separate Peace* (Knowles, 1960), a call to the publisher brought us a packet of book reviews as well as information from several other school districts who had battled and won censorship cases related to the book. When *Bridge to Terabithia* (Paterson, 1977) was the target in a fifth-grade classroom in our district, the teacher and I called Katherine Paterson, who talked to us at length about why she wrote the book and how she might help with the case. We found that those we contacted were very willing to help us as we defended the books they had written and published.

NCTE has published a document entitled *The Students' Right to Read* (updated 1982), and in 1991 NCTE and IRA jointly published *Common Ground* (see appendix A). These two brochures are readily available and inexpensive. *The Students' Right to Read* offers not only an articulate statement about the necessity of student choice, but also covers procedures for selecting and defending books. *Common Ground* offers action plans and strategies at the local, state, national and international levels for getting involved in battling censorship before a challenge occurs. The pamphlet also includes a valuable list of names and addresses of organizations that are interested in fighting censorship.

The American Library Association offers a kit each year as part of celebrating Banned Book Week. The 1996 kit cost $28.00 and contained posters, bookmarks, and resources for informing students, faculty, and community members about censorship. In addition, several books have been written which provide insight into and resources for the censorship battle. My students and I found two books which were helpful in examining the scope of censorship. *Banned in the U.S.A.* (Foerstel, 1994) includes a comprehensive look at several aspects of censorship, information about book-banning cases, and interviews with frequently banned authors such as Blume, Cormier, and Paterson. *Banned! Book Censorship in the Schools* (Rogers, 1988), is written to and for students to help them understand issues related to censorship and student choice.

Not with a Bang, but a Whimper

Censorship, and a fear of censorship, have created classrooms of disempowered teachers and disenchanted readers. In many cases, the bang of powerful, heated discussions around a piece of literature that has challenged everyone's thinking has been reduced to whimpered, staid responses to teacher-directed questions. I fear classrooms where students read a very limited, safe selection of books. I fear the kind of fellow citizens they will make. As a teacher and a citizen, I would rather risk a censorship issue so that my students and I could have a discussion about personal values and responsibility after reading a book such as *Fair Game* (Tamar, 1993) than run the risk of denying students the opportunity to express their concerns and thoughts. Such represssion could have far worse implications. I wouldn't want to see my students' names in an article headlined, "Pensacola school struggles to recover from October sex scandal" (*Orlando Sentinel*, 1996).

As a reader, I'm glad that my notion of what it might mean to survive didn't only come from reading Stevenson's *Kidnapped*, but has been expanded over the years by books such as *I Know Why the Caged Bird Sings* (Angelou, 1970); *The Book of Ruth* (Hamilton, 1988); *She's Come Undone* (Lamb, 1992); and *Freak the Mighty* (Philbrook, 1993). I have examined my life by looking into the mirrors held to my face by poets and playwrights, by artists and musicians, and I have come away from each encounter stronger for having been there. Do we want less for our students?

When I was a high school English teacher, I made it a goal for students in my classes to encounter at least a thousand new books during our time together. I knew what I hoped they were learning: life seen through the perspective of only one book could be harmful, but the perspectives gained from a thousand books—a thousand writers—would only make them more willing to look for other voices and perhaps take the risk of adding their own. The writer who invited Jason to become a reader and a writer was Stephen King; for Terri, it was Maya Angelou; and for Rachel it was Scott O'Dell. Each then went on to read hundreds of other writers. Shouldn't all our students have the same opportunity to find a reading/writing mentor who leads them to a lifetime of words and books?

Works Cited

Applebee, A. (1989). *A study of book-length works taught in high school English courses.* (Report 1.2). Washington, DC: National Endowment for the Arts.

Brown, J., & Stephens, E. (1995). *Teaching young adult literature: Sharing the connection.* Belmont, CA: Wadsworth Publishing.

Foerstel, H. N. (1994). *Banned in the U.S.A.: A reference guide to book censorship in schools and public libraries.* Westport, CT: Greenwood Press.

Hamburg, J. (1996, June 9). Pensacola school struggles to recover from October sex scandal. *The Orlando Sentinel*, p. 1.

Huck, C. (1977). Literature as the content of reading. *Theory into Practice, 16* (5), 363–371.

Kaywell, J. (1993). *Adolescent literature as a complement to the classics.* Norwood, MA: Christopher-Gordon.

Kaywell, J. (1995). *Adolescent literature as a complement to the classics II.* Norwood, MA: Christopher-Gordon.

Kaywell, J. (1997). *Adolescent literature as a complement to the classics III.* Norwood, MA: Christopher-Gordon.

Rogers, D. J. (1988). *Banned! Book censorship in the schools.* New York: Messner.

Simmons, J. (1991, Winter). Censorship in the schools: No end in sight. *The ALAN Review 18* (2), pp. 6–8.

Resources

American Library Association. (1996). Banned Books 1996 Resource Guide. Mailing Address: Banned Books Week, Office for Intellectual Freedom, American Library Association, 50 East Huron, Chicago, IL 60611 (phone 1-800-545-2433/4223 or fax 1-312-280-4227).

National Council of Teachers of English, 1111 W. Kenyon Road, Urbana, IL 61801-1096 (phone 1-800-369-6283 or fax 217-328-9645).

———

For literature references, please see "Reference List of Literary Works."

16

In the Case of King

▼

What May Follow

ANNE E. POOLER & CONSTANCE M. PERRY

▼ ▼ ▼ ▼

*. . . but Ms. Yarrow claimed that Norman had
made the cut across his hand himself and his
partner had done the one over his eyebrows for
him. They had done this, she said, after pushing
her back into Unit 12 of the Railroad Motel, breaking her nose and four of her fingers, fracturing
nine bones in her left foot by stamping on it repeatedly (they took turns, she said), pulling out
wads of her hair, and punching her repeatedly in
the abdomen. The short one then raped her, she
told the IA shooflies. The broad shouldered one
had tried to rape her, but hadn't been able to get it
up at first. He bit her several times on the breasts
and face, and then he was able to get an erection,
she told them, "but he squirted all over my leg
before he could get it in . . . ."*

Stephen King, *Rose Madder*

This is where censorship in schools usually begins, with offensive words, graphic violence, sexually explicit acts, or a
paragraph read out of context. Many a teacher has been
caught off balance at a school board meeting or parent conference
with a demand for censorship of literature in the classroom. What do
you do? These kinds of situations must be handled with great care.
They are delicate, volatile, highly charged, and consequential for teachers and students, both individually and collectively, both in the short-
term and as they affect long-term efforts at reform and innovation.

To help you think through the issues involved in such cases,
let's look briefly at the definition of censorship, the nature of controversial issues, your rights and responsibilities as a teacher in addressing a potential censorship issue in literature, and then explore a censorship case study.

The world of the mind is the world of ideas. Your role as a
teacher is to constantly nurture students to help them extend the
boundaries of their minds, to challenge them to see the world in

different ways, to explore the joys of the mind, and to become open-minded thinkers and innovative artists. Often working against these purposes, censorship is based on moral judgments that may run the gamut in a community. A teacher's job is to find the equilibrium that allows a balance between constantly challenging the boundaries of thought *and* accommodating the values of a particular community.

A wide range of materials in schools can be seen as controversial or worthy of censorship. Why does one community ban certain material in schools that another may allow? For a variety of reasons, including the back-to-basics movement, K–12 schools regularly face the criticism that our schools are failing to prepare students. The belief that our society is at a moral low, the increased power of the religious right, and the censorship of specific materials go hand-in-hand with such criticism.

You may well be familiar with specific books that have been attacked, including *Of Mice and Men* (John Steinbeck), *Catcher in the Rye* (J. D. Salinger), *The Bell Jar* (Sylvia Plath), *The Adventures of Huckleberry Finn* (Mark Twain), *Bridge to Terabithia* (Katherine Paterson), *Forever* (Judy Blume), and *Cujo* (Stephen King). These books have been challenged because they focus on death, are sexually explicit, contain profanity, or deal with mysticism or Satanism. Even the *American Heritage Dictionary* has been under attack.

In more than 40 percent of the cases reported, censors were successful in restricting or removing materials (Scales, 1990). To that figure should be added restrictions resulting from widespread self-censorship, where teachers limit their curriculum in an attempt to avoid confrontation with the censors (Scales, 1990). This may be the most serious censorship of all. A teacher brings to the classroom her own intellectual curiosity and her ways of seeing the world. She is best at her job when she can use her personal intellectual energy to ignite the minds of students. Self-censorship means she becomes dependent upon a curriculum often developed by a committee to satisfy others—the community, the school board, or other groups at large.

Many teachers try to avoid controversy—sticking to safe, non-controversial materials—but struggle to figure out just what fits in that category, given the many definitions of "controversy" in a society. A number of Stephen King's books, as well as those by other authors, have been judged as not safe. Many students are then denied exposure to materials that a teacher believes would capture their interest in reading. Teachers then feel guilty for having abandoned materials they believe produce generally positive outcomes for students (Davis, 1996).

Rights and Responsibilities

Just what rights and responsibilities do teachers have in choosing appropriate material whether controversial or not? A basic academic right is encompassed in the First Amendment of our Constitution: "Congress shall make no law respecting an establishment of religion, or prohibiting the free exercise thereof; or abridging the freedom of speech, or the press, or the right of the people peaceably to assemble, and to petition the Government for a redress of grievances."

Supreme Court Justice William O. Douglas elaborates on this first amendment right:

> The First Amendment was designed "to invite dispute," to "create dissatisfaction with conditions as they are," and even to stir "people to anger."
> The First Amendment was not fashioned as a vehicle for dispensing tranquilizers to the people. Its prime function was to keep debate open to "offensive" . . . people . . . . By reason of the First Amendment . . . speakers and publishers have not been threatened or subdued because their thoughts and ideas may be "offensive" to some.   Douglas, Miller v. California, June 6, 1973, 43 U.S. 15, p. 145. (Pally, 1991)

Academic organizations, among others, have supported the first amendment. For example, a committee of the National Council for the Social Studies expressed that teachers have the right to do the following:

- participate in the development of curriculum and the selection of teaching materials;
- select for classroom study controversial issues (literature) that relate to the curriculum, and are appropriate to the maturity, intellectual and emotional capacities of the students;
- [have access to or create] a written policy approved by the local Board of Education which:
  a. clearly states the right of students to learn and of teachers to teach.
  b. provides guidelines and safeguards for the study of controversial issues.
  c. details and insures fair procedures for investigating criticism of the study of controversial issues. (Academic Freedom Committee, 1991)

Rights are accompanied by responsibilities, and in choosing materials for classroom use, teachers must recognize these responsibilities. As long as students are minors, the school does act in loco parentis; some materials may not be appropriate for children of certain ages. Showing R-rated films in ninth grade without parental permission is one such example. In addition, materials must fit within the approved curriculum, and if they are potentially controversial because of profanity or sexual explicitness, the materials must be evaluated as worthy literature. These responsibilities contain no absolutes, and that may well be why literature is regularly challenged by parents, students, or other community members.

In order to explore the issue of censorship of school curriculum materials, put yourself in the place of the teacher in the following case study. It represents what can and has happened in censorship disputes across the country.

Assigning Stephen King: Learning the Hard Way

Pat, a tenth-grade English teacher in a suburban middle class community, is in her second year of teaching. Pat brings two passions to her work. One is to introduce fine literature and the second is to introduce the joys of reading to her students (some of whom have been identified as "reluctant readers"). In a short period of time she has established a good rapport with students and has received positive evaluations from her supervisors. Parents seem to enjoy the variety of experiences their children have in her class.

One of the contemporary authors she enjoys is Stephen King. She knows that students like him and can identify with his characters. She wishes to use his writing to teach such literary techniques as characterization, plot, setting, imagery, and point-of-view. On a second level, she believes King is a master at looking at moral and ethical questions of humanity and redemption. Pat knows that King has been a controversial author in some school systems across the country and knows that she needs to follow the right procedures in assigning his works to avoid controversy later on.

Pat wants to assign the book *Carrie*. First, she develops her rationale for choosing the book:

1. The story concerns an adolescent who is definitely an outsider to peers and parent, a situation her adolescents can relate to.

2. King's deft touch of detailed description, which can help students' writing.

3. Like other King books it is written on different levels—at one level a great story and at a deeper level, full of metaphors for life.

4. The monster in *Carrie* can stand for the greater "monsters" of contemporary life. (see Beahm, 1995)

Pat discusses her choice with her department chair, James, who refers to the pamphlet *Common Ground* (1991). This resource was developed by the National Council of Teachers of English/International Reading Association (NCTE/IRA) Joint Task Force on Intellectual Freedom and outlines strategies to follow before a challenge arises regarding selection of classroom material (appendix A). Pat and James feel it is important to review these procedures because King's works have been challenged in other communities.

In following NCTE/IRA guidelines provided in *Common Ground*, Pat finds the print and nonprint materials selection policies and procedures and complaint policies on file in the main office. She and James meet with the principal, Ms. Shore, to discuss her selection. Together they review the system selection policy and agree the book has merit. Additionally, Pat agrees to help students find an alternative book to read if the students or parents object to reading Stephen King's *Carrie*.

Pat assigns the book, and two weeks later a parent calls the chair of the school board complaining about the horrible book his daughter is forced to read. It contains offensive language, and describes life situations that the parent believes are inappropriate for adolescents. The chair tells the superintendent, Mr. Izod, to "take care of it." Mr. Izod informs Ms. Shore, the principal, about the complaint and the principal indicates she was aware of the assignment as the teacher and department chair had followed correct procedures for choosing the assignment. Mr. Izod instructs Ms. Shore to have the teacher change the assignment. Ms. Shore convinces Mr. Izod to allow her to call a meeting that includes the parent, Pat, and the department chair, James, to try to explain how and why the challenged materials were selected.

At the meeting, the parent is provided with the rationale for assigning *Carrie*, but he still objects. However, when he is made aware that there is an alternative assignment option, he feels it is appropriate for his daughter to do the alternative assignment. The meeting ends with an alternative being chosen.

Prior to the meeting, however, the parent has shared his concerns with a number of community members. Although now he feels comfortable with the resolution, enough people in the community, some of whom do not have students in the school, continue to call school board members with concerns and complaints about "the kind of stuff" that is being taught. The situation escalates into a community brouhaha when a small but vocal group strongly objects to allowing King's book to be assigned. At the next school board meeting a number of concerned citizens insist that the school not allow *Carrie* to be included in the curriculum. Pat speaks in favor of the book as does her department chair. The school board members listen and indicate they have a policy in place to review challenged materials. It is agreed that the review process is to be followed, which results in a favorable decision by committee for continuing the assigned reading of *Carrie*. Superintendent Izod informs the school board of the findings. Pat thinks the issue is finally settled.

The vocal community group is not satisfied with this decision. They organize and speak vehemently against the committee's recommendation at the next school board meeting. They point to the violence and "the moral decay of our times," linking these social conditions to the ideas put into students' heads by books such as King's. This vocal group convinces the school board in a five-to-four decision to demand the removal of *Carrie* from the curriculum.

What, if Anything, Went Wrong?

Following policies and procedures may not be enough. Whenever a vocal minority threatens to rule the day, work needs to be done to publish procedures, more fully inform interested parties, debate salient issues, and involve more people within and beyond the school.

Even though proper procedures were followed, *Carrie* was banned because of pressure from a small, vocal minority. Other activities could have encouraged the board to resist the pressure. The teachers and administrators involved could have (1) educated the school board by providing them with the book, as well as reviews of and rationales for its use; (2) created a broader community dialogue in support of intellectual freedom to discuss the issues involved and to mobilize the support in advance of the challenges. As suggested in *Common Ground*, you can do this by discussing intellectual freedom at faculty meetings and at parent–teacher meetings. In doing so, you educate other people to speak up at school board meetings in favor of the challenged books.

Stephen King, a former high school English teacher and a contemporary author, is read by millions. Many educators believe his books can capture the interest and minds of young readers. His works are lightning rods for potential censorship challenges, but educators equipped with solid rationales, a clear understanding of their students, with knowledge of the mores of their community, and a dose of courage can encourage students to understand their own tastes as readers through exposure to King.

Pat, from the case study, has decisions to make. Will she press the issue and ask for reconsideration, garnering support and educating the school board along the way? Will she stay quiet until she has a continuing contract (tenure)? Will she never dare choose literature that could prove controversial again? Whatever Pat decides, her experience has been an unfortunate one. She has learned that the best time to think about censorship is before you need to think about it. Still, the issues and consequences were deeper and more far-reaching than she had ever anticipated, which left her, her teaching, and her students in a kind of limbo. Pat and her colleagues were also left without the means to engage in further dialogue with those citizens who had objections to *Carrie.*

Final Thoughts

We encourage you to discuss this hypothetical case in your next faculty meeting. We also encourage you to maintain a regular dialogue with colleagues and community, keeping academic rights and responsibilities in mind. That is an important way for you to know your community's mores and in turn for the community to be open to the merits of literature that may be controversial. Such activities will prevent vocal minorities from catching others unprepared; in the case presented here, such actions may well have resulted in the school board upholding the use of *Carrie.* Whether it is Stephen King or another author, classroom teachers need to be proactive.

Works Cited

Academic Freedom Committee of the National Council for the Social Studies. (1991). Academic freedom and the social studies teacher. *Social Education, 55* (1), 13–14.

Beahm, G. (Ed.). (1995). *The Stephen King companion.* Kansas City, MO: Andrews and McMeel.

Davis, W. (1996). *Impact of the new religious right on public schools.* College of Education: University of Maine.

NCTE/IRA Joint Task Force on Intellectual Freedom. (1991). *Common ground.* See appendix A, this volume.

Pally, M. (1991). *Sense and censorship: The vanity of bonfires.* New York: Americans for Constitutional Freedom.

Scales, P. (1990). Library censorship is not justified. In L. Orr (Ed.), *Censorship: Opposing viewpoints* (pp. 126–132). San Diego, CA: Greenhaven Press.

For literature references, please see "Reference List of Literary Works."

17

Be Prepared

▼

Developing a Censorship Policy for the Electronic Age

ABIGAIL C. GARTHWAIT

Free societies . . . are societies in motion, and with motion comes tension, dissent, friction. Free people strike sparks, and those sparks are the best evidence of freedom's existence.

—Salman Rushdie

▼ ▼ ▼ ▼ ▼

Mr. Kimball: "My students had a blast today comparing some reviewers' vocabulary choices as they wrote about Desperation *and* The Regulators. *They offered significant insights into reviewers' motivation as well as their own."*

<http://www.desperation.com/reviews.html>

Ms. Saks: "I couldn't have been more pleased when Jeremy (of all kids!) asked if he could do extra research last week. Unfortunately, our library media center didn't have any print information about R. L. Stine. But fortunately, our librarian started him on an Internet search and he actually found the answer to his pressing question: 'What's the most horrifying thing that ever happened to R.L. Stine?' He's so proud of himself."

<http://place.scholastic.com/goosebumps/index.htm>

Jenny: "Horror stories fascinate me!! I love being scared by a book I'm reading especially when I'm curled up in a comfy chair in my own home. By the way, I've started an e-mail correspondence with this nice young man who feels the same way. . . ."

Student comment

For today's classroom, the Internet offers vast learning opportunities, and students and teachers are finding they can extend their appreciation of popular artists like Stephen King and popular genres such as horror through this electronic resource. But what would happen if one of Mr. Kimball's students gains access to a Web site carrying explicit photographs of intentional carnage? Or if Jeremy finds a way to order expensive spin-off goods and charges them to his parents? Or if Jenny ends up being stalked by a young man who wasn't so nice after all? Will consequences of isolated incidents destroy Internet access for all students? Headlines such as the following could delay or totally sideline a school's access to global networks: "Web how-to for grenades leaves children injured." (Amsterdam, 1996, cited in Maine's *Bangor Daily News*) If, however, you hold the Internet responsible—as this headline does—you could also hold your mail carrier responsible for delivering an illegal chain letter. Other authors in this collection have dealt with how to develop and debate acceptable print media in schools (see Allen, chapter 15; Pooler and Perry, chapter 16). My primary concern is with the electronic medium.

The electronic age brings with it new censorship issues, on which schools and districts must take a proactive stand. For decades now, selection policies for library and classroom materials have been articulated, affording a manner of protection against biased lobbying efforts, assertive religious organizations, or aggressive corporate parties. Traditional selection policies may also provide a structure for school response, should any material be challenged. But the Internet opens up a whole new area of concern. There is no online guidance from master teachers or expert librarian–researchers, and students have nothing to guide their Internet use.

The major difference between an Acceptable Use Policy (AUP) and a Selection Policy is that the latter deals with material that is purposefully evaluated and selected to fit the school's educational goals. School library media specialists and teachers exercise care and professional judgment in selecting the most balanced, well-rounded, and unbiased material in order to avoid spending precious resources on poorly written and/or inaccurate material. (Teachers don't invest hours in a read-aloud unless they are convinced of its quality.) An Acceptable Use Policy, on the other hand, merely informs a community about which materials may be accessed.

Guidelines for establishing AUPs and censorship issues were central concerns of the Reading Stephen King Conference. Workshops on the subject were attended by people from many states, as well as by teachers and librarians in Maine. The issues were of particular interest to Maine because of a recent agreement reached between the state's largest phone company (NYNEX) and Maine's Public Utilities Commission, which made the Internet accessible to every school and library in the state. The rapid push in technology has left many educators' heads spinning. The danger, of course, is that educators will be vulnerable to the whims of various interest groups, some of which believe that unlimited electronic access to information is a bad thing.

One of the best ways to be prepared for the challenges ahead is for schools to formally adopt an Acceptable Use Policy. Such a policy may make censorship less common, as well as provide support to students whose constitutional rights are endangered. AUPs take a positive stand that will assist in protecting districts from uninformed or irrational diatribes and attempts to limit Internet access.

Free Speech in Cyberspace and Community Concerns

Without adequate policy preparation and a suitable knowledge base, some staff members may react inappropriately when they become aware of the multifaceted Internet. As an example, look at the fascinating case of Paul Kim. In 1995, Paul was a high school student in the state of Washington. He participated in extracurricular activities, was a top scorer for the National Merit Scholarship, earned nearly a 4.00 average, and scored close to perfect on the SATs. On his own time and without using school equipment, he set up a parody of his high school home page, spoofing what he saw as the prevailing adolescent preoccupation with sex. He also provided links to relevant, publicly accessible pages. At the advice of his guidance counselor, Paul removed the pages from public Internet access and was assured that there would be no further administrative repercussions. Nevertheless, without Paul's knowledge, the principal wrote letters to all the colleges that he had applied to and rescinded her earlier recommendation. Paul was unaware of her actions until one university admissions officer phoned him to find out the real story behind the retraction!

Paul was, however, accepted at Columbia, and his home page (Kim, 1997) contains a link to what he calls his "bit of trouble." The American Civil Liberties Union became involved, and the case was settled out of court for $2,000. Apparently no compensation was awarded for distress and violation of Paul's constitutional and civil rights, although the Supreme Court has repeatedly upheld that a student's rights do not stop at the school door.

The big issue here is control. In the past, schools could generally rest assured that good, professional opinion led to the acquisition of all material used inside school walls. In addition, teachers felt that they had some handle on the ideas that students were sharing with each other. Once a computer is plugged into the Internet, there certainly isn't that same level of control.

The issues are complex, and there are no easy answers. No one wants their own children or those in their classrooms to be "harmed," but notions of what causes "harm" can vary substantially. What one parent might consider harmful, another might dismiss. Can ideas be considered unhealthy? Just because a student reads deeply about socialist reform issues doesn't mean that she will become a machine-gun-toting anarchist. At what age are students capable of understanding and dealing with weighty issues? Certainly, I wouldn't want many kindergartners I know making decisions about consequences or punishments concerning playground problems. Age and developmental levels are important considerations. That's why I wouldn't want an elementary school student wandering around in newsgroups such as <alt.sex.bestiality>. Yet, how long can we reasonably expect to shield our students from the "real world"?

The Internet is so new in schools that the legal system has not yet established the standard of care which should be exerted to protect students. This standard will only come about through an accumulation of court cases. In the meantime, schools will be operating in a rather vague and uncertain legal environment.

What are some areas that have caused concern to some people?

- Psychotics preying on children and young adults via e-mail and/or chat rooms.
- Hate mail or harassment.
- Lack of quality control due to ease of publication of inaccurate material. (For instance, someone could write a seemingly credible article on chemistry experiments and put it on the Internet in three minutes. A professional journal may toss it immediately, recognizing that the combination of ingredients is dangerous.)
- Confidentiality of student records. (Casual "water fountain" gossip can instantly be a major disaster if it's distributed throughout the network.)
- Perceived "addictive" quality of the Internet. (Combined with TV and Nintendo, computers will keep children from playing creatively or going outside any more.)
- Ease of purchasing. (Children might financially obligate their parents or the school with order-now, pay-later items.)
- Exposure to violent material.
- Exposure to pornography. (And whose definition will you use?)
- Commercial nature of the Internet. (For example, it contains alcohol advertisements.)

As a teacher, you will hear the concerns above voiced many times. Be sure that you are prepared for the possible event that a parent may not want the Internet in the school *at all*. Our position is that although parents have the right to raise their children as they see fit, they do not have the right to dictate the education for all children and young adults in the school. If their child is not to use the Internet, they should make that clear with the child and send a note to school to that effect.

One of the thornier issues to be solved is whether the school will expect parents to sign an agreement that their child may use the Internet. What are the practical considerations and repercussions of a few students being denied Web access because their parents have heard horror stories? How will teachers deal with twenty-two students who are working on Internet research and two students who are not allowed to use the Internet but are sitting right next to them? Does this widen the gap between the information haves and have-nots?

Developing Acceptable Use Policies

In the preceding section I have articulated the rationale for a proactive Acceptable Use Policy. What general components are involved?

Most Acceptable Use Policies Include the Following:

- A clear statement of purpose about why the district is providing the Internet to its staff and students (e.g., to support curriculum and other educational services). Usually a district's purpose is not to allow general unlimited Internet access any more than it would support watching daily soap operas or TV channel surfing during school time.

- Language which often speaks about "maximizing the benefits and minimizing the risks" of Internet use.

- A statement about using "appropriate language." Caution: A court of law may see a similar statement as unclear and "overly broad."

- A statement about not harassing anyone for any reason and what to do if a user is harassed.

- A statement about abiding by copyright laws.

- A statement about not accessing or attempting to access another person's account.

- A statement about the consequences of misuse.

- A statement about vandalism, or malicious intent to cause harm to the network.

- A place for the signature of the student or staff member who agrees to Internet use as stated in the policy.

Some Acceptable Use Policies Include the Following:

- A statement about increased productivity within the district due to telecommunications.

- Rules about staff distribution of confidential student information. It might seem natural to be corresponding with the guidance counselor via e-mail, but e-mail is not guaranteed to be private.

- A disclaimer regarding loss of data on the school or district network.

- A place for the signature of the student's parent (or guardian) to indicate that the policy has been read and understood and that the parent allows the student to use the Internet as outlined.

- A division of Internet uses into a variety of levels, separating private e-mail from group use and both of these from students' research uses.

- A statement that only students' first names will be used on school-published Web pages and that children's pictures will not be used without parents' written permission. Young children are taught not to talk to strangers, but if their picture, name, and life story are published on the school's Web pages, they are, in essence, talking to a whole world of strangers.

- A sponsoring teacher's signature. (This is something that I would not recommend, as it places individual teachers directly in the path of a lawsuit.)

Whenever access to information is denied, free-speech issues are involved. In such a new area as Internet use, many of the issues have little legal precedent. Web pages should be viewed in a similar manner as articles regarding fair-use copyright law. For an excellent and understandable discussion of many of these issues, see Nancy Willard's (1996) Web pages, *A legal and educational analysis of K–12 Internet Acceptable Use Policies.*

Be clear about what you are expected to do if a student feels that her or his account has been unfairly canceled as a consequence of what an authority perceives as a misuse. There should be a clearly stated avenue of recourse. Note that some advisors feel that an account cannot be suspended if a student is in the process of protesting a revocation of an account.

Importance of Process

Many people consider the actual process of building an Acceptable Use Policy to be at least as important as the final product. Employees

of public institutions would do well to remind themselves of the value
of obtaining many levels of input. It is wise, though, to begin our
"homework" before the public eye is trained on us. Learn what might
be considered harmful. Know who the potential censors might be in
your community; know their issues. It's possible that the strongest
voices may not come from concerned parents but from an organized
group which desires to dictate school policies based on its own narrow agenda.

It might be a help to work through foundational topics by addressing pertinent questions, such as the following:

- Is Internet access a right or a privilege? This question lies at
  the heart of many policy decisions.

- Is there value in students doing "exploratory" Internet activities (Net surfing, skimming along the surface)? Math teachers know the value of giving students time to "play" with
  new manipulatives before they involve them in more struc-
  tured activities. Will this theory work on the Internet? Is recreational net surfing a poor use of school time and resources?

- How private is e-mail? (Attorneys have been equating e-mail
  examination with "just reason" locker searches. Are teachers "allowed" to read notes being passed in class?)

- Should the school prohibit counselors and other staff from
  sending confidential reports and other sensitive material via
  e-mail?

- Should students use the Internet only with signed parental
  permission?

- If your district decides to require parental signatures, how
  will this be managed on a daily basis? Will the library media
  specialist or computer lab coordinator be required to know
  whether every student in the school has a signature on file?

- Should prohibitions such as e-mail harassment be included
  in an AUP? (Should they be addressed because of the ease of
  occurrence and potential anonymity in electronic communi-
  cations, or should they not be included because in-place laws
  cover this issue?)

- Should the consequences be spelled out? Usually the amount
  of restricted time on the network is specified. Some districts
  state that any violation of the policy results in losing access
  for a year. Should a warning be issued, or is the act of signing
  the policy considered the warning?

- Who holds the ultimate legal responsibility for students? Generally it's the school board. The superintendent is generally
  placed in the role of overseer supported by a building level
  guide.

Once your school and community have become involved in
the process of creating a document which addresses censorship issues,

it's time to look at other concerns, such as what to do about student-run Internet "ventures" for profit. Some schools state up-front that they are not responsible for unauthorized monetary obligations undertaken by staff or students. Some districts do not allow political fundraising or other political actions other than writing to elected officials. Many schools are pondering whether to allow dial-up Internet access via a school server from home. Should it be available for teachers as well as students?

Even after the policy is developed and approved, the work of technology leaders is not over. They will need to educate the parents, the students, and the rest of the staff. It will also be helpful to recognize that an AUP is a living document. As technology develops, so must the AUP. Reserve the right to change it.

What You Should Know about Filtering Software and Hardware

There is a beguiling aspect to Net censorship. Concerned parents and teachers may be tempted to think, "Ah, for x (sum of money) I can completely protect my children from all the horrors I've read about on the Internet." But this seeming elixir of safety is a mere illusion. There are numerous reasons not to use software or hardware that blocks out sites that may possibly be objectionable. First, we should be protective of our precious liberties regarding free speech and access to information. Allowing censors to encroach in small ways lays the foundation for an "infobahn police force" (Rheingold, 1995). Second, in education, one of our weightiest charges is to teach children and young adults how to make good decisions. Last year I watched as a fifth-grade boy was searching the Civil War on the Internet in conjunction with a history fair. He typed into the search text box the word SLAVERY and was rewarded with an enormous number of hits that he needed to sort through. As he looked for relevant Web pages, he examined each title and accompanying introductory words. So focused on the topic at hand, he easily by-passed "Uncle Robert's Leather Shop" with its seductive wording involving sexual bondage. Since it wasn't relevant to his topic, he skipped right by it. He was using evaluative skills during that research session—isn't that what we want to teach?

You should also know that filtering software (such as CyberPatrol, Net Nanny, or Cybersitter) isn't particularly effective. On one hand, adolescents may be particularly keen to be able to find something that an authority figure has just told them was blocked. (Blocks and filters can act like a thrown gauntlet.) On a practical note, filtering software will fail to block out some sites, and it may not allow important material through that should be accessible. If the filter is set to screen out Web sites using the word "sex," will students find the information they are looking for on AIDS, the life cycle of a flea, or the poetry of Anne Sexton? Furthermore, no device can filter out inaccurate, misleading, or inferior sites.

Another point against using filtering software is that the costs are high in dollars, either because of an initial charge and sometimes because of monthly updating fees. As fast as some of the censors are finding offensive sites and putting them on the block-out list, the purveyors are finding new ways around such a block. Indeed, the Net was originally constructed so that if a packet of information met with a roadblock the carriers were to find any way around it.

Filtering and blocking software may be viewed as violations of civil liberties. And if we look at filtering and blocking through a legal lens, precedence can be found that any Internet provider who attempts to block "offensive" material may be more liable should a user stumble across an "objectionable" site. It has been said that a Beware-of-the-Dog sign indicates the owner is already aware of a dangerous dog and therefore should be more liable.

Checklist for Becoming Knowledgeable about School Internet Use

If you are at a loss as to how to proceed, consider the suggested steps outlined below. Double-check that you haven't left out important elements. It's possible that your school or district is already in the throes of working through this process and has found a different order to be effective.

—— **Become well informed**: Organize an all-out information-collecting effort and form a committee involving school leaders and policy makers. Learn what the technology can and cannot do; thoroughly understand both the hardware and software. **Collect** varying examples of policies around the country (see Resources). Include your own school's Selection Policy for Library and/or Classroom Materials. Don't try to shortcut by adopting another district's policy.

—— **Distribute copies** among the committee members and ask that they come prepared to discuss pros and cons of the various documents. **Begin discussion** with a thorough philosophical statement of educational beliefs and purposes. List pros and cons for each issue or characteristic that committee members bring to the table.

When the committee is comfortable with a draft, present it to a broader-based committee: students, the staff of all involved schools, and key community members. This is important because you may have a great policy that is totally unenforceable or unwieldy to use daily. Begin by stressing the positive elements. A committee member from the local public library would probably be valuable, too. Keep the lines of communication open. Requesting public input early on goes much further toward building community trust than developing your district's policy in secret.

—— **Hold a public hearing** after the next draft is ready. (Be sure that spelling and grammar are checked and that no areas are left murky!) Give demonstrations, and pass out readings. **Listen** to public concerns and answer questions.

—— Take the recommended policy draft to your **school board** for final approval.

—— Present numerous opportunities to train the remainder of the staff and students and to educate the public. Place a high value on **appropriate and professional training**. The job isn't complete even after the policy has been passed. Simply placing it in the school handbook doesn't guarantee compliance.

—— If your policy is complex, **post a short, clear list** understandable to your student population near all computers with Internet access.

There is no guarantee that being effectively prepared will protect you and your school from problems or challenges. But allowing yourself to be taken by surprise will almost surely cause distress.

In his speech at the Reading Stephen King Conference, Stephen King spoke eloquently about his views on censorship and reading. You may wish to send your students to the Web page review, but visit it first, and find out if your school has an Acceptable Use Policy.

Works Cited

For Net newbies, the Web sites listed below may be accessed by opening up your favorite browser and typing the URL (Uniform Resource Locator) into the location or address field. All of the sites listed were accessed by the author on 14 March 1997.

Kim, Paul. "The Life and Times of Paul K. Kim." (8 February 1996).
    http://www.cc.columbia.edu/~pkk11/
    (letter from ACLU) 25 May 1995.
    http://k12.cnidr.org:90/paulkim.html

Stephen King Talks about *Desperation and The Regulators*." Penguin. 1996.
    http://www.desperation.com/kingtalks.html

"R. L. Stine Goosebumps on the Web." Scholastic. 1996.
    http://place.scholastic.com/goosebumps/index.htm

Rheingold, Howard. "Why Censoring Cyberspace is Dangerous & Futile."
    (August 1995).
    http://www.well.com/user/hlr/tomorrow/tomorrowcensor.html

"Web how-to for grenades leaves children injured. (Amsterdam)." *Bangor
    Daily News* (Maine). 19 October 1996: A3.

Willard, Nancy. "A Legal and Educational Analysis of K–12 Internet
    Acceptable Use Policies." 1996.
    http://www.erehwon.com/k12aup/legal_analysis.html

Resources

About Stephen King

Nomura, Ed. "Stephen King." (7 March 1997).
    http://phrtayl0.ucsd.edu/~ed/sk/

Osborne, Kate. "Stephen King: I want to mess with your life." *SALON
    Daily Clicks: Media Circus.* (1996).
    http://www.salon1999.com/media/media961015.html

Acceptable Use Policies

"Armadillo's WWW Server: Acceptable Use Policies." 18 April 1996.
    http://chico.rice.edu/armadillo/acceptable.html

The Texas Education Network (TENET). "Acceptable Use Policies."
    17 January 1996.
    http://www.tenet.edu/tenet-info/accept.html

Whitley, Peggy. "Internet Acceptable Use Policies." Kingwood College
    Library. 13 June 1996.
    http://www.nhmccd.cc.tx.us/groups/lrc/kc/usepolicies.html

Free Speech

"Bill of Rights and Responsibilities for Electronic Learners." EDUCOM
    Review. May/June 1993.
    http://www.sfasu.edu/bill.html

Cyberspace Law Center. "Freedom of Expression Resources." 1995.
    http://www.cybersquirrel.com/clc/expression.html

Kadie, Carl M. "Applying Library Principles to Public and Academic
    Computers." Computers, Freedom, and Privacy. 26 March 1994.
    http://www.eff.org/CAF/cfp94.kadie.html

National Council of Teachers of English. 1996. *Guidelines for selection of
    materials in English Language Arts Programs.* Stock #19778.
    Urbana, IL: NCTE. Cost of brochure $1.00 or $7.00 per 100. Order
    from: 1111 W. Kenyon Road, Urbana, IL 61801-1096.

Censorship

Burton, Paul F. "Controlling Access to the Internet." 10 October 1996.
    http://dis.strath.ac.uk/people/paul/Control.CDA.html

"A Dozen Reasons Why Schools Should Avoid Filtering." *From Now On.*
    5 (5) March/April 1996.
    http://www.pacificrim.net/~mckenzie/mar96/whynot.html

National Council of Teachers of English. Censorship Packet (no charge).
    Call NCTE Headquarters: 1-800-369-6283 or 217-328-3870. Fax:
    217-328-9645.

Ross, W., & Bailey, G. D. "Creating safe Internet access." *Learning and
    leading with technology*, pp. 51-53.

Reference List of Literary Works

Allison, Dorothy. 1992. *Bastard Out of Carolina*. New York: Dutton.

Angelou, Maya. 1970. *I Know Why the Caged Bird Sings*. New York: Random House.

Austen, Jane. 1996. *Pride and Prejudice*. 1813. Reprint, New York: Penguin.

———.1990. *Emma*. 1815. Reprint, New York: Bantam.

Beowulf. 1968. Translated by Kevin Crossley-Holland and introduced by Bruce Mitchell. New York: Farrar, Straus and Giroux.

Blatty, William Peter. 1971. *The Exorcist*. New York: Harper Row.

Blume, Judy. 1970. *Are You There God? It's Me, Margaret*. Englewood Cliffs, NJ: Bradbury Press.

Borland, Hal. 1963. *When the Legends Die*. New York: Bantam.

Brontë, Emily. 1979. *Wuthering Heights*. 1847. Reprint, New York: Penguin USA.

Browne, Claude. 1965. *Manchild in the Promised Land*. New York: Signet.

Burgess, Anthony. 1963. *A Clockwork Orange*. New York: Norton.

Carroll, Jim. 1978. *The Basketball Diaries*. New York: Penguin.

Cather, Willa. 1941. *O Pioneers*! Boston: Houghton Mifflin.

Contemporary Authors: New Revision Series. 1989. Detroit: Gale.

Dickens, Charles. 1948. *Great Expectations*. 1861. Reprint, New York: Dodd, Mead.

———.1972. *The Pickwick Papers*. Edited by R. L. Patten. 1837. Reprint, New York: Penguin.

———.1990. *A Tale of Two Cities*. 1859. Reprint, New York: Vintage.

Dickinson, Peter. 1988. *Eva*. New York: Dell.

Douglass, Frederick. 1960. *Narrative of the Life of Frederick Douglass: Written by Himself*. 1845. Reprint, Cambridge, MA: Belknap Press.

Eliot, George. 1968. *Silas Marner*. 1861. Reprint, New York: Lancer.

———. 1980. *The Mill on the Floss*. 1860. Reprint, New York: Viking Penguin.

The Epic of Gilgamesh. 1989. Translated with an introduction by Maureen Gallery Kovacs. Stanford, CA: Stanford University Press.

Evans, Nicholas. 1995. *The Horse Whisperer*. New York: Delacorte Press.

Fielding, Henry. 1987. *Joseph Andrews*. 1742. Reprint, New York: Methuen.

Fowles, John. 1969. *The French Lieutenant's Woman*. Boston: Little, Brown.

Goldsmith, Oliver. 1924. *The Vicar of Wakefield*. 1766. Reprint, New York: Macmillan.

Greene, Bette. 1991. *The Drowning of Stephan Jones*. New York: Bantam.

Gunther, John. 1949. *Death Be Not Proud*. New York: Harper and Row.

Hamilton, Jane. 1988. *The Book of Ruth*. New York: Doubleday.

Hawthorne, Nathaniel. 1955. *The Scarlet Letter*. 1850. Reprint, New York: Washington Square.

Hergesheimer, Joseph. 1924. *Balisand*. New York: Knopf.

Hess, Joan. 1995. *Miracles in Maggody: An Arly Hanks Mystery*. New York: Penguin.

Hesse, Hermann. 1971. *Narcissus and Goldmund*. 1930. Reprint, New York: Bantam.

Hinton, S. E. 1979. *Tex*. New York: Delacorte Press.

Homer. 1950. *The Complete Works of Homer: The Iliad, The Odyssey*. Translated by Andrew Lang, Walter Leaf, Ernest Myers, and S. H. Butcher. New York: Modern Library.

James, Henry. 1984. *The Portrait of a Lady*. 1881. Reprint, New York: Penguin.

———. 1957. *The Turn of the Screw*. 1898. Reprint, New York: Dutton.

Kazantzakis, Nikos. 1953. *Zorba the Greek*. New York: Simon and Schuster.

Kesey, Ken. 1962. *One Flew over the Cuckoo's Nest*. New York: Viking.

Keyes, Daniel. 1966. *Flowers for Algernon*. New York: Harcourt, Brace and World.

King, Gary C. 1992. *Blood Lust*. New York: Signet.

Knowles, John. 1960. *A Separate Peace*. New York: Macmillan.

Koontz, Dean. 1990. *The Bad Place*. New York: Putman.

———. 1993. *Dragon Tears*. New York: Pocket.

Lamb, Wally. 1992. *She's Come Undone*. New York: Simon and Schuster.

Lasky, Kathryn. 1996. *Memoirs of a Bookbat*. San Diego: Harcourt Brace.

Lesley, Craig. 1984. *Winterkill*. Boston: Houghton Mifflin.

Malamud, Bernard. 1980. *The Natural*. New York: Avon.

McCammon, Robert. 1987. *Swan Song*. New York: Pocket.

———. 1987. *Stinger*. New York: Pocket.

———. 1991. *Mine*. New York: Pocket.

Melville, Herman. 1962. *Moby-Dick*. 1851. Reprint, New York: Macmillan.

Miller, Jason. 1982. *That Championship Season*. New York: MGM/UA Home Video. Film.

Milton, John. 1971. *Paradise Lost*. Edited by A. Fowler. 1667. Reprint, New York: Harlow, Longman.

Mitchell, Margaret. 1936. *Gone with the Wind*. New York: Macmillan.

Morrison, Toni. 1987. *Beloved*. New York: Knopf.

Norris, Frank. 1986. *The Octopus*. 1901. Reprint, New York: Penguin.

————. 1976. *The Pit*. 1903. Reprint, New York: Buccaneer Books.

————. 1950. *McTeague*. 1899. Reprint, New York: Holt, Rinehart and Winston.

Oates, Joyce Carol. 1995. *Zombie*. New York: Dutton.

O'Brien, Tim. 1990. *The Things They Carried*. New York: Penguin.

Paterson, Katherine. 1977. *Bridge to Terabithia*. New York: HarperCollins.

Philbrick, Rodman. 1993. *Freak the Mighty*. New York: Scholastic.

Salinger, J. D. 1945. *Catcher in the Rye*. Boston: Little, Brown.

Sebestyen, Ouida. 1994. *Out of Nowhere*. New York: Orchard Books.

Shakespeare, William. 1974. *The Riverside Shakespeare*. Edited by G. Blakemore Evans. Boston: Houghton Mifflin.

Shelley, Mary Wollstonecraft. 1988. *Frankenstein*. 1818. Reprint, New York: Bedrick/Blackie.

Sparks, Beatrice, ed. 1979. *Jay's Journal*. New York: Times Books.

Spenser, Edmund. 1977. *The Faerie Queene*. Edited by A. C. Hamilton. 1596. Reprint, New York: Longman.

Steinbeck, John. 1937. *Of Mice and Men*. New York: Penguin.

Stevenson, Robert Louis. 1942. *Kidnapped*. 1886. Reprint, New York: Dodd, Mead.

Stowe, Harriet Beecher. 1981. *Uncle Tom's Cabin*. 1852. Reprint, New York: Bantam.

Sweeney, Joyce. 1994. *The Tiger Orchard*. New York: Laurel Leaf.

Tamar, Erika. 1993. *Fair Game*. San Diego: Harcourt, Brace.

Twain, Mark. 1951. *Adventures of Huckleberry Finn*. 1884. Reprint, New York: Globe.

Updike, John. 1963. *The Centaur*. New York: Knopf.

Virgil. 1987. *The Aeneid*. Edited by R. D. Williams. Boston: Allen and Unwin.

Walker, Alice. 1983. *The Color Purple*. New York: Washington Square Press.

Waller, Robert James. 1992. *The Bridges of Madison County*. New York: Warner Books.

Books by Stephen King

Bachman, Richard [pseud.]. 1996. *The Regulators*. New York: Dutton.

————. 1982. *The Running Man*. New York: Dutton.

King, Stephen. 1974. *Carrie*. Garden City, NY: Doubleday.

————. 1975. *Salem's Lot*. Garden City, NY: Doubleday.

————. 1977. *The Shining*. Garden City, NY: Doubleday.

————. 1978. *The Stand*. Garden City, NY: Doubleday.

———. 1978. *Nightshift*. Garden City, NY: Doubleday.

———. 1979. *The Dead Zone*. New York: Viking.

———. 1980. *Firestarter*. New York: Viking.

———. 1981. *Cujo*. New York: Viking.

———. 1982. *Different Seasons*. New York: Viking.

———. 1983. *Christine*. New York: Viking.

———. 1983. *Pet Sematary*. Garden City, NY: Doubleday.

———. 1983. *Cycle of the Werewolf*. Westland, MI: Land of Enchantment.

———. 1985. *Skeleton Crew*. New York: Putnam.

———. 1986. *It*. New York: Viking.

———. 1987. *Eyes of the Dragon*. New York: Viking.

———. 1987. *Misery*. New York: Viking.

———. 1987. *The Tommyknockers*. New York: Putnam.

———. 1988. *The Dark Tower: The Gunslinger*. New York: New American Library.

———. 1989. *The Dark Tower 2: The Drawing of the Three*. New York: New American Library.

———. 1989. *The Dark Tower 3: The Waste Lands*. New York: New American Library.

———. 1989. *The Dark Half*. New York: Viking.

———. 1990. *Four Past Midnight*. New York: Viking.

———. 1991. *Needful Things*. New York: Viking.

———. 1992. *Blood Lust*. New York: Signet.

———. 1992. *Gerald's Game*. New York: Viking.

———. 1992. *The Wastelands*. New York: New American Library/Dutton.

———. 1993. *Dolores Claiborne*. New York: Viking.

———. 1993. *Nightmares and Dreamscapes*. New York: Viking.

———. 1994. *Insomnia*. New York: Viking.

———. 1995. *Rose Madder*. New York: Viking.

———. 1996. *Desperation*. New York: Viking.

———. 1997. *The Green Mile*. New York: Plume.

———. 1997. *The Dark Tower 4: Wizards and Glass*. New York: Plume.

King, Stephen, and Peter Straub. 1984. *The Talisman*. New York: Viking.

Books for Children and Young Adults

Aiken, Joan. 1989. *Give Yourself a Fright: Thirteen Tales of the Supernatural*. New York: Delacorte Press.

Black, J. R. *Shadow Zone Series*. New York: Bullseye Book/Random House.

Conrad, Pam. 1990. *Stonewords: A Ghost Story.* New York: HarperCollins.

Cooper, Susan. 1986. *The Selkie Girl.* New York: Macmillan.

Courtney, V. (Adapter), and G. Goddard (Creator). *The Skeletal Warrior Series.* New York: Random House.

Deary, Terry. *Horrible Histories Series.* New York: Scholastic.

Duncan, Lois. 1981. *Stranger with My Face.* New York: Laurel Leaf/Dell.

Fitzgerald, John D. 1973. *The Great Brain Reforms.* New York: Dial.

Fleischman, Paul. 1980. *The Half-a-Moon Inn.* New York: HarperCollins.

Foster, Alan Dean. 1974. *Star Trek Log One.* New York: Ballantine.

Goldin, Stephen. 1979. *Trek to Madworld.* New York: Bantam.

Hayes, Geoffrey. *Graveyard Creeper Mystery Series.* New York: A First Stepping Stone Book/Random.

Haynes, Betsy. (Creator). *The Bone Chillers Series.* New York: Harper Paperbacks.

Howe, James. *Bunnicula Series.* New York: Avon Camelot.

Hunter, Mollie. 1975. *A Stranger Came Ashore.* New York: HarperCollins.

———. 1988. *The Mermaid Summer.* New York: HarperCollins.

Jacobs, David. *The Bug Files Series.* New York: Berkley Books.

King, Jane. *The Ghoul School Series.* New York: Minstrel Book/Pocket.

Levy, Elizabeth. *Something Queer Series.* New York: Yearling/Dell.

Locke, Joseph. *Blood and Lace Series.* New York: Bantam.

Lunn, Janet. 1985. *The Root Cellar.* New York: Puffin/Viking Penguin.

McKissack, Patricia C. 1992. *The Dark-Thirty: Southern Tales of the Supernatural.* New York: Knopf.

Mahy, Margaret. 1982. *The Haunting.* New York: Macmillan.

———. 1989. *The Blood-and-Thunder Adventure on Hurricane Peak.* New York: Yearling/Dell.

Mooser, Stephen. *The Creepy Creature Club Adventure Series.* New York: Young Yearling/Dell.

Osborne, Mary P. *The Magic Tree House Series.* New York: A First Stepping Stone Book/Random House.

Pascal, Francine. (Creator). Sweet Valley Twins Series. Lakeville, CT: Greycastle Press.

Piasecki, Jerry. 1995. *Laura for Dessert.* New York: Skylark/Bantam.

———. 1995. *Teacher Vic is a Vampire . . . Retired.* New York: Skylark/Bantam.

Pike, Christopher. *Spooksville Series.* New York: Minstrel/Pocket.

Sleator, William. 1988. *The Duplicate.* New York: Dutton.

Spenser, M. D. *The Shiver Series.* Plantation, FL: Paradise Press.

Stine, R. L. 1994. *My Hairiest Adventure.* New York: Scholastic.

———. 1996. *The Beast from the East.* New York: Scholastic.

————. 1996. *Ghost Camp*. New York: Scholastic.

————. 1996. *Nightmare in 3-D*. New York: Pocket.

————. 1997. *Beware, the Snowman*. New York: Scholastic.

————. 1997. *Killer's Kiss*. New York: Pocket.

————. *Fear Street Series*. New York: Scholastic.

————. *Ghosts of Fear Street Series*. New York: Pocket.

————. *Give Yourself Goosebumps Series.* New York: Scholastic.

————. *Goosebumps Series*. New York: Scholastic.

————. *Graveyard School Series*. New York: Skylark/Bantam.

Stone, Tom B. 1994. *The Skeleton on the Skateboard*. New York: Skylark/Bantam.

Snyder, Zilpha Keatley. *The Castle Court Kids Series.* New York: Bantam Doubleday Dell Books for Young Readers.

Wright, Betty R. 1994. *The Ghost Comes Calling*. New York: Scholastic.

————. 1995. *Out of the Dark*. New York: Scholastic.

Wrightson, Patricia. 1989. *Balyet*. New York: Macmillan.

Yolen, Jane. 1991. *Greyling*. New York: Philomel/Putnam.

Appendixes

A

Common Ground

▼

Speak with One Voice on Intellectual Freedom and the Defense of It

COMMON GROUND

The National Council of Teachers of English *and* The International Reading Association

Speak with One Voice on Intellectual Freedom and the Defense of It

Prepared by the NCTE/IRA Joint Task Force on Intellectual Freedom:

James E. Davis, Chair
Lorri Neilsen, Co-chair
Joyce Armstrong Carroll
Marie M. Clay
Millie Davis
Mabel T. Edmonds
Alan E. Farstrup
Shirley Haley-James
Janie Hydrick
Miles Myers
Jesse Perry
Wendy L. Russ
John S. Simmons
Robert C. Small, Jr.
Anne Tarleton
Judith N. Thelen
Geneva Van Horne
M. Jerry Weiss

NCTE/IRA Joint Statement on Intellectual Freedom

All students in public school classrooms have the right to materials and educational experiences that promote open inquiry, critical thinking, diversity in thought and expression, and respect for others. Denial or restriction of this right is an infringement of intellectual freedom.

Official policy of the International Reading Association (IRA) supports "freedom of speech, thought, and inquiry as guaranteed by the First Amendment of the Constitution of the United States," and the National Council of Teachers of English (NCTE) "supports intellectual freedom at all educational levels." Because of these almost exactly similar positions against censorship, the two associations, both advocates of literacy education and concerned with the issues that affect it, have formed a joint task force on intellectual freedom. One of the many goals of the NCTE/IRA Task Force on Intellectual Freedom is the development of this document to heighten sensitivity about censorship concerns and provide a resource for communities facing challenges to intellectual freedom.

The First Amendment of the U.S. Constitution guarantees freedom of expression:

"Congress shall make no law respecting an establishment of religion, or prohibiting the free exercise thereof; or abridging the freedom of speech or of the press; or the right of the people to assemble, and to petition the Government for a redress of grievances."

So does Article 19 of the United Nations Declaration of Human Rights:

"Everyone has the right to freedom of opinion and expression; this right includes freedom to hold opinions, without interference, and to seek, receive, and impart information and ideas through any media and regardless of frontiers."

Principles

The following principles of access, diversity, and fairness translate the ideal of the First Amendment into classroom reality:

Prepared by the Joint Task Force on Intellectual Freedom of the National Council of Teachers of English and the International Reading Association: James E. Davis, Chair, Lorri Neilsen, Co-chair, Joyce Armstrong Carroll, Marie M. Clay, Millie Davis, Mabel T. Edmonds, Alan E. Farstrup, Shirley Haley-James, Janie Hydrick, Miles Myers, Jesse Perry, Wendy L. Russ, John S. Simmons, Robert C. Small, Jr., Anne Tarleton, Judith N. Thelen, Geneva Van Horne, M. Jerry Weiss.

1. The education community should actively support intellectual freedom within the United States and among all nations.

2. Intellectual freedom in education is sought through fostering democratic values, critical thinking in teaching and learning, open inquiry, and the exploration of diverse points of view.

3. Educational communities should prepare for challenges to intellectual freedom with clearly defined procedures for the selection and review of educational materials and methods.

4. To preserve intellectual freedom in the classroom, educational communities, using professionally responsible criteria, should be free to select and review classroom curricula and materials that meet the needs of a diverse student population. Selection and revision of materials and methods does not necessarily mean endorsement or promotion; an educator's freedom to choose responsibly to meet student needs is a form of intellectual freedom.

What To Do: Action Plan/Strategies

Local Level

As a matter of regular practice, and before a challenge arises:

- Check to see if there are print and nonprint materials selection policies and procedures and complaint policies (including forms) on file. If there are no policies, participate in developing them and in having them adopted by the school board. Circulate policies frequently to faculty, administrators, and parents.

- Prepare, seek, and collect rationales for the use of specific curricular materials and practices.

- Discuss with immediate supervisor the selection of all class texts and nonprint media and the development of reading lists and nonprint media.

- Stay in touch with district supervisory personnel on matters of curricular practices and materials selection.

- Create a dialogue with the broader community in support of intellectual freedom to discuss the issues involved and to mobilize support in advance of challenges.

- Find alternate choices for students who wish to "opt out" of an assignment.

- Save selected written student responses to works assigned to illustrate the diversity of responses to literature.

■ Discuss with local book salespeople their company's current position on exclusion, abridgement, and adaptation in published texts, as well as in those in preparation. Integrity requires that publishers prominently note "abridgements."

■ Engage students in discussions about and activities related to intellectual freedom.

■ Establish a professional library that includes publications related to intellectual freedom in a special section of the media center or teachers' lounge.

■ Discuss intellectual freedom at faculty meetings and parent-teacher meetings.

■ If your system engages in collective bargaining, propose the inclusion of an intellectual freedom clause as a "working condition" of the next collective bargaining agreement.

■ Work with your local councils of NCTE and IRA and with your librarians to address issues of intellectual freedom and to develop local resources.

■ Stay informed about groups whose goal it is to remove books and other curricular materials from schools (e.g., Eagle Forum, Concerned Women of America, Focus on the Family, American Family Association, Citizens for Excellence in Education.)

■ Keep a file of reviews of and rationales for use of specific instructional materials.

After a challenge has been made:

■ Try to resolve the challenge informally at the building level. Make an appointment to meet with the complainant to explain how and why the challenged materials were selected.

■ Be sure a third person is present at all meetings.

■ If the complainant wants to continue to challenge the material after this meeting, provide him or her with a request-for-review form.

■ If a completed request-for-review form is submitted, make sure the district policy for review is strictly adhered to.

■ Inform the community of the challenge and conduct the review process openly.

State/Provincial Level

Remember that many local tactics apply at the state/provincial level.

■ Join and work with your state/provincial affiliates of IRA and NCTE. Get the topic of "intellectual freedom" on programs and in resolutions.

■ Form a state coalition for intellectual freedom, including, for example, IRA, NCTE, American Library Association (ALA) affiliates, as well as artists' organizations, booksellers, video dealers, and American Civil Liberties Union (ACLU) representatives.

■ Participate in state adoption procedures and encourage the inclusion of intellectual freedom criteria in state adoption policies. Have on file state textbook and materials adoption criteria.

■ Become acquainted with people in the state/provincial department of education office on professional practices.

■ Solicit information on materials selection and curricular practice from state supervisors in English, reading, elementary school, middle school, and high school.

■ Collect and make available pertinent literature from other organizations such as the Association for Supervision and Curriculum Development (ASCD), National Association of Secondary School Principals (NASSP), National Association for Elementary School Principals (NAESP), and American Association of School Administrators (AASA), and work with these organizations on initiatives for intellectual freedom.

■ Propose intellectual freedom as a topic for state meetings of IRA, NCTE, ALA, National School Boards Association (NSBA), or National PTA meetings.

■ Stay informed of new state or provincial legislation affecting intellectual freedom. Support intellectual freedom legislation, and work to have such legislation enacted.

National Level

■ Become familiar with national organizations that deal with intellectual freedom.

■ Gain information about resources that NCTE and IRA have available for dealing with issues of intellectual freedom.

- Gain an understanding of teachers' and citizens' rights in matters of intellectual freedom.

- Provide information and suggestions on the issue of intellectual freedom to organizations such as the U.S. Department of Education, Education Commission of the States (ECS), and National Governors' Association (NGA).

- Encourage the inclusion at national conferences of programs dealing with intellectual freedom.

- Join national and international organizations such as NCTE, IRA, ALA, and the National Coalition Against Censorship (NCAC).

International Level

- Cooperate with international organizations that deal with issues of intellectual freedom (e.g., United Nations Educational, Scientific and Cultural Organization [UNESCO], International Federation of Library Associations and Institutions [IFLA], and PEN International).

- Support international policies against censorship.

- Encourage inclusion of intellectual freedom sessions at international conferences.

- Work with organizations of teachers in other countries to promote intellectual freedom.

- Promote statements of intellectual freedom as a basic human right.

- Work with organizations in other countries to promote intellectual freedom.

Groups Interested in Fighting Censorship

American Association of School Administrators (AASA)
 1901 North Moore Street, Arlington, VA 22209
 703/528-0700   *Contact: Gary Marx*

American Association of University Professors (AAUP)
 1012 14th Street, NW, Suite 500, Washington, DC 20005
 202/737-5900

American Civil Liberties Union (ACLU)
 132 West 43rd Street, New York, NY 10036   212/944-9800

American Library Association (ALA)
Freedom to Read Foundation
50 East Huron Street, Chicago, IL 60611   312/280-4224 or
800/545-2433, ext. 4224   *Contact: Anne Levinson*

Association for Supervision and Curriculum Development (ASCD)
1250 North Pitt Street, Alexandria, VA 22314-1403
703/549-9110

Education Commission of the States (ECS)
707 17th Street, Suite 2700, Denver, CO 80202-3427
303/299-3692

International Federation of Library Associations and Institutions (IFLA)
PO Box 95312, 2509 CH The Hague, Netherlands

International Reading Association (IRA)
800 Barksdale Road, PO Box 8139, Newark, DE 19711-8139
302/731-1600   *Contact: Wendy Russ*

National Association of Elementary School Principals (NAESP)
1615 Duke Street, Alexandria, VA 22314 703/684-3345

National Association of Secondary School Principals (NASSP)
1904 Association Drive, Reston, VA 22091 703/860-0200

National Council of Teachers of English (NCTE)
1111 W. Kenyon Road, Urbana, IL 61801
217/328-3870   *Contact: Millie Davis*

National Coalition against Censorship (NCAC)
2 West 64th Street, New York, NY 10023   212/724-1500

National Governors' Association (NGA)
Hall of States, 444 North Capitol Street, NW
Washington, DC 20001   202/624-5300

People for the American Way
200 M Street, NW, Suite 400, Washington, DC 20036
202/467-2381   *Contact: Mark Sedway*

Student Press Law Center
1735 I Street, NW, Suite 504, Washington, DC 20006
202/466-5242

PEN American Center
568 Broadway, New York, NY 10012   212/334-1660

UNESCO
7, Place de Fontenoy, 75700 Paris, France

U.S. Department of Education
400 Maryland Avenue, SW, Washington, DC 20202
202/708-5366

Bibliography of Resources

General Statements

Burress, Lee, and Edward Jenkinson. *The Student's Right to Know.* Urbana, IL: National Council of Teachers of English, 1983.

Donelson, Kenneth L. *The Student's Right to Read.* Rev. ed., Urbana, IL: National Council of Teachers of English, 1972.

"Free to Learn: A Policy Statement on Academic Freedom and Public Education," State of Connecticut Controversial Issues Policy, 1981. Reprinted in *Protecting the Freedom to Learn* by Donna Hulsizer, People for the American Way, 1989, p. 47.

IRA Censorship Statement, International Reading Association, Intellectual Freedom Committee, 1985.

"Library Bill of Rights," American Library Association, 1980.

"Statement on Censorship and Professional Guidelines." Urbana, IL: National Council of Teachers of English, 1982.

Current Intellectual Freedom Climate

American Library Association. *Information, Freedom and Censorship: World Report.* Chicago, IL: 1991.

Gabler, Mel, and Norman Gabler (with James C. Hefley). *What Are They Teaching Our Children?* Wheaton, IL: SP Publications, 1985.

Noble, William. *Bookbanning in America.* Middlebury, VT: Paul S. Erickson Publisher, 1990.

People for the American Way. *Attacks on Freedom to Learn.* Washington, DC, Annual Report. n.d.

Schlafly, Phyllis, ed. *Child Abuse in the Classroom.* 2nd ed. Alton, IL: Pere Marquette Press, 1985.

Weiss, M. Jerry. "A Dangerous Subject: Censorship." *ALAN Review 15* (1988): 59–64.

What to Do

Burress, Lee. *Battle of the Books.* Metuchen, NJ: Scarecrow Press, 1989.

Davis, James E., ed. *Dealing with Censorship.* Urbana, IL: National Council of Teachers of English, 1979.

Demac, Donna A. *Liberty Denied: The Current Rise of Censorship in America.* New York: PEN American Center, 1988.

Hoffman, Frank. *Intellectual Freedom and Censorship: An Annotated Bibliography.* Metuchen, NJ: Scarecrow Press, 1989.

Hulsizer, Donna. *Protecting the Freedom to Learn: A Citizen's Guide.* Washington, DC: People for the American Way, 1989.

International Freedom Committee Young Adult Services Division. *Hit List: Frequently Challenged Young Adult Titles: References to Defend Them.* Young Adult Services Division, American Library Association, 1989.

Jenkinson, Edward B. *The Schoolbook Protest Movement: 48 Questions and Answers.* Bloomington, IN: Phi Delta Kappa Educational Foundation, 1986.

Karolides, Nicholas J., and Lee Burress, eds. *Celebrating Censored Books!* Urbana, IL: National Council of Teachers of English, 1985.

Marsh, David. *50 Ways to Fight Censorship & Important Facts to Know about the Censors.* New York: Thunder's Mouth Press, 1991.

National School Boards Association. *Managing the Controversy.* Alexandria, VA: National School Boards Association, 1989.

Office for Intellectual Freedom of the American Library Association. *Intellectual Freedom Manual.* 3rd ed., 1989.

Reichman, Henry. *Censorship and Selection: Issues and Answers for Schools.* Chicago, IL and Arlington, VA: American Library Association and American Association of School Administrators, 1988.

Shugert, Diane P., ed. "Rationales for Commonly Challenged Taught Books" (entire issue). *Connecticut English Journal* 15:1, Fall 1983.

West, Mark I. *Trust Your Children: Voices against Censorship in Children's Literature.* New York: Neal-Schuman Publishers, 1988.

Censorship Isn't a Problem Anymore, Is It?

Do you know what the censors are saying. . .

"I hope I live to see the day when, as in the early days of our country, we won't have any public schools. The churches will have taken them over again and Christians will be running them."

—The Reverend Jerry Falwell
(Donna Hulsizer, *Protecting the Freedom to Learn*)

"Until textbooks are changed, there is no possibility that crime, violence, venereal disease, and abortion rates will decrease."
—Mel and Norma Gabler
(Donna Hulsizer, *Protecting the Freedom to Learn*)

"Modern public education is the most dangerous single force in a child's life: religiously, sexually, economically, patriotically, and physically."
—The Reverend Tim LeHaye
(Dave Marsh, *50 Ways to Fight Censorship*)

Teachers Aren't Affected by Censorship, Are They?

Have you ever heard or said . . .

- I'm afraid to use this book because some parents will object.

- I've heard that film caused trouble before.

- I read this book aloud to the class, but I changed some of the words.

- Our drama group can't do that play; the language might offend someone.

- I know my students want to talk about that issue. I don't dare let them.

- Inviting this author to our school will just cause trouble.

- I would love to order this book/tape/film for my school, but I won't even bother. The administration would never give me the money for it because they'll find something objectionable.

- I never ask my kids to write responses to what they read. That's an invasion of their privacy.

- My class doesn't visit that museum on field trips because of some nudity in the artwork there.

"The book...is an exquisite example of human genius. Where it flourishes, man flourishes. Where it withers, humanity withers. The book is strong. It can endure for a thousand years and more, but there exist those who would put out its eyes, blacken its words, reduce it to a gray heap of ashes, lock it in chains, and let generations live and die in darkness."

—Harrison E. Salisbury, in a lecture at the Library of Congress, 1983

"No book is safe from the censors. What they fear is an open exchange of ideas. They're worried that once you slip onto the raft with Huck and Jim, or watch Henry Miller banging against the soft walls of the universe, or experience James Baldwin's Amen Corner, *it may change you. And they're right."*

—Dave Marsh, *50 Ways to Fight Censorship*

"School children are one of the largest captive reading audiences in the world today. Because of the high cost of textbook publishing, relatively small interest groups can influence the content of textbooks throughout the U.S. It has become a very politicized process."

—Sherry Keith, author, *Politics of Textbook Selection*

"Schools should teach children how to think, not what to think. To study an idea is not necessarily to endorse an idea."

—Connecticut State Department of Education
1981 policy on academic freedom
(National School Boards Association,
Censorship: Managing the Controversy)

"I would ask you to reconsider your decision for the sake of your students, the ideals of education and knowledge, and also the freedom of speech and thought. We shall not be protecting our youth if we swathe them in ignorance, nor shall we earn or deserve their respect, if we cannot place enough trust and faith in them to reason and respond on their own behalves."

—George Braziller; publisher of the book *365 Days*,
in a letter to the chair of the Baileyville, Maine,
school committee that had removed the book
from the library.

B

Excerpt from A Teacher's Guide to Selected Horror Short Stories of Stephen King

A TEACHER'S GUIDE TO SELECTED HORROR SHORT STORIES OF

STEPHEN KING

from the anthologies
Night Shift, Nightmares and Dreamscapes,
and *Skeleton Crew*

prepared by
M. Jerry Weiss
Jersey City State College, Emeritus

with
Arthea J. S. Reed, Ph.D.,
Univ. of North Carolina at Asheville
and
W. Geiger Ellis, Ed.D,
Univ. of Georgia, Emeritus

Suggestions for Teaching

Before Reading the Stories

■ Introduce the genre of horror and suspense with a film, such as *The Haunting, The Phantom of the Opera,* or *Psycho.* Have students identify and analyze the elements of suspense and horror in the film.

■ Orally read a horror story, such as Edgar Allan Poe's "The Tell-Tale Heart" to the class. Discuss why it is so horrifying.

■ Compile a collection of horror and/or suspense stories with which the students are familiar.

During Reading Activities

As an introduction to a unit on horror and suspense, small groups of students can each read a different Stephen King selected short story, and discuss and write about the stories using the questions and activities below. After reading, discussing, and writing about the King stories, students can read one or more of the classic works suggested in the bibliography. Students can utilize their knowledge of the genres of horror and suspense learned from reading the King stories to analyze the classic fiction.

Students can keep a response journal, recording their reactions to the stories. They can select their own topics or respond to the questions below.

The response journal might be followed up with students working in reading groups. Students who have read the same story can share their ideas and thereby gain other insights into the story.

These questions are appropriate to discuss or write about after reading any of the suggested short stories:

■ What is the nature of evil?

■ What is the embodiment of evil in the story?

■ How does King develop the suspense in the story?

■ What elements of surprise are built into the story?

■ Who is the protagonist? Is she or he a victim? How does King make you empathize with the protagonist?

■ Who or what is the antagonist? When do you discover who the antagonist is? How do you feel after you discover this?

Prepared by M. Jerry Weiss, Jersey City State College, Emeritus; with Arthea J. S. Reed, Ph.D., University of North Carolina at Asheville, and W. Geiger Ellis, Ed.D., University of Georgia, Emeritus.

Questions and Activities for Suggested Short Stories

Each of the selected short stories listed below is appropriate for classroom use, and the questions and activities are designed for the indicated short story. The questions should allow students to respond to the stories orally or in writing. They may be used with the entire class or with small groups of students. Teachers may find other stories in the three anthologies that are appropriate for their particular students.

Stories from *Night Shift*

"JERUSALEM'S LOT" (pp. 1–34)

1. As a writing technique King uses a series of letters to explain what is happening in Chapelwaite. How effective is this technique as he spins his haunting tale?

2. The eerie setting is established early in the story. Describe your reaction to Calvin's comments about townspeople stating: "What was said, sir, was that anyone who would live in Chapelwaite must be either a lunatic or run the risk of becoming one." (p. 3) What do you think is going to happen?

3. What does Charles learn about his ancestry from Mrs. Cloris? What does Charles learn about the house?

4. Explain Mrs. Cloris's statement, "Some die not. . . some live in the twilight shadows Between to serve–Him!" (p. 7)

5. Why do you think King tries to involve all of one's senses in describing Jerusalem's Lot? How effective is he?

6. Charles states that he thinks he knows why "Jerusalem's Lot is a shunned town." (p. 11) What reasons can you give for this possible conclusion?

7. What is a "Satan's Mass"? (p. 12)

8. How does Mrs. Cloris explain the evil things that have happened since Charles and Calvin have arrived? What does she recommend? If you were in their place, would you leave? Explain. What history about Chapelwaite does she offer?

9. King wants to increase the sense of horror as Charles and Calvin explore the house. What do they discover in the cellar?

10. What is meant by "nosferatu–the Undead?" (p. 21)

11. What does Calvin seem to indicate when he writes: "It seems we wait in the deceptive Eye of the Storm?" (p. 21)

12. What evidence is there that "blood calls to blood?" (p. 23) What does this mean?

13. Describe the horror that takes place when Calvin and Charles return to the church.

14. What part does James Boon play in "Jerusalem's Lot?"

15. How does King conclude this tale? What twists are added to the tale? What do you think might happen next?

"GRAVEYARD SHIFT" (pp. 35–51)

1. In ten words or less, describe Hall at the beginning of the story.

2. What element of horror does King use to introduce the tale?

3. On page 37, King skillfully establishes the setting and action for the tale. If you were Hall, would you accept the job offer? Explain your answer.

4. What do you think Hall's premonition is that involves Warwick? (p. 38)

5. How does King appeal to all of the reader's senses as he describes the setting and circumstances? How effective is the author?

6. Wisconsky describes the rats, "It almost seems like they think. You ever wonder how it'd be, if we was little and they were big?" (p. 39) To what extent does this enable the reader to foresee the structure of the action within the story?

7. What horrible thing happened to Ray Upton? What is the reaction among the workers?

8. As the story develops, what is the relationship between Hall and Warwick? How does Hall confront Warwick with town ordinances? What is the effect?

9. What do the men discover in the sub-cellar?

10. How does King skillfully end the story? What is your reaction to his technique?

"NIGHT SURF" (pp. 52–60)

1. What seems to bond the young people together? What are your feelings about these people?

2. What is "A6"? Compare it to similar diseases throughout history.

3. How do you explain the Bernie-Susie relationship?

4. What has changed since "A6"?

5. What would be your thoughts and activities if you and five friends were the last inhabitants on earth?

"I AM THE DOORWAY" (pp. 61–73)

1. What, in your mind, are the achievements as a result of space flights? What is the cost for a space flight program? What are your

personal feelings about maintaining such a program? What tragedies and near tragedies have taken place over the years of the U.S. space flight programs?

2. What happened to Arthur as he came down from his space flight? How has this affected him? What was the shocking discovery he made about his itchings?

3. What does Arthur mean when he says "I am the doorway?" (p. 61)

4. What leads Arthur to his final decision?

"GRAY MATTER" (pp. 105–116)

1. What is the setting for this story? Why is it so important?

2. How does Henry react to Timmy's plea?

3. What is the horrible tale Henry tells the others as they are carrying the beer to Richie's? What are their reactions? What are yours?

4. How do you explain the end of the story?

5. How does King draw the reader's senses into this grotesque tale?

"STRAWBERRY SPRING" (pp. 171–180)

1. What is "strawberry spring"? (p. 171) How does this become a part of the story?

2. Listen to a recording of "Love is Blue" or "Hey, Jude" or "Scarborough Fair" to get a sense of the times—the late 1960s. Also, note that Stephen King is an avid radio and rock-and-roll fan.

3. Who is "Springheel Jack"? (p. 171)

4. Research information about Jack the Ripper.

5. On page 179, King has a paragraph that refers to "draft protesters," a "sit-in where a well-known napalm manufacturer was holding interviews." Find information about the late 1960s in newspapers and magazines to see how common such situations were. Why did people feel this way? Could such activities happen today? Explain.

6. What is your reaction to the ending of the story?

"THE LAST RUNG ON THE LADDER" (pp. 279–290)

1. King enjoys using children in his stories. How does he capitalize on their secrets and curiosities in this tale?

2. How effective is the transition from the results of jumping into the hay to the news item Larry has about his sister?

3. Why did the contents of the letter move Larry?

4. What are your feelings about Larry?

"THE MAN WHO LOVED FLOWERS" (pp. 291–296)

1. How would you best describe the young man? If you were in a position to make a television program based on the story, what actor could best play this part? What criteria did you use to make this decision?

2. How do the radio news items contrast with the season and the young man's feelings?

3. What was meant by the statement, "His name was love"? (p. 296)

"THE WOMAN IN THE ROOM" (pp. 313–326)

1. Why is the man who is visiting his mother in the hospital upset by the thought of the "cortotomy"? (p. 314)

2. Find out as much as you can about Michael Crichton's *The Terminal Man* and Ken Kesey's *One Flew Over the Cuckoo's Nest*. How do these works inform King's story?

3. King makes an unusual comparison as he describes patients walking slowly in the hospital hall. "It is the walk of people who are going nowhere slowly, the walk of college students in caps and gowns filing into a convocation hall." (p. 315) What is your reaction to this comparison?

4. The doctor says, "Your mother can no longer count time in terms of seconds and minutes and hours. She must restructure those units into days and weeks and months." (p. 320) What do you think he means?

5. What is your reaction to what Johnny does to help his mother out of her condition? Do you think mercy killing is ever justified? Explain.

Stories from *Nightmares and Dreamscapes*

"SUFFER THE LITTLE CHILDREN" (pp. 81–92)

1. Why do you think Miss Sidley picks on her students?

2. How might you explain how she seems to know what her students are thinking or doing?

3. Why is Robert her major nemesis?

4. What does Robert mean when he says, "There's quite a few of us."? (p. 87)

5. Why does Miss Sidley bring a gun to school? Do you think she was justified in using it? Explain your response.

6. How would you explain the ending of the story?

"THE DOCTOR'S CASE" (pp. 551–581)

1. Explain the title of this story.

2. What is meant by "I might as well set it down before God caps my pen forever"? (p. 551)

3. Identify Lestrade, Watson, and Holmes.

4. Why does Lestrade bring Holmes into the case?

5. Who solves the murder? How?

6. Compare this story with a Sherlock Holmes mystery by Arthur Conan Doyle and note the differences in the characters of Dr. Watson and Holmes.

Stories from *Skeleton Crew*

"WORD PROCESSOR OF THE GODS" (pp. 307–325)

1. What did the title suggest to you before you read the story?

2. Describe the word processor Jon created. Why did he build it?

3. Would you prefer Jon or Seth as a friend? Give your reasons.

4. The Jon we meet at the end of the story is somewhat different from the Jon at the beginning. Discuss how he has changed and what events have made him different.

5. What is Nordhoff's role in this story?

6. Can you justify Richard using the EXECUTE button the way he did? Explain your answer.

"THE MAN WHO WOULD NOT SHAKE HANDS" (pp. 326–344)

1. How does the author build suspense in this story?

2. What is meant by "IT IS THE TALE, NOT HE WHO TELLS IT"? (p. 326)

3. Who are George Gregson's fifty-three "good friends who saw me through my time of trial"? (p. 327) How is this an example of the use of irony?

4. What events lead to Brower never shaking hands? How does George learn of these events?

5. Compare this story with King's novella, "The Breathing Method" in *Different Seasons.*

"THE REAPER'S IMAGE" (pp. 363–370)

1. Who is the reaper in this story? Where is he seen?

2. What kind of place is the Samuel Claggert Memorial Private Museum?

3. Describe the characteristics of Mr. Carlin and Johnson Spangler. What kind of person is each one?

4. What does the author tell us about Delver Mirrors?

5. Do you like the ending? Give your reasons. Continue the story with an additional episode.

"UNCLE OTTO'S TRUCK" (pp. 427–443)

1. King cautions readers, "Most of you . . . will not believe." (p. 427) How does he make this a believable story?

2. The author compares the final break-down of Uncle Otto's truck with the "wonderful one-Hoss shay" (p. 429) in Oliver Wendell Holmes's poem "The Deacon's Masterpiece." Based on that poem, write your own description of the truck's demise.

3. What observations led to the narrator's suspicion that Uncle Otto murdered his partner? How? Why?

4. Give some examples of how King uses humor in this tale.

After Reading Activities

Drama

■ Have a small group of students develop a classroom dramatic presentation of one of the stories for the class.

■ Sponsor a Stephen King Storytelling Festival. Students can sign up to tell their favorite tale. This can be either a group project, where several participate in telling a story, or an individual project. The emphasis is on oral interpretation and making the story come alive. Adaptations are permissible.

■ Do a class "campfire" in which each small group of students tells their story utilizing good storytelling techniques. Students should orally capture their listeners' attention as King captures his readers' attention.

Media

■ "Inner Sanctum" was a popular radio program. Several cassette recordings have been made and are commercially available. Play one or two of these and compare them with the King stories you have read. Adapt one King story for a similar radio program. Present the adaptation via the school public address system or make a recording for use in another class.

■ View one or two "Twilight Zone" videotapes. How well do you think Stephen King's short stories could be adapted for this series? Try choosing one story and make a film/videotape or screen adaptation.

■ Several of Stephen King's novels have been made into movies. Choose one from the following list and make a comparison between the book and film versions: *Carrie, Misery, The Shining, Dolores Claiborne, The Shawshank Redemption* (based on "Rita Hayworth and the Shawshank Redemption" in *Different Seasons*), or *Stand By Me* (based on "The Body" in *Different Seasons*).

Writing

■ Encourage students to write their own horror stories. By using a copy machine or word processor, publish a horror story collection. Some students might serve as editors and illustrators. This would be a great Halloween project.

■ Using one or more of King's short stories as models, write a horror story in which suspense builds and there is an element of surprise.

■ Write a first paragraph for a suspense/horror story that captures the readers' attention in the way King does.

■ Setting the scene is important in horror and suspense. Discuss King's settings and develop one of your own for a horror or suspense story.

Reading

■ Read what Stephen King has written about evil and analyze the story you have read applying his comments.

■ Compare King's plots to the plot of any other horror or suspense story you have read. Discuss why King is such a popular writer.

Technology

There are several electronic newsgroups for fans of Stephen King. Have students monitor a group and then post a question or new topic for discussion. Some newsgroups include: alt.books.stephenking; alt.fan.authors.stephenking; alt.horror. Stephen King homepages can be found on the internet by searching via Stanford's Yahoo search engine. Try http://www.csif.cs.ucdavis.edu/~pace/king.html as a starting point.

Extending Students' Learning

Activities

■ Have students write a critical review of one of King's short stories. Discuss how the author builds the suspense and introduces the horror. Examine how he deals with evil, captures the readers' attention, and utilizes elements of surprise. Submit your review to the school literary journal or newspaper.

■ Read about the lives of other horror or suspense writers. Compare their fears to the fears King writes about in his own words.

■ Read what King says about writing. Read other authors' comments on writing. What similarities and differences do you find?

Bibliography: Suggestions for Additional Reading

Brontë, Charlotte. *Jane Eyre.* New York: Signet Classic, 1960. Afterword by Arthur Zeiger.

Brontë, Emily. *Wuthering Heights.* New York: Signet Classic, 1957. Introduction by Susan Fromberg Schaeffer.

Collins, Wilkie. *The Woman in White.* New York: Signet Classic, 1985. Introduction by Frederick R. Karl.

Conrad, Joseph. *Heart of Darkness* and *The Secret Sharer.* New York: Signet Classic, 1983. Introduction by Albert I. Guerard.

_____. *Tales of Unrest.* New York: Penguin Classic, 1991.

Cuddon, J. A., ed. *The Penguin Book of Ghost Stories.* New York: Penguin, 1984.

_____, ed. *The Penguin Book of Horror Stories.* New York: Penguin, 1984.

Dickens, Charles. *Selected Short Fiction.* New York: Penguin Classic, 1976. Introduction by Deborah A. Thomas.

Doyle, Sir Arthur Conan. *The Adventures of Sherlock Holmes.* New York: Penguin, 1981.

_____. *The Sherlock Holmes Mysteries.* New York: Signet Classic, 1987. Introduction by Frederick Busch.

Hardy, Thomas. *The Distracted Preacher and Other Tales.* New York: Penguin Classic, 1979. Introduction by Susan Hill.

_____. *Jude the Obscure.* New York: Signet Classic, 1980. Afterword by A. Alvarez.

Hawthorne, Nathaniel. *Selected Tales and Sketches.* New York: Penguin Classic, 1987. Introduction by Michael J. Colacurcio.

Jackson, Shirley. *The Haunting of Hill House.* New York: Penguin, 1984.

_____. *We Have Always Lived in the Castle.* New York: Penguin, 1984.

James, Henry. *The Turn of the Screw and Other Short Novels.* New York: Signet Classic, 1995. Introduction by Perry Meisel.

Kafka, Franz. *The Transformation ("Metamorphosis") and Other Stories.* New York: Penguin Classic, 1992. Edited and Translated by Malcolm Pasley.

Kaye, Marvin, ed. *The Penguin Book of Witches and Warlocks: Tales of Black Magic, Old and New.* New York: Penguin, 1991.

Poe, Edgar Allan. *The Portable Poe.* New York: Penguin, 1977. Edited by Philip Van Doren Stern.

_____. *The Science Fiction of Edgar Allan Poe.* New York: Penguin Classic, 1976. Introduction by Harold Beaver.

Ryan, Alan, ed. *The Penguin Book of Vampire Stories.* New York: Penguin, 1988.

Shelley, Mary. *Frankenstein.* New York: Signet Classic, 1963. Afterword by Harold Bloom.

Skal, David J. *The Monster Show: A Cultural History of Horror.* New York: Penguin, 1994.

Stevenson, Robert Louis. *Dr. Jekyll and Mr. Hyde.* New York: Signet Classic, 1987. Introduction by Vladimir Nabokov.

Stoker, Bram. *Dracula.* New York: Signet Classic, 1965. Introduction by Leonard Wolf.

Wells, H.G. *Selected Short Stories.* New York: Penguin Classic, 1979.

Wilde, Oscar. *The Picture of Dorian Gray and Selected Stories.* New York: Signet Classic, 1962. Foreword by Gary Schmidgall.

Winter, Douglas E. *Stephen King: The Art of Darkness.* New York: Signet, 1986.

Woolrich, Cornell. *Rear Window and Other Stories.* New York: Penguin, 1994.

_____. *Waltz Into Darkness.* New York: Penguin, 1995.

Program of Events for the Reading Stephen King Conference

READING STEPHEN KING

**ISSUES OF CENSORSHIP,
STUDENT CHOICE,
AND THE PLACE OF POPULAR
LITERATURE IN THE CANON**

A Conference to be held
Friday, October 11, and
Saturday, October 12, 1996
at the University of Maine
Orono, Maine

Reading Stephen King: Issues of Student Choice, Censorship, and the Place of Popular Literature in the Canon

Sponsored by The University of Maine College of Education

Friday, October 11th and Saturday, October 12th, 1996

Program of Events

Welcome! The following events are designed to help you explore Stephen King's work, and the issues it raises, based upon your needs and interests as a student, scholar, parent, teacher, or community member. Feel free to attend any sessions that interest you.

A few notes that will help everyone enjoy the conference more:

■ If you are lost or confused, look for student workers wearing bright red "I read banned books!" tee-shirts. They can help you navigate the campus and conference events.

■ Conference organizers are wearing bright orange stickers on their nametags. They are also happy to assist you.

■ Please wear your nametag at all times. It is your "ticket" to many conference events. Space is limited, and we want to ensure that paid participants receive seats at all events.

■ Throughout the conference, we will be drawing names for autographed copies of Stephen King books, gift certificates, and other goodies. Make sure your name is in the pool of names to be drawn by filling out our Stephen King Reader's Survey at registration.

■ Please provide Stephen King with the same respect for his privacy he receives from others in his hometown. **No requests for autographs or book signings throughout the conference events, and no flash photography during Mr. King's talk. These policies will be strictly enforced.**

Free time?

Why not take a walking tour of campus and view Stephen King's old haunts as a student? "King of the Campus," a map highlighting landmarks from King's time as a student, is included in your conference materials. If you have additional time, you may want to try the "IT" tour or "King Landmarks" driving tour also included in this packet.

The University of Maine Bookstore in the Memorial Union (open Friday afternoon only) has a display of King's books. The University Library has a display of King artifacts from the Special Collections Department, which houses many of King's original manuscripts from his works in progress.

Special

We want to thank the steering committee of Rosemary Bamford, Ed Brazee, Phyl Brazee, Kelly Chandler, Robert Cobb, Virginia Nees Hatlen, Ethel Hill, Kay Hyatt, Jan Kristo, Paula Moore, Tom Perry, Brenda Power, Susan Russell, and Jeff Wilhelm for their hard work over the past 18 months in putting the conference together.

Thanks also to the local bookstores which did in-house displays, events, and discounted books, especially Betts Bookstore, Borders, BookSource, and Mr. Paperback, and to the National Council of Teachers of English for censorship guides.

Schedule of Events

Friday, October 11

Noon - 3 p.m. Registration (Maine Center For the Arts)

3:15-4:30 p.m. Concurrent Sessions (see below)

Concurrent sessions on Friday and Saturday are designated as Literary Criticism, Censorship, Teaching Practice or Youth Strand. These designations are to help you understand the general themes of the presentations. But use these designations only as a guide—you are welcome to go to any sessions that interest you.

5:30-7:00 p.m. Creepy Cuisine Banquet (Wells Conference Center)

7:30-8:30 p.m. Keynote Address by Stephen King (Hauck Auditorium, Memorial Union)

Introduction by Burton Hatlen, Professor of English and Interim Dean of the College of Arts and Humanities

Concurrent Presentations

CS = Censorship, TP = Teaching Practice, LC = Literary Criticism, YS = Youth Strand

Friday, 3:15-4:30

1. Censorship Issues in the Electronic Era (CS)

Gail Garthwait (Asa Adams Elementary School and University of Maine, Orono, ME), Debe Averil (Bangor High School, Bangor, ME), Debbie Locke, and Kathy Foss
   This panel of local library media specialists will discuss roles of educators and parents, student responsibilities on the Internet, acceptable use policies and freedom in cyberspace, and potential problem areas. 202 Shibles Hall

2. Covert Censorship (CS, TP)

Ruth Farrar (Bridgewater State University, Bridgewater, MA)
   Analysis of children's literature reveals the preponderance of a single approach to conflict resolution. Following a brief introduction, participants will work in small groups to examine award-winning children's literature and identify the value systems within the books through a series of workshop exercises. 1912 Lounge–Memorial Union

3. What Students Have to Say about Censorship and Student Choices (TP, CS, YS)

John D'Anieri and Students from Noble High School (Berwick, ME)
   What happens when students study censorship as part of a student-centered reading and writing curriculum? Through an interactive panel discussion, high school teacher John D'Anieri and his students will talk about what they learned from developing this unit together. Bangor Lounge–Memorial Union

Saturday, October 12

8:30 a.m. Coffee, Pastry and Juice Available in Corbett Lobby

9:00 a.m.-10:30 a.m. Plenary Session: *When Stephen King (and Controversy) Come to School* (101 Corbett Hall)

   Jeff Wilhelm, University of Maine, Moderator

10:45-Noon Concurrent Sessions (see below)

Noon-1:30 p.m. Luncheon: Stephen King's Field of Dreams and Nightmares (Wells Conference Center)

This testimonial luncheon is a salute to Stephen King's love of baseball. Join in the fun of hot dogs, Crackerjack, (root) beer and stories at the open mike of reading King's work.

1:45-3:00 p.m. Concurrent Sessions (see below)

4. Critical Theory Colloquium (LC)

All three of these presentations will examine provocative issues in Stephen King's work through the lens of critical theory. There will be time for questions and discussioin among the presenters and the audience. Old Town Lounge–Memorial Union

Canonical Ambivalence in Stephen King

Emily Hegarty (Suffolk University, Boston, MA)

Randall Flagg: The Master and the Other

Felicia Beckmann (University of Missouri–Columbia)

Absent without Leave: Stephen King's Stand

Stephen Glickman, (University of Colorado, Boulder)

5. Before and After the Fall: The Passage from Childhood to Adulthood in Stephen King's It (LC)

Burton Hatlen, University of Maine
In addition to a literary analysis of the passage through adolescence in *It,* Burton Hatlen will talk about his experiences as a mentor, friend, and colleague of Stephen King's over the past 30 years. Peabody Lounge–Memorial Union

6. King's Works and the At-Risk Student: The Broad-Based Appeal of a Canon Basher (TP,YS)

John Skretta (Northeast High School, Lincoln, NE)
John Skretta works almost exclusively with high school students who receive special education services. In this presentation, he will demonstrate why Stephen King's works are especially relevant to and popular with his students. South Lown–Memorial Union

7. Why *Goosebumps* Is Good for Your Kids (TP, CS, YS)

Jonathan Wilhelm (Lorain, OH)
Jonathan Wilhelm is "Mr. Hatbox," creator and host of an award-winning children's program on Cablevision. In this presentation, he will argue that R.L. Stine's "Goosebumps" series is a valuable learning tool for students, parents, and teachers. FFA Lounge–Memorial Union

8. Religious Imagery in Desperation, The Regulators, and The Green Mile (LC)

Tyson Blue (Rochester, NY)
Prominent King scholar Tyson Blue will present an analysis of imagery in Stephen King's latest work, demonstrating the thematic ties that bind these three books together. Sutton Lounge–Memorial Union

9. **"When *It* Comes to the Classroom" (TP, YS)**

Ruth Hubbard (Lewis and Clark College, Portland, OR) and Kim
Campbell (Riverdale High School, Portland, OR)
    It. That frightening horror that fashions many a teacher's worst
nightmares. *It*, of course, is a novel by Stephen King, but it also represents popular culture to these presenters. This workshop considers the
role of popular culture in one high school classroom. North
Lown–Memorial Union

10. **Reading and Writing Workshop for Youths (YS)**

Karen Johnson, Facilitator (University of Maine)
    This workshop for teens will include the reading and discussion of
Stephen King's brief story "Here There Be Tygers" from *Skeleton Crew*,
and conversation about Stephen King's style, what makes horror
writing appealing, and how students can use his work as a model for
their own. Davis Room–Memorial Union

Saturday Concurrent Sessions

10:45 a.m.-noon

1. **Anatomy of a Book Censorship (CS, YS)**

Molly Sinclair, Stuart Hardy, Joseph Corcoran, and Marla Ferris
(Strong, ME)
    The censorship battle over *Bastard Out of Carolina* at Mount
Abrams High School has recently received national attention. Join the
teachers involved as they discuss the controversy through four differ-
ent lenses–procedural, academic, personal and legal. Bangor
Lounge–Memorial Union

2. **Increasing Literacy and Diversifying the Canon: The Use of
Stephen King's Short Works in the Classroom (TP, YS)**

Timothy Westmoreland (University of Massachusetts at Amherst) and
Debra Westmoreland (Amherst-Pelham Regional School District,
Amherst, MA)
    What is a good starting point for integrating King's work into a
school reading program? Timothy and Debra Westmoreland will
demonstrate how they were able to include King's short works in their
high school curriculum. South Lown–Memorial Union.

3. **Killing the King or Facing Medusa: The Ethical Power of Evil in
Literature (TP, LC, YS)**

Brian Edmiston (The Ohio State University)
    Facing and reacting to evil in literature is a productive venue for
ethical dialogue. In this presentation, noted drama educator Brian

Edmiston will argue that by identifying with evil perspectives in King's work and other literature, we may begin to accept our own capacity for hatred, anger, lust and other "deadly sins." North Lown–Memorial Union

4. Dealing with Censorship and Controversial Issues: Rights and Responsibilities for Educators (CS, TP)

Anne Pooler, University of Maine
How do we define controversy? And what are the legal and ethical issues we need to deal with when controversy emerges in our schools? In this practical and interactive session, Anne Pooler will share what teachers need to know and do when using controversial texts. 202 Shibles Hall

5. Colloquium on Popular Fiction in the Classroom (TP, LC)

Blending the theoretical and the practical, these three presentations will explore how and why popular fiction can be used successfully in the college classroom. 1912 Lounge–Memorial Union.

Why Teach Popular Literature? Bunjee Jumping, Cinderella Structures, and the Primal Routes of Literacy

Quentin Eastman (University of New Hampshire, Durham, NH)

A Course for all Reasons: Reading and Writing Popular Fiction

Anita Kurth (University College, Bangor, ME)

Behind Closed Doors: Stephen King in the College Classroom

Amy Conrad (University of Rochester, Rochester, NY)

6. Colloquium on Connecting King to the Classics (LC)

These three presentations suggest connections between King's work and the canon. Following the formal talks, there will be time for the presenters and the audience to explore how to build on popular interest in King as a bridge to the classics. Nutter Room–Memorial Union

Poe versus King: The Chilling Path into the Canon

Sandra Chervinsky (Merrimack College, North Andover, MA)

(De)Constructing the Good/Evil Dualism: American Gothic Fiction, Psychic Tensions, and the Face of Fear

Sarah Morgan (Colby College, Waterville, ME)

Stephen King: The Shakespeare of the Twentieth Century

Theresa Seward (Williams College, Williamstown, MA)

7. A Combustible Combination: A Thematic Unit on Censorship and Composition (CS, TP)

Mary Segall (Quinnipiac College, Hamden, CT)
This presentation offers an approach to reference writing for high school and college students around censorship issues. Using sources as far-ranging as MTV and Jerry Falwell, the focus is on student investment in research and writing. FAA Lounge–Memorial Union

8. If Students Own Their Learning, What Do Teachers Do? (TP)

Curt Dudley-Marling (York University, Toronto, Canada)
This presentation will use examples from classrooms at all levels to complicate the notion of student ownership. Curt Dudley-Marling seeks to help teachers live more comfortably with the uncertainties, ambiguities, and contradictions that attend the practice of offering students control over their learning. Peabody Lounge–Memorial Union

9. Morality in the Horror Fiction of Stephen King (LC)

James Anderson (Johnson and Wales University, Warwick, RI)
This presentation will consider the criticism of King's work because of the violence often included in it. James Anderson will argue that King's basic themes deal with the need for moral and ethical behavior in modern society, using horror to show the corruption of a world without ethics. Davis Lounge–Memorial Union

10. Reading and Writing Workshop for Youths (YS)

Kelly Chandler, Facilitator (University of Maine)
This workshop for teens will include the reading and discussion of Stephen King's brief story "Here There Be Tygers" from *Skeleton Crew*, and conversation about Stephen King's style, what makes horror writing appealing, and how students can use his work as a model for their own. Sutton Room–Memorial Union

1:45-3:00 p.m.

1. Be Prepared: Protecting Yourself and Your School by Writing a Censorship Policy (CS)

Gail Garthwait, Asa Adams Elementary School and The University of Maine
A practical, informative session that will provide everything you need to know about crafting a censorship policy (print and non-print) for your school. Gail Garthwait, an experienced library media specialist, will guide you in developing a first draft. 202 Shibles Hall

2. One Book Can Hurt You . . . But a Thousand Can't (TP, CS)

Janet Allen (University of Central Florida, Orlando, FL)
This session will examine the irresponsibility that arises when we limit the reading possibilities for students. Using the claims of recent

censorship cases as a base, former Maine teacher Janet Allen will look at what children don't learn when these rich texts are unavailable to them. South Lown–Memorial Union

3. The Horror Is Only Skin Deep: Parents and Students Deconstruct the Stephen King Text (TP, YS)

Holt Littlefield (Stevens High School, Claremont, NH) and Students and Parents from Stevens High School)
The presentation team for this lively multimedia session includes high school students, parents, and a teacher, Holt Littlefield. In addition to discussing possible uses for King's work in the high school curriculum, the workshop will consider the following questions: when we deny access to King's books, are we censoring theme or content? North Lown–Memorial Union

4. Establishing Student Choice: The Place of Individualized Reading Programs in Traditional Secondary English Programs (TP)

Kathryn Ford (Coe-Brown Northwood Academy) and Robert Pingree (Concord High School, Concord, NH)
Reading programs which place student choice at their center can encourage students to become more active, careful readers. This presentation offers a workshop format with resources, lists, getting-started techniques, and personal anecdotes. 1912 Lounge–Memorial Union

5. Screams and Whispers: Redemption through Friendship in Selected Works of Stephen King (TP, LC, YS)

Sandy Brawders (University of Maine)
Join Sandy Brawders and the "Bump in the Night Players" for a rousing reader's theater presentation on redemption through friendship in King's work using a dramatic visual, auditory and kinesthetic means. Especially appropriate for teens and their teachers. Bangor Lounge–Memorial Union

6. Perspectives on Censorship (CS, YS)

Two students and a graduate instructor will present viewpoints on censorship and its effects on schools. Following the individual talks, there will be time for audience discussion–guaranteed to be lively–about this important issue. Nutter Room–Memorial Union

Bringing Truth to America's Youth

Aaron Cooper (University of Nebraska)

Censorship and the Purpose of Education

Danielle Mahlum (University of Wyoming)

Censorship: A Student Perspective

Doug Mowbray (Ridge, NH)

7. Critical Theory Colloquium (LC)

Three presentations offer new perspectives on King's work using provocative theoretical angles. Discussion will follow, with time for the presenters and audience members to explore connections across the three talks. Davis Lounge–Memorial Union

Raising the Dead: Teaching Theory through Non-canonical Texts

Miriam Heddy Pollock (New York University, New York, NY)

Stephen King and Prototype Theory

Kristine McCrady (Arizona State University, Tempe, AZ)

Teaching Stephen King as Rhetoric and the (Unknown) Student Body

Jeffrey Hoogeveen (University of Rhode Island)

8. King in the Classroom: Students Read *Pet Sematary* (TP, YS)

Mark Fabrizi (North Branford (CT) High School)
Mark Fabrizi will show how he uses *Pet Sematary* with his high school students to explore the themes of death, religion, and loss of loved ones in a way that students find accessible and interesting. FFA Lounge–Memorial Union

9. How Patrick Buchanan Would Read Stephen King (LC, CS)

Ed Ingebretsen (Georgetown University, Washington, DC)
Using excerpts from his current book-in-progress, *Creating Subjects, Making Monsters,* Ed Ingebretsen will argue that narratives of horror derived from Gothic fantasy help shape post-Buchanan political realities.

10. Stephen King's Women (LC)

Kathleen March (University of Maine)
In this interactive presentation, Kathleen March will consider the cases of Dolores Claiborne, Rose Madder, and Ruth (from *Insomnia*) in framing King's view of contemporary women and their plight. Peabody Lounge–Memorial Union

The Screening Room

The following films adapted from Stephen King's work will be shown in the Mahogany Room at Wells Commons on Saturday, October 12:

10:00 a.m.-noon	*Dolores Claiborne*
1:30-3:30 p.m.	*Stand by Me*

Editors

Kelly Chandler is a doctoral student in literacy education at the University of Maine. The author of numerous articles on secondary reading programs, she is currently completing a qualitative dissertation study of the readers of Stephen King's work.

Brenda Miller Power is associate professor of literacy education at the University of Maine. She is the founding editor of *Teacher Research: The Journal of Classroom Inquiry.*

Jeffrey D. Wilhelm is assistant professor of literacy education at the University of Maine, where he teaches courses in adolescent reading, drama, secondary methods, and research. He is the author of *Standards In Practice: Grades 6–8*, published by the National Council of Teachers of English.

Contributors

James Albright is a veteran high school teacher from State College, Pennsylvania. He is currently enrolled in the doctoral program for literacy, language, and culture at Pennsylvania State University.

Janet S. Allen is professor of secondary English education at the University of Central Florida. She taught high school English for more than twenty years in northern Maine. Her most recent book is *It's Never Too Late: Leading Adolescents to Lifelong Literacy*.

Rosemary A. Bamford is professor of education in reading and language arts at the University of Maine. She is also the site coordinator for Reading Recovery for the College of Education's trainer site. She has made presentations at numerous conferences and has written extensively on children's literature and literacy education.

Kimberly Hill Campbell is the teaching principal at Riverdale High School, Oregon. She is an adjunct instructor at Lewis and Clark College and has published numerous teacher research studies chronicling her work with high school English students.

Michael R. Collings is professor of English at Pepperdine University. He is the author of over seventy books, including seven on Stephen King, the most recent being *The Work of Stephen King*. Another new book, *Scaring Us to Death: The Stephen King Phenomenon,* is in press.

Curt Dudley-Marling is professor of education at York University in North York, Ontario. The author of many books and articles on whole language theory and practice, he is currently the co-editor of *Language Arts.*

Mark A. Fabrizi began teaching English at North Branford High School after earning a master's degree from the University of Pennsylvania. He has published two short stories and a poem and was a finalist in the 1996 Poet-of-the-Year competition of the New England Association of Teachers of English.

Abigail C. Garthwait is a doctoral student in literacy education at the University of Maine. She is also a librarian at Asa Adams School in Orono, Maine, where she has been a state and regional leader in integrating technology into library programs.

Roberta F. Hammett is a veteran high school teacher from State College, Pennsylvania. She is currently enrolled in the doctoral program for literacy, language, and culture at Pennsylvania State University.

Ruth Shagoury Hubbard is associate professor of language, learning, and culture at Lewis and Clark College in Portland, Oregon. Her seventh book, *A Workshop of the Possible: Nurturing Children's Creativity in the Classroom,* was published in 1996.

Stephen King, the world's bestselling novelist, lives with his wife, the novelist Tabitha King, in Bangor, Maine.

Janice V. Kristo is professor of education in reading and the language arts at the University of Maine. She has written four books in the areas of children's literature and literacy education.

Constance M. Perry is professor of curriculum, instruction, and foundations in the College of Education, University of Maine, Orono. She has a special interest in the ethical context of teaching in today's schools.

Anne E. Pooler is associate dean of education and associate professor of social studies education at the University of Maine. As a classroom social studies teacher and administrator, she has dealt with various situations involving controversial issues and censorship.

John Skretta is a teacher of at-risk students at Northeast High School in Lincoln, Nebraska. He teaches in a district pilot program that is committed to helping struggling students meet graduation requirements through an interdisciplinary, highly personalized, and student-centered "school-within-a-school" program.

Michael W. Smith is co-editor of *Research in the Teaching of English*. He directs the Department of Learning and Teaching in the Graduate School of Education at Rutgers University.

*This book was typeset in Antique Olive and Melior by
Doug Burnett and Electronic Imaging.
The book was printed on 50-lb. Finch by Port City Press.*

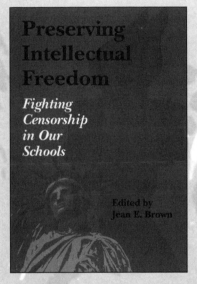